Albert Guérard

Educator, writer, critic, and citizen of the world, Albert Guérard celebrates this year the fiftieth anniversary of his becoming a teacher in America. In the course of his continuing search for fundamental values, his experiences of half a century have rewarded him not only with uncommon learning, but with a broad human wisdom. He has shared that wisdom in four books — of which *Testament of a Liberal* is the fourth to appear — and which he groups together under the title, "What the Teacher Learnt." Among Mr. Guérard's many other books are *Beyond Hatred*, *The France of Tomorrow*, and *Europe Free and United*. He served in the OSS during World War II, and on the Hutchins Committee to Frame a World Constitution; he is Professor of General and Comparative Literature and Lecturer in French Civilization (Emeritus) at Stanford University.

Testament of a Liberal

ALBERT GUÉRARD

Testament of a Liberal

HARVARD   UNIVERSITY   PRESS

CAMBRIDGE,   MASS.:   1 9 5 6

To Stanford University
the Home of my Spirit

THE WINDS OF FREEDOM BLOW

By Albert Guérard

Beyond Hatred
The France of Tomorrow
Europe Free and United

WHAT THE TEACHER LEARNT

. *Personal Equation*
. . *Education of a Humanist*
. . . *Testament of a Liberal*
. . . . *Bottle in the Sea*

Contents

PART I

The Things That Are Caesar's

I	A Liberal?	3
II	Culture vs. Cultures	16
III	Civilization and Culture	28

PART II

Political Freedom

IV	The Coming Victory of Liberty	41
	i. The Manifesto	
	ii. Post Mortem	
V	Politics and Government	57
VI	Democracy and Its Rivals	68
VII	What Can Be Done?	82
VIII	Justice: Virtue, Art, and Technique	108
IX	Politics at Its Worst: International Relations	128
X	The Snare of Leadership	142

PART III

Free Enterprise

XI	Confusions	155
XII	Monoliths	165
XIII	Modest Proposals	176
XIV	Drastic But Not Subversive	187
XV	Can Ethics Be Ruled Out?	197
XVI	If This Be Treason . . .	209
	Appendix: Syllabus of the Principal Errors of Our Times	221

Foreword

INTENTIONS,   APOLOGIES,

ACKNOWLEDGMENTS

This is my testament, or, more exactly, my testimony, with-out benefit of the Fifth Amendment. It is not a textbook, it is not a treatise, and it is not intended to make friends or influence people.

For the relief of my own conscience, I found it worth writ-ing. The problem is why you should find it worth reading. Solely as an exercise in free thought, and there is no thought worthy of the name that is not free. Free does not mean lawless: thinking has its stringent rules. Free does not mean independ-ent: our minds are conditioned. Freedom means honesty, which in its turn is inseparable from self-respect: never to profess, never to accept anything as true, unless you are intimately con-vinced that it is so.

When fear is simply the awareness of danger, it is realistic, reasonable, and salutary; and it implies no loss of dignity. It is only when fear leads to capitulation that it becomes debasing. Freedom from such craven fear is the most precious of all free-doms, and by a *Liberal* I mean a man liberated from that canker. The fear of persecution; the fear of ostracism; the fear of ridi-cule. This last is the most insidious: we cannot ignore the opinion of our fellow men. Writers in particular need a public and must strive to please. So every author needs a Dale Carnegie at his elbow. André Gide told a searching explorer of his works: "What a pity I did not have the benefit of your criticism before I wrote my books!" But there is one case in which this does not apply: the case of a personal confession. Here sincerity is the only rule. I must present myself as I am, "with my warts," as my master Montaigne put it. Unsound judgment? Ill temper? Poor taste? I cannot otherwise. This book is not the blurred composite picture of many minds — my own, and those of my friendly advisers. It is not a dignified *Portrait of the Author as Nicholas Murray Butler*. If there were in these pages any capitulation to good manners, the whole benefit of the experiment would be lost.

I am different, because I am a man, and all men are different. My readers are welcome to note, and regret, and deplore the differences. This book, and the larger enterprise of which it is a part, is directed against enforced conformity: it is not an attack on common sense. For if every individual is unique, he is also 99.44% human. I am not a rebel by nature. I find it agreeable to agree. I am a born, trained, and practiced fellow traveler. If you invite me, I shall go with you, not one mile, but twain. But I reserve the right to part company at any moment, courteously, and in the hope of meeting again. This, I take it, is the American Way of Life. I have no desire *"d'épater le bourgeois,"* to horrify the Rotarian. My very pleasant experiences with the Rotarians have taught me that they were *inépatables*: they receive the most outrageous paradoxes with an understanding smile. I have no dramatic talent: I could not play any part, even my own. So against the advice, gratefully acknowledged, of trusted friends, I have deliberately left in this book because they were part of myself thoughts and phrases which they found objectionable. My one hope is to induce free thought in others; and the only way in which this can be achieved is by keeping my own thought scrupulously free.

This is the record of a long life, and the reflections of at least sixty years. Allusions to the current scene must be read in that light. I am a student of history, not a politician or a journalist. I have few illusions about the "momentary momentousness" of the men, slogans, and issues of the present day. I never believed that our civilization would perish because a Senator was riding roughshod over our most cherished liberties. Unburied, he is forgotten; but he was of some importance, as the symptom of an ever-recurring danger. If a people ceases from eternal vigilance, a Napoleon, a Hitler, a Franco, a Huey Long will always be at hand. I have no desire to magnify particular episodes: I am conscious of the underlying, the ever-present peril. We thought thirty years ago that there would never be another Mitchell Palmer; but the next generation may well have its own Herbert Brownell. The type is perennial.

When I wrote the essay which is the core of this book, "The Coming Victory of Liberty," the outlook was dark indeed. Civilizations have perished before, because they refused to take thought in time. Today, we are in a springlike mood; the cold war is thawing away, and we are forgetting the winters of our discontent. I am ready for the new cheerfulness. I am eager to sing the lovely medieval lyric as lustily as any man:

> Sumer is icumen in:
> Lhude sing cuccu!

But there is no permanent victory except in death. Life and liberty demand, life and liberty *are,* unceasing mental strife. It is quite possible that by the time these lines appear in print, mankind will be reclothed in its rightful mind; that we shall have ascended, with a great national hero, from "No substitute for victory" to "War must be outlawed now." Then we shall be free to face nobler problems than mass murders. But as I am penning this farewell, the outlook is still dubious, many actual facts are still tragic. The Supreme Court, our last hope, has not yet discovered that its duty is to uphold the Constitution, not to suspend the First Amendment during the present emergency. As an adolescent, I was deeply stirred by the Dreyfus Case: *one man* was imprisoned unjustly, and we felt our safety, our dignity, were in jeopardy. Today, there are hundreds who have suffered persecution, scores who have been sentenced to jail, for no act of violence or treason, but for heretical thought.

If I have not shunned the reproach of paradox — many a paradox is but an unrecognized truism — I have deliberately

courted the accusation of platitude. There is nothing in these
pages that has not been said, and immeasurably better said, by
Rabelais, Montaigne, Descartes, Voltaire; by Milton, Locke,
Jefferson, John Stuart Mill, and Herbert Spencer. If I stand
against the national state, the party system, the profit motive
and the sectarian church, I know I am one of an innumerable
company. Every one in his senses condemns jingoism, partisanship, selfish greed and fanaticism. But after squaring our conscience, we do lip service again to the same ancient idols. This,
like my other farewell books, is directed against the middle-
roader, the man who sings *Excelsior!* with inspired mien, and
swoops down from those starry heights to a realistic down-to-
earth "deal"; the Laodicean, "rich and increased with goods,"
and neither cold nor hot. Naïve? No doubt; but at any rate not
lukewarm.

Many years ago,[1] I announced a farewell volume, to be entitled *Bottle in the Sea.* Like the "positively last appearances"
of Sarah Bernhardt and Buffalo Bill, my last bow has become
something of a habit, and my single *Bottle* has turned into an
array of four. The series is called "What the Teacher Learnt."
I am dimly contemplating a much larger series: "What the
Teacher Failed to Learn."

The four books, *Personal Equation, Education of a Humanist, Testament of a Liberal, Bottle in the Sea,* should be considered as a single work. But each has a different field, is presented from a different angle, and can be read independently.
There are, inevitably, principles which underlie all four, and
which have to be reiterated in each. Less excusable is the repetition of historical instances, parables, and even phrases — perhaps a score of them. I hope the reader will not be discourteous
to old acquaintances such as Monsieur Josse, *The Emperor's
New Clothes*, and the mathematician Laplace. Who knows?
They may improve on the second or third meeting. I do not
apologize: I repeated certain things deliberately, because I

[1] In Kunitz and Haycraft, *Twentieth Century Authors* (New York,
1942), pp. 583-584.

thought they were worth repeating. They fill at most a dozen pages in nearly a thousand. I should like to quote, not in every book, but in every chapter, the words of George Washington: "As a citizen of the great Republic of Humanity at large." I am not quite sure that certain anthropologists, and most Daughters of the American Revolution, would fully realize the import of that phrase, even if they were to read it fifty times.

I must express my deep gratitude to those fortresses of free thought and free speech, *The Southwest Review* and *The Pacific Spectator*. Many passages in the following pages first appeared in these two fearless magazines. As a rule, these passages were reorganized and entirely rewritten for this book, which is intended to be a book, and not a chance bundle of essays. One, however, "The Coming Victory of Liberty," is reproduced verbatim from the Autumn 1951 number of *The Southwest Review*. It brought me so many messages of sympathy that it reached the dignity of a minor document. I may have attempted forbidden paths, and better men than I have suffered for lesser offenses. But in my straying from the prescribed track, I have met delightful company.

ALBERT GUÉRARD

PART I

The Things That Are Caesar's

CHAPTER I

A Liberal?

The vanity of all labels appears most glaringly when a label is pinned on you. I have been called a liberal and a humanist, and I have courteously acknowledged the intended compliments. But both terms are exceedingly vague. They have that confused richness of meaning which makes you sigh for the holy simplicity of the unthinking. Both have a tinge of the ineffectual: the work of the world is done by coarser hands. Both have overtones of superciliousness. A conscious liberal or a conscious humanist (not that the terms are synonymous) knows that he is not as other men are, even as this member of the common herd, this crackpot, this Babbitt, or this profiteer. And smugness is damnation.

I have to accept the terms as roughly true. But one thing the teacher has learnt in his half-century of pedagogical endeavor: roughness, for all its bluff vigor, can be the most insidious enemy of thought. Never speak roughly, and above all strive never to think roughly. There is more peril in a rough truth than in a refined delusion. For a refined delusion, carried to the extreme point of refinement, is self-refuting. A rough truth tends to get rougher, more hopelessly entangled with errors and lies; and its core of rightness breeds self-righteousness, which drugs the intellect and perverts the will. A rough truth is bound to seek the support of rough force: in the vernacular, to get tough and crack down on its opponents. A rough truth roughly enforced means fanaticism, the never-failing source of most human ills. This book is a running battle against rough truths. Among them, at random (*roughly*), I may cite: that all men are created equal; that the will of the majority should prevail; that we are bound to fight for our country, right or wrong; that sturdy individualism is the first of all the manly virtues. They are not false, but they are crude. They need to be, not swept away, but challenged, tested, and purified.

Instead of a *liberal*, I might choose to call myself an *intellectual*. The term was minted, at the time of the Dreyfus Case, to bring disrepute on the champions of justice: this would confer upon it a patent of nobility. Throughout my career as a teacher and writer, I have insisted on the primacy of thought: the whole dignity of man, according to Pascal; the very proof of man's existence, according to Descartes. Thought is capable of no evil that more thought cannot cure. I do not deny the validity of practical sense and of the mystic experience: but both must submit to the check of thought. Not everything that works is right; not every vision is of God. Goodness itself is subject to the rule of clear honest thinking: the Catholic Church does not hold children responsible for their sins until they have reached "the age of reason."

Reason therefore, careful orderly thinking, is the indispensable instrument. But it is only an instrument: it does not provide the fundamental data, it does not define the final goal. Without, we encounter a universe which, in terms of our finite minds, is *absurd*; within, our aspirations are ever reaching beyond the capacity of our thought. To turn a tool into an end is a common delusion. There are many such idols: the army, the letter of the law, the machinery of the constitution, the tricks of the market place, the techniques of the various arts. Intellectualism as an absolute faith belongs to that class of heresies. I have often said that we should be "rationalists — within reason." To me Reason is not a goddess, but a servant. Reason is not a mechanism functioning in the void: it is a constant and scrupulous adjustment between our yearnings, which Reason cannot fathom, and the brutal facts, which Reason can neither explain nor deny. The rational is only that infinitesimal part of the real that has been reduced to human order. Reason is at the helm, but it is our aspirations we steer by. And if steering means shaping our course by the stars, it means also keeping clear of rocks and shoals.

If I had to adopt a label, I should call myself a searcher, or better a seeker. The *quest* is a paradox. Its object cannot be defined until it has been reached; and in human terms this can never come to pass. But the quest itself implies faith in its object: the words of Pascal apply not to one sacred figure only, but to all aspects of the truth: "Thou wouldst not be seeking me, if thou hadst not already found me." The quest is at the same time utopian and dynamic. The goal is beyond our reach; yet it determines the *sense* of our lives.[1]

What is a liberal? In politics, liberalism is a chameleon: it changes colors from country to country and from generation to generation. *Liberal* has become almost as elusive as *Democrat* is in American parlance: no one could hope to reach an unclouded understanding of democracy from the tenets, the methods, and the antics of the Dixiecrats combined with Tammany Hall. Perhaps it would be better if all party names were strictly conventional, without any suspicion of ideological nonsense: like the term *Gueux* for the Dutch rebels against Spain, Whigs and Tories in eighteenth-century England, *Sans-Culottes* in revolutionary France, Locofocos and Mugwumps in our own tradition.

The Liberal Party in Great Britain had a long and honored career before it became a recalcitrant ghost. And it did stand for many kinds of freedom: for Free Churches against the Establishment, for free speech and free education, even for the political freedom of subject nationalities, within the Empire as well as without. It only balked at Free Thought and Free Love in the narrower sense of the terms. It was attached also to a *liberal* economy — individualism, free trade, *laissez faire*, unrestrained competition. Even in its heyday, however, it was less an association of men with a great and definite common purpose than a shifting and uneasy coalition of many traditions and many interests: old Whigs like Sir William Harcourt clashing with Radicals like Sir Charles Dilke, pious Nonconformists

---

[1] A student of mine once defined a great thinker as a "plumber of perilous depths." A splendid if somewhat equivocal title. I have no claim to such profundity. But Albert Einstein proudly accepted his membership card in the Plumbers' Union.

aghast at the outspoken atheism of Bradlaugh, merchants and manufacturers fighting the landed gentry while sharing with the squires their faith in the sanctity of private property. Add to this cauldron, for a whole generation, the Irish Home Rulers, who had little in common with their Liberal allies, and the increasing force of Labor before it had evolved, confusedly, a social philosophy of its own. At its best, English Liberalism enlisted my cool sympathy, never my whole-hearted allegiance. There is hardly any man who was so consistently right as John Stuart Mill, unless it be John Locke: but the colorful wrongheadedness of Disraeli, Ruskin, and even Carlyle, had a more searching appeal. English Liberalism was irremediably drab. I am willing to be a fossil of the eighteenth century; I refuse to be a fossil of the nineteenth.

The French *Philosophes,* whom I proudly count among my masters, were not "liberals" in politics: they believed in the Enlightened Despot. It was the reactionary *Parlements* (Courts of Justice) that attempted to check progress in the name of liberty. The Revolution was the triumph of Liberty: Samson the executioner wore a Liberty cap, and Madame Rolland sighed on the scaffold: "O Liberty! How many crimes are committed in thy name!" Liberty and Napoleon, of course, were not on speaking terms. Under the Restoration, the word "liberalism" was used with English overtones: it meant a strictly constitutional monarchy, the need for a French 1688. Its hero was La Fayette, its philosopher Benjamin Constant: a political creed might fare worse. By comparison with the rule of the elder Bourbons, the bourgeois regime of Louis-Philippe was *liberal*: as a matter of fact, its principles were exactly those of our modern Republicans. In the minds of the king and of his right-hand man Guizot, however, sound liberalism was identical with their own authority and their own interests. More rapidly than in middle-class England, liberalism died of congenital dullness. "France was bored."

After 1860, the Second Empire followed, haltingly, a "liberal" trend. The iron-fisted regime (*un gouvernement à poigne*) found it advisable to put on velvet gloves. But the autocratic principle, Caesarian democracy, was not abandoned, and the last plebiscite, in May 1870, failed to dispel that ambiguity. Under the Third Republic, liberalism never was an organized party, but a pallid shade of opinion, on the whole conservative. It defended "the essential liberties" against the Jacobines, for whom *liberties* in the plural could hardly be distinguished from *privileges*. In a country where *Radical* has long come to mean trimmer and timeserver, it is not strange that *liberal* should be a polite version of *reactionary*. For the semanticist, politics is as perverse a realm as Alice's Wonderland. Do we not defend "democracy" in close alliance with Franco? Have we not hailed a military *coup d'état* in Guatemala as a victory for the "free world"?

Liberal in America is often equated with *Progressive*. The latter term was applied to the Populist movement, to the abortive campaigns of Theodore Roosevelt, Robert La Follette, and Henry Wallace, and, more loosely still, to the constructive efforts of Woodrow Wilson and Franklin D. Roosevelt. Progress, of course, is even more question-begging than liberty. Certain it is that the two are not synonymous. Progress of a kind may be imposed from above, as it was by Peter the Great or by the colonial powers, including our creditable record in the Philippines. Liberty may be legitimate resistance to such a method of progress: Aguinaldo thought he stood for liberty.

There is a familiar caricature of the liberal in modern American politics, and, like many caricatures, it has a cruel element of truth. The Liberal is too sensible to make up his mind, and too cautious to face a responsibility. He clings obstinately to the middle of the road: unable to choose between two lines of traffic, he creates a hazard for both. In scriptural language, he is a Laodicean. If such an unfavorable connotation could attach to what should be a noble ideal, it is because liberty is a negative conception. In the fields where liberty does exist, a pure liberal, a liberal who is nothing else, is a vacuity. What matters most for the individual and for the community, is not liberty itself, but what you plan to do with it. It would be highly desirable if the liberty of the murderer were restricted just before he had a chance of committing his crime. The liberty of erecting skyscrapers and increasing the suicidal congestion of our cities is one which needs to be sternly restrained.

I am a *Liberal* in the same sense as I am a *Respirationist.* I need air to breathe, and if I am stifled, I shall fight for "the freedom of my lungs," even if I have to smash a window pane. I know that there are well-intentioned persons bent on rationing my air supply, and blending it with a gas of their own: on the spiritual plane, breathing demands eternal vigilance. But *Respirationism* is merely a defensive rule of life. My one desire is to take it for granted that I am free to breathe and free to think. I do not want to be constantly obsessed with the fear of stifling. Again, the essential point is not to assert my freedom, but to make intelligent use of it.

The discussion of religious problems will be found in the fourth volume of this series, *Bottle in the Sea.* But political, social, and religious questions have many elements in common and are hard to disentangle. Indeed, the main thesis of this purely political essay is that our practical activities should be ruled by a religious faith. If we were to reduce the field of religion to the organized churches — a dangerous confusion of thought — liberalism in that domain would have little sense: there can be no liberal orthodoxy. I had the opportunity of studying the "Liberal Catholicism" of Lamennais, who finally had to leave the Church, of Montalembert and Lacordaire, who, within the Church, fought a long and losing battle. I came to see the wisdom of Pope Pius IX, when he said: "Anathema on any one who should maintain that the Sovereign Pontiff can and must be reconciled with progress, liberalism and modern civilization!" This is truer still, although less obvious, of the sects which have pared their theology to the bone. A faith with a few stark dogmas is less capable of compromise than one richly wreathed with traditions and legends. A liberal Catholic is less absurd than a liberal Calvinist.

This is not the place either to discuss liberty from the metaphysical point of view. In pure logic, liberty has no standing: scientific determinism in its rigor, and the conception of an eternal, omniscient, omnipotent God are equally destructive of liberty. You may retort: "Then logic be damned!" and I shall not demur. Liberty might well be a mere *as if*, veiling the abysses of our ignorance: I am persuaded myself that the area of freedom is infinitesimal compared with that of necessity. But the sense that we are capable of a choice is the very foundation of our mental and spiritual life. If you remove it, right and wrong, good and evil, love and hate vanish into the inane, and we, as persons, disappear likewise. Infinitesimal, the realm of liberty? So be it, but of infinite significance to us, and of infinite price. What matters it if, in the boundless universe, I am but an atom of an atom? The one thing certain is that *I am*.[2]

The idea of liberty is compatible either with an optimistic or with a pessimistic view of human nature. At one extreme, we find the Utopian anarchism of the Rousseauists. If all restraints were removed, if the artificial laws which constitute society were abolished, man would recover his innocence and his happiness. All we need, Voltaire commented, is to go on all fours.[3] For the pessimist, man is evil: according to Taine, a lustful and ferocious gorilla. The one certain good in this brutal world is power: power to survive, power to conquer, power to rule. On this assumption, the wise course is to allow free competition in the struggle for life: the fittest will emerge. Now the State is an association for the protection of the incompetent: the self-reliant should assert his independence against "his enemy the State." This liberalism with a somber Darwinian tinge was that of the Manchester School: "Devil take the hindmost." With different ideologies, it belongs also to the world of the Bismarckians and the Nietzscheans. It is the very antithesis of Christianity, which was from the first the religion of the meek. Many political and economic liberals, however, are curiously

---

[2] It has often been remarked that we feel most free when we are most *determined*, i.e., when we know the reason why. In history, the men with the strongest will power were those who denied the freedom of the will: Stoics, Mohammedans, Calvinists, Jansenists, early Communists. Freedom is not chance or caprice.

[3] But in his *Social Contract,* conceived before he had had the revelation of Rousseauism, Jean-Jacques enacted a code of democratic tyranny, and begat Robespierre.

optimistic at heart. Like Mandeville, they hold that "private vices," such as ruthless greed, may turn into "public benefits." With Adam Smith, they believe that a Guiding Hand will harmonize the welter of self-seeking into a common good. Free competition, however, which is the freedom they cherish above all others, is not conducive to liberty. Under such a dispensation, the many would soon be enslaved; and the rulers themselves, constantly haunted by fear, would not be truly free.

In defiance of determinism, fatalism, and predestination, then, we move and act as though we had some freedom of choice. And that freedom implies an inevitable corollary: we have our share — again limited but all-important — of moral responsibility. We are men because of this freedom; and this freedom is inherent in thought. The inorganic world is not free. Creatures of instincts and reflexes are not free. Robots are not free. Men swayed unthinkingly by mass prejudices are not free. "By thought ye shall seek the truth; and the quest shall make you free." At this exact point, Liberalism and Humanism are one.

The coercion of thought is therefore an abridgment of man's essential liberty and a lowering of his dignity. I'd rather be in jail and keep the liberty of my mind, than be "free" to buy and sell to my heart's content while bartering away my integrity. For every human being, there is a hierarchy of values. Freedom of thought is to me what chastity is to the nun, physical courage to the warrior: not the whole of life, but a *sine qua non*.

Nonconformity is more than man's first privilege: it is man's highest duty. Not that I feel compelled to oppose every one at every point: *contra omnes in omnibus*. On the contrary, I take pride in being a congenital fellow traveler; I am sure I shall boast of it repeatedly in these pages. I like society, and the more varied the better. I am not ashamed to share opinions with the Man in the Street, and even with the Man in Wall Street. I am a more *catholic* American than most: I agree with everything that the Republicans have to say of the Democrats, and vice versa.

But this is the Land of Liberty, and I belong to the Free

World. My assent or my consent must be won by persuasion. If I am told that I must be free on the lines prescribed by the Attorney General, by various Congressional committees, even by Congress as a whole, I can only shrug my shoulders: this is too absurd to deserve discussion. Such tyranny may have to be taken tragically: men's lives are constantly wrecked by it; but it cannot be taken seriously. As a liberal and as a humanist, I reserve the right to follow my own line of thought. I shall keep on believing that two and two are four, and that Synghman Rhee is a ruler of questionable wisdom, even though a Cao-Daist or a Rosicrucian, a Jacobin or a Jacobite, should happen to agree with me. If this be contempt of Congress, make the most of it. The alternative would be self-contempt, which is much harder to face.

Franklin Roosevelt, who had a nimble mind in a crippled body, could swing with masterly ease from "freedom of" to "freedom from": translators found it hard to follow his flight. There is a marked difference between freedom of thought, and freedom from thought. The latter is by far the more comfortable: for thinking, born of pain, refines, but does not destroy, pain. Many sedatives have been devised to allay the malady of thought. The crudest is the one suggested by Pascal, in whom the pangs of thought reached tragic intensity:"Carry on religious practices: it will stupefy you." The cleverest is the devising of systems: systems turn spiritual anguish into a circular, effortless, innocuous motion. The pleasantest and most effective is success. When all is well with us, why think at all? It might disturb a delicate balance, for thinking is a subversive activity. As the English, in the eighteenth and nineteenth centuries, had reached preëminence in commerce, industry, politics, and war, they evolved the national dogma, curiously at odds with the facts, that it was un-English to think. (They never dared to say that it was un-Scottish.) Thinking was the vice of the *logical* French or the pedantic Germans. America, attaining in our own times an even more enviable degree of wealth and power, declared all *isms* to be foreign fads and perversions. Who in his senses would question the essential rightness of a society whose only harrowing problems are to find a parking space and a baby sitter? So our national schools of psychology, from Pragmatism to Behaviorism, are devoted to the minimizing or denial of thinking.

No contented herd has ever been known to think. Neither do the angels suffer from that affliction. But man is neither angel nor beast. So humanistic liberalism is capable of quiet defiance. It is a rule of life for the gentle, but not for the poor-spirited. It has in it a touch of stoic pride. As a code of *noblesse oblige,* it would be exposed to the charge of superciliousness, if it were not so freely open to those of scant learning and humble station. The French speak of *les professions libérales.* If the distinction between free and unfree, liberal and servile occupations were made hard and fast, it would become an obnoxious absurdity. The difference is deeper and more subtle. I have known men in the most respected professions who were by no means liberal in spirit. I have met humanistic liberals of the purest type among Parisian workingmen at the time of the Dreyfus crisis. I doubt not that many are to be found in the ranks of American labor: it has been my misfortune not to have come into contact with them.

The very essence of the liberal professions is that they rise above the notion of pelf. Priest, teacher, judge, lawyer, doctor, may receive compensation "so that they be free from worldly care." But no man worthy of his high calling will measure his skill according to his fee. There are no second-class surgical operations, no sacraments at bargain rates. The member of the liberal profession is free, not only from the tyranny of lucre, but from any authority which, in his chosen field, would attempt to bend his spirit. A surgeon must follow his own judgment. And although some lawyers do evince an uncanny dexterity in casuistry, one who for profit would consciously cheat justice deserves to be disbarred. The member of the most orthodox church does not teach what he is made to teach, against his own conscience; if he preaches a dogma, it is because he wholeheartedly believes in it. He may, like the soldier, be subject to material discipline; but he remains the master of his soul.

This double freedom exists among those whom we are
pleased to call the common people. I counted among my friends
at Stanford a cobbler from Martinique who was in every respect a gentleman. He was paid: the laborer is worthy of his
hire. But the relations between us were of man to man, and the
service counted for more than the pay. I have often noticed
with what pleasure people who had done some little job for me
would say: "No charge!" It was the magic password into the
liberal fellowship. The craftsman has his pride, like the artist.
He works for a customer, whom he must satisfy; but he will not
play fast and loose with his professional conscience. Such liberal conditions cannot easily prevail among people who are cogs
in a huge machine, from the highest paid technician to the
merest common laborer. But they are not debarred from the
liberal fellowship: their work done, they recover their freedom.
I am sure there are "humanistic liberals" at the work bench and
even on the assembly line: but to find one among the hucksters
would strike us as a miracle. Wherever they live and whatever
they do, men like my Stanford cobbler are the core of the Free
World, a commonwealth of the spirit, without a constitution
and without a territory.

We also use the word *liberal* in terms of finance: "a liberal
allowance." Here it is not the amount of money that is decisive,
but the spirit in which the money is tendered. The spendthrift
may not be more liberal than the niggard, but simply more of a
fool. The illiberals, a few years ago, jeered at "a quart of milk
for every Hottentot"; they showed themselves ready to pour
hundreds of billions into armaments, because that was "tough
and realistic." In this narrower but very legitimate sense, *liberal*
means *generous*. Generous not merely in terms of cash; but even
more in terms of understanding and sympathy. To be illiberal
is to be grudging and mean. The climax of the illiberal spirit
was reached by Calvin Coolidge, after the first great crusade to
make the world safe for democracy: "They hired the money,
didn't they?" — a palpable truth so mutilated that it became
more hateful than a lie. The irremediable curse of partisan politics is not wastefulness and incompetence, but meanness. A

society is not in a wholesome state when smearing becomes its chief concern, when the press and the air waves are filled with venomous denunciations, when principles are derided as "starry eyed," when long-range interests are denounced as unrealistic. To the liberal, there may be some excuse for crudity; there is none for meanness.

Of all freedoms — and more than four could be listed — the essential one is freedom from fear; for it is fear that paralyzes thought, and poisons even the plain and stodgy "freedom from want." The word *fear* is ambiguous. We must distinguish between the fear which is the reasonable anticipation of danger, and the vague fear that preys on the mind. The first is a warning light upon our path, the second spreads darkness. Man should be prudent, but not timorous. Evil is to be faced with open eyes; if it can not be averted, it should be stoically endured, never condoned. The fight is ennobling; defeat itself is not degrading. It is not death, but the fear of death, that is abjection. For the liberal, terror and torture are unwelcome facts, but they are not arguments. This means, against Margaret Fuller, that we are not required to accept the universe. As Pascal, Vigny, and — *longo intervallo* — Henley *Invictus* have taught, we are free to spurn the material world at the very moment when it is crushing us. I shall not bow down before the blind fury of the hurricane; and if I were told that back of the physical scourge, there is a cosmic spirit of vindictiveness, I should despise it all the more: brutal power is merely crude, vengeance is mean. But such a supposition is absurd: to believe in Hell is blasphemy.

If we are free from morbid fear, we shall also be free from unreasoning hate: for we hate only that which we obscurely dread. We do not hate a typhoon, a disease, a wild beast: we try to keep out of their way. Hate is bred by our own confusion: we hate in our enemy that which is struggling for mastery in our own hearts. In cruder terms: what we hate most in others is our own caricature. It reveals to us the Yahoo or the Hun that we are trying to ignore or conceal. We hate heretics worse than infidels, because they offer a more insidious temptation.

We hate rivals, because they have so much in common with us: pride, toughness, materialism, faith in *their* manifest destiny, reliance upon coercion to enforce a certain "way of life."

Both hatred and fear are the fruit of division and doubt. The man or the nation that is generous because self-assured cannot hate. That is why, in happier days, I borrowed from David Starr Jordan what I thought was the highest conception of America: *the land where hatred expires.* At this point, humanistic liberalism stops, and religion proceeds. Liberalism is freedom from hate, religion is love. As in this Christian land love is considered soft, and toughness is praised as the highest virtue, it is safer to be content with the negative phrasing: liberalism transcends hatred.[4]

Finally, we speak of "a liberal education": here again, *liberal* and *humanistic* come very close together. I wish we all could secure such an education on the same delightful terms as Richard Steele: "To love her," he said of Lady Elizabeth Hastings, "was a liberal education." A liberal education does not consist in acquiring fashionable skills and prejudices: horsemanship, the proper tie, and the threefold gospel of Mr. T. S. Eliot, so as to be fit for the society of gentlemen: this is snobbishness in ideal purity. The method suggested by Matthew Arnold, "getting to know the best that has been thought and said in the world," is only a means. By such a standard, Socrates would be far less *cultured* than, let us say, Paul Elmer More. But "through this knowledge," Arnold expects us to turn "a stream of fresh and free thought upon our stock notions and habits": a liberal education is an instrument of liberation. It takes us beyond fear and beyond hatred. It is a quiet and constant challenge to all the taboos. It may be summed up in the single word: *Why?* and more aptly still, in the great refusal to be bluffed or coerced out of our responsibility: *Why not?* This to me is the American, because it is the human, way of life.

[4] Cf. *Beyond Hatred: The Democratic Ideal in France and America* (London and New York, 1925).

CHAPTER II

Culture vs. Cultures

$\mathscr{I}$ had trained myself to be in France a teacher of English civilization. Fate, in the shape of Miss Wilhelmina Macartney — my Lady Elizabeth Hastings — decreed that I should become, in America, a teacher of French civilization. Civilization, or culture? From the first, I was struck with the ambiguities of both terms, and with the uncertainty of their boundaries. What I called, after Guizot and Buckle, history of civilization was known in German as *Kulturgeschichte*. The twenty-one civilizations of Arnold Toynbee might just as well be termed cultures. I have recently read an excellent volume of *Essays on Chinese Thought*: it is part of a series entitled "Comparative Studies in Cultures and Civilizations." I have no hope to teach the learned world, once for all, how the terms should be used. But it was my duty to find out how I was using them myself. In the process, certain conceptions had to be brought into sharper focus. Others did fade away altogether. Which was clear gain: for our minds are cluttered up with hesitant ghosts.

In my youth, the word *culture* in the Western languages denoted a thorough education, intended to develop harmoniously the innate capacities of the mind, and to serve as a guide for well-disciplined action. Culture was not necessarily linked with material progress: the sages of remote ages, and particularly the Greek philosophers, were thought of as men of high culture. It was not denied that an uncultured mind could possess magnificent possibilities, just as the jungle has more fertility than many a well-tilled area. But this potential wealth is to a large extent wasted until civilization — thought, purpose, effort — is brought to bear.

This is the conception of culture which was sponsored, and

splendidly exemplified, by Goethe. Matthew Arnold gave it currency in the English language; and as it became current, its freshly minted sharpness of outline was to some extent blurred. Arnoldian culture was closely followed by its own caricature: a blend of snobbishness and pedantry. It must be constantly borne in mind that for Arnold, as well as for Goethe, culture was "the pursuit of our total perfection." *Pursuit* implies purpose; *total* implies balance; *perfection*, which is unattainable, implies that culture is not an achievement but a quest. Culture then is not a commodity that can be purchased and then locked away among our own stores: this is a form of fetishism which is not special to pseudo culture; it has prevailed in all ages, and is rife with us today. It is of the same kind as literalism and ritualism in religion, or flag-waving in citizenship: spin your prayer wheels, buy the Hundred Best Books, and you shall be saved. Boston at the end of the nineteenth century was singled out as the pattern of such *culture*. H. G. Wells, a lusty vulgarian, made fun of that bloodless community: not even a hothouse, but a museum of glass flowers. The fact that William James, Henry Adams, and George Santayana belonged to that frigid circle seems to have escaped the critics.

When Edward Burnett Tylor published in 1871 his great book on *Primitive Culture*, the title came with the tang of a paradox, but it was not an absurdity. The work was subtitled *Researches into the Development of Mythology, Philosophy, Language, Art and Custom*. No one doubts but all these activities belong to the domain of *culture* (still in the singular): even *custom*, in the sense of *good manners*. What Tylor did establish was that efforts in those fields were not restricted to our own times, or to those luminous ages in the past whose achievements remain our most precious possessions. The cultural urge, in forms which offer a high degree of elaboration, exists among people whom we consider primitive.

This should lead us to recast our notion of the primitive. Rousseau's primitive man is a myth; and Rousseau himself came very near admitting it. In the interminable chain from animality to our present happy and glorious condition, the ancient primitives, and those arrested communities which survive today as living fossils, are infinitely closer to us than they are to the brute. Anthropology, in the sense it has acquired since Tylor, might well be a needed antidote to Boston superciliousness. Just as Molière's Alceste preferred an uncouth folk song to an inane sophisticated sonnet, we have come to appreciate the spirited cave drawings of the Magdalenian period and the vigorous carvings of West Africa far above the banal perfection of Andrea del Sarto. What we find in such works of primitive art, as well as in the efforts of gifted children, is a striving to understand, to explore, to create. Primitive societies were once dynamic. If they reached the stage of frozen pseudoclassicism — the end of the quest, the perfect equilibrium which means death — that is a peril which threatens all ages. The blight upon such arrested societies is not their primitiveness, for freshness is a promise: it is their premature senility.

The word *culture*, however, assumed in anthropology and sociology a meaning antagonistic to the Goethean: not striving, but acquiescence; not originality, but conformity. The responsibility for the change does not rest entirely with Tylor and his disciples. It goes back to the eighteenth century, and the revolt of the Obscurantists against the Enlightenment. It was at that time that the doctrine of unconscious growth was evolved, in order to minimize or undermine the faith in determined effort. According to that school, planning and questing alike are vanity. There are no sudden deaths in Nature, and there can be no new departures. It is a delusion to hold that a poet of genius named Homer deliberately composed the *Iliad*: Homer is a myth, and the *Iliad* matured obscurely out of a thousand ballads. It is foolishness to believe that men, consciously and at a definite time, can write a constitution or found a city: the sole legitimate constitution is an inchoate mass of precedents, the only valid city planner is the cow whose random track, in the course of generations, turns of its own accord into a well-beaten path and ultimately into a well-paved street. This is the doctrine of Joseph de Maistre, who prophesied with superb assurance that the proposed city of Washington would never be built. Above all, it was the creed of Edmund Burke, who fanatically denounced the French Revolution because it strove to apply intelligence to human affairs. Burke chose to forget that England had gone through two revolutions, and had produced a number of lucid, vigorous treatises on government, before she could afford to relax into the safety and comfort of *unthinking*.

In the scientific nineteenth century, the natural sciences were pressed into service. Change was not denied: indeed it was affirmed as a cardinal principle, under the name of evolution. But such a change required aeons. Lyell, in geology, discredited the notion of catastrophe, in the same way as Burke had shown the ineptitude of revolution. The word *organic* came into favor: a beautiful romantic metaphor which has drugged many a sober scientist. Society was founded not on a *Social Contract* which the parties could amend at will, but on a mass of material conditions, traditions, habits, mores, so huge, so cohesive, that it was beyond the power of any man or any generation perceptibly to alter it. Thoughts, beliefs, rules of conduct, institutions, ceremonies, symbols, which were the human expression of these deep realities, partook of the same character: they could be modified only in accordance with their secret inner law, and with geologic gradualness.

To this *organic* complex, in which interdependence and continuity were the essential factors, the anthropologists attached the name of *culture*. Its manifestations obviously differed in time and space: there is no single human culture, there is an infinite variety of cultures. The term applies most definitely to the primitives, ancient or contemporary, because their way of life seems to us unaffected by purposive thinking: they rest content in Burke's haven, the wisdom of prejudice. But, more questionably, the word *culture* was applied also to vast historical or geographical groups: *periods* in history, *nations* at the present time. There was a medieval culture. There is a Chinese culture: ask Messrs. Mao Tse Tung and Chou En Lai. There was most definitely a German culture, and Hitler, not Goethe, was its prophet. In America, we call it our "Way of Life."

I shall not insist upon the absurdity of using the word *cul-*

ture, i.e., deliberate cultivation, to denote the result of unconscious growth and unreasoning acquiescence. Such contradictions in terms are all too familiar: we keep referring to "a Catholic nationalist," "an orthodox Protestant," "a Christian soldier," as though the terms thus coupled were not wholly incompatible. I am not grudging my tribute to the vast amount of investigation done by the anthropologists and its fascinating results: studies in cultures are among my favorite readings. But anthropology is a science, and in science the facts presented must have some relevancy, and this requires a body of thought: a mere collection of curiosities will not do.

Now there is much in anthropological thought that strikes me as sound. I firmly believe that no single human activity can be wholly dissociated from all the others: that is why *Homo Œconomicus* was such an inane fallacy. I believe also that human thought is neither eternal nor instantaneous: it exists *in time*, and the boldest dreams have their roots in the past. Voltaire called his universal history an *Essay on Manners*, and he recognized the formidable power of tradition, explicit or barely conscious, under the name of *custom*. I am not therefore attacking anthropology, but the current — the passing — doctrine of *cultures*.[1] To this doctrine I have two objections. The first is that it enormously exaggerates the homogeneity of the cultural group. The second is that it turns an acceptable statement of fact — "There are preëxisting collective forces which condition our thought and action" — into a commandment: "Thou shalt accept this particular determinism."[2] I mean this *Testament* to be a practical book: do not believe that I am indulging in the discussion of tenuous theories. I am attempting to understand what is meant by *un-American*. And this is essential if we want to preserve "life, liberty, and the pursuit of happiness."

[1] Two very learned ladies, Ruth Benedict and Margaret Mead, personally assured me that the mystic-romantic conception of cultures as organism is waning.

[2] The formula "acceptance of a determinism" was coined by Maurice Barrès. The *determinism* was summed up as *"la terre et les morts"*: the soil and the dead.

I am no Pico della Mirandola, no Arnold Toynbee (and, I may add with modest pride, no Oswald Spengler either). But certain things I do know by experience, at first hand; others I know pretty definitely, at second-hand no doubt, but not without critical inquiry. And through this knowledge, imperfect as it is, I feel able to turn a stream of fresh and free thought upon what I am told, not only of Middletown, but of the Zuñi Indians and the Trobrianders.

When I came to this country, I was told very definite things about *The French*, which I knew positively not to be so. I have been tempted to write, ironically, an *Essay on France and the French* which would be a catalogue of popular (and learned) misconceptions. I have been restrained by the fear that it might be taken at its face value and become a best seller. In most of my books, from *French Civilization in the Nineteenth Century* (1914) to *Education of a Humanist* (1949), I have had to fight against those loose, ubiquitous and indestructible phantoms, *the Soul of France, the French Character* — and I have fought in vain. I am weary of repeating that Rabelais was not Calvin, that Molière was not Pascal, that Voltaire was not Rousseau; that Guizot, Lamennais, Lacordaire, Victor Cousin, Michelet, Proudhon, Veuillot, worlds asunder, were the flowers of the same society. At every turn, in every generation, I found Frenchmen who agreed with certain foreigners better than with some of their compatriots. "Rather Hitler than Blum!" was not an isolated blasphemy: with variations, it had echoed through the ages.

There were in France a few moments of almost miraculous unanimity: the voluntary abandonment of feudal privileges on August 4, 1789, Armistice Day on November 11, 1918. They were few, and they were fleeting: sober dawn brought misgivings. Collective life is made up, not of unanimities, but of tensions. This is true not merely of national "cultures": it is true also of those abstractions which, although not formally organized like the nations, are actually more real, the *Periods*: the atmosphere, the *Zeitgeist* of the eighteenth century is something more vital than the governments of Sir Robert Walpole or Cardinal Fleury. Definite periods, of repose or of revolution, are rare: human annals are a tale of endless confusion. But even in the periods which seem to possess an organic unity of their own, their apparent harmony is due to discipline, not to free consent. Much as I admire Henry Adams, I think his *Mont-Saint-Michel and Chartres* is a brilliant satire rather than a serious contribution to history: he used his retrospective Utopia as a foil to show up the ambiguities and contradictions of his own time, just as Tacitus gave an idealized picture of the Germans in order to criticize imperial Rome. As a matter of plain fact, men in the Age of Faith were even more tragically divided in their minds than we are. At the dawn of French literature, we find the *Song of Roland*, with a faith that is stark and pure — although it is a paradoxical compound of Odinic prowess and Christian humility; and by the side of that stern epic, we have *The Pilgrimage of Charlemagne*, a tale as irreverent as Voltaire's *Pucelle*. At the height of the medieval period, we are told of children flocking to a crusade: the little ones whom Jesus loved felt destined to redeem His tomb; but we also encounter the shipowners who offered them free transportation, and sold them to the Saracens. In the uneasy dusk of that Age of Faith, we see Gilles de Rais the pervert and aesthete fighting by the side of St. Joan.

What struck me about all those alleged unanimities was that most of them were enforced, and some of them by means of utter ruthlessness. The Church had a short way with heretics: "Kill them all! God will recognize His own!" On the miniature stage of Geneva, Calvin was no less stern in repressing dissent. The massacre of the Huguenots on the Night of St. Bartholomew's was a great purge of subversives; and as such it was hailed by all the rightminded from the Pope down. "One faith, one law, one king": that Hitler-like formula had been invented two centuries before Louis XIV: but he did his best to turn it into a fact, and the liberal or pluralistic Edict of Nantes was revoked. The Revolution imposed Fraternity as well as Liberty: "Be my brother, or I'll kill you." Rosas was an admirable defender of the Argentine Way of Life when he had all schoolchildren open their classes with the chant: ¡*Mueran los salvajes, inmundos, asquerosos Unitarios!*[3] I wish Clemenceau the journalist had been free to sum up the policy of Clemenceau the dictator: "All good Frenchmen are unanimously in favor of my policy: fight to the bitter end. Those who differ are traitors, and will be shot." [4]

In the course of history, organic unity, unconscious harmony, impressed me not as realities but as dreams; and — the old phrase inevitably springs to mind — "not even beautiful dreams." So I began to wonder whether they did exist in the realm explored by the anthropologists. We are informed that the primitives punish with the utmost rigor every infringement of the taboos: which proves that the taboos are not self-enforcing. Investigators will duly note outward conformities, since these are the facts they are looking for. They do not pause to consider that the conformities may be as shallow as they are obvious. Some members of the community may believe heart and soul in the enforced orthodoxy and its ritual. Others may conform out of sheer passivity; some out of self-interest; some out of cowardice. Many dissent at heart, but do not care to fight: even Rabelais and Descartes, those heroes of thought, strove to keep on the safe side of the stake, and accepted, with crossed fingers, "the French Way of Life." Are there no mute inglorious Rabelais and Descartes among the Samoans and the Trobrianders? Even in the most backward tribes, there are a few who dare to rebel: a later generation may hail them as emancipators and martyrs.

For submission to a cultural determinism is by no means inevitable. Evidently it is safer to conform. When it comes to the law of gravity, we'd better accept the universe. But you never know whether a taboo is a law of nature or a superstition

[3] "Death to the savage, obscene, disgusting Centralists!"
[4] Perhaps the best example of a *culture* that never attained organic unity is that of the Jews. With the Torah as an inflexible rule, and God jealously watching over His people, the annals of the Jews offer a lurid tale of strife, rebellions, relapses into idolatry. The Prophetic Books are a splendid testimony to the constant strain of dissent. And the Jews of today, whether in Israel or in the Diaspora, are not more united than their remote ancestors.

until you try the experiment. Kapiolani, in December 1824, descended into the crater of Kilauea, to defy the Fire Goddess Pele; and Pele ceased from troubling.

The *organic* trend of thought, so dear to the anthropologists, might lead us into sheer absurdity. Two can play at that game. We might be told, in the same spirit: "Never remove a diseased appendix, a tumor, even a callus: they are natural growths, and Nature knows best." This is no heavy-handed irony: it is exactly on a level with the doctrine: "Do not interfere with native cultures: you would destroy their spontaneous and age-ripened vital equilibrium. Do not deprive African or Polynesian tribes of their fetishes, taboos, human sacrifices, cannibalism, slavery." If Burke were living today, he would prophesy that it spells destruction for India to root out the caste system, the pariahs, the sacred cows, suttee, purdah, child marriages: India will find herself "deculturized," an anaemic body without a soul. China is rushing toward the abyss: the Chinese elected to cut off their pigtails and to unbind their women's feet. All Christian missionaries, all carriers of Western thought, all advocates of democracy, are wholesale murderers of the spirit. A convert like Chiang Kai-shek can only be a monster: he has cut himself off from all that had been for aeons the spiritual life-stream of his people. England and France are both engaged in Westernizing West Africa: England by creating autonomous governments patterned after her own, France by giving the natives full and free access to the French community: but there are anthropologists who shake their heads at both methods alike. Even Governor General Eboué, himself a perfect example of cultural assimilation, was of two minds on the subject: at times his thought was human and rational, at times it worked on anthropological lines.[5]

[5] A striking example of the "anthropological" attitude was offered in New Zealand by Professor Ralph Piddington, of Auckland University. New Zealand's treatment of the Maoris has been a model of fairness. The equality promised them in 1840 remains the rule. They mingle at all levels with European society. Some have risen high in the professions, and received knighthoods. All wrong, said Professor Piddington. The best would be for Maoris and Europeans to live side by side, but separately, recognizing and respecting their differences. This resembles in

Unanimity and stagnation are two names for a single disease, the arteriosclerosis of a society. The living facts (I, too, am a believer in biology!) are infinite variety and constant striving. The heresy I am denouncing is *cultural totalitarianism*: every one within the group — be it tribe or nation — should believe in the same myths, cherish the same traditions, observe the same taboos. Such a condition (we call it *hundred-per-centism*) is obviously not natural; it has to be enforced; and every totalitarianism turns into a tyranny. The liberal attitude, on the contrary, the creed and rule of the Free World, is *pluralistic dynamism*. In every society, primitive as well as sophisticated, there are many strains of descent, biological and cultural, many trends, conscious or obscure, many divergent desires. A collective Way of Life is rather a *modus vivendi*: not a rigid, all-embracing code, but a constant adjustment of conflicts.

This is true not of the social group merely, but of the individual as well. Every man has in his heart and mind multitudinous traditions and aspirations. We all belong to all the ages. There are in us predatory and possessive instincts which are paleolithic. Most of us have a Greek philosophy, a Roman conception of law, a Judeo-Hellenic religion, a political system which goes back to 1688 or 1789, an economic thought arrested in 1776 (*Wealth of Nations*) or in 1847 (*Communist Manifesto*). Only our technology is of the latest pattern. And we belong also to the ages to come, for the present is lighted (dimly) and shaped (feebly) by our hopes. No man, in the most homogeneous community, is exactly like any other man: cultural personalities are as unique as thumbprints. And no man conforms, in all things and from hour to hour, to a single formula. The truculent Senator or the Tycoon who attend church on Sunday morning live in a different cultural climate on Monday morning; and on Monday night, still another aspect of their personalities may emerge.

---

spirit our Southern compromise: "equal but separate accommodation." It leads straight to South Africa's *Apartheid*. The interesting point is that this anthropological proposal created a storm of protest on the part of the Maori community.

In man, tribe, or nation, we have to take into account the dead weight, the inertia, the momentum: that is why I have no faith in sudden and total conversion, in revolution, in Utopia through victory. But we must be aware also of the adventurous urge, the creative power, the dynamism. The data, the actual facts at any moment, cannot be ignored: without ores, there could be no metallurgy. But purposive energy is not less essential: without metallurgy, there would be no usable metals. And it is metallurgy that discovers the ores; tomorrow, it might succeed in extracting magnesium from the sea rather than from the earth. In other words, for every man or nation the essentials are not traditions and taboos, but life, liberty, and the pursuit of happiness. And this most orthodox formula defines *culture* according to Goethe and Matthew Arnold, rather than *cultures* according to the anthropologists of yesterday. For blind attachment to the past is not life, but stagnation and death. Unreasoning acceptance of cultural patterns is the reverse of liberty; and the "pursuit of happiness" comes close to Arnold's "pursuit of our total perfection."

After voicing my disagreement with certain distortions of anthropology, I want to affirm in closing this section my sense of the great services, practical as well as theoretical, that this young science has rendered. First of all, it has created in us a new respect and a new sympathy for certain forms of life widely different from our own. It made us realize that the "primitives" need not be "savages," that the "uncivilized" have "culture." They have asked themselves the essential questions, and offered elaborate answers. The true primitives, in the contemptuous sense of the term, are the men who care not at all about religion and society, and who think only of their own pleasures and profits.

Then anthropology works beautifully, and ironically, in reverse. An exotic culture which offers a definite pattern is a fascinating and sobering caricature of our own. It makes it plain that we too have blind traditions, fetishes, taboos, castes, sacred cows. We can easily imagine a super-anthropologist from Mars or Altruria puzzled and entertained by our systematic yet non-rational behavior. As in other branches of studies, the *comparative* is the path to the *general*. It leads us from literatures to literature, from religions to religion, from cultures to culture.

Above all, I believe that anthropology is wise in warning us: "Do not attempt, suddenly, forcibly to impose a new culture — your own — upon an alien people. The result will be fierce resistance; and, if resistance collapses, an inner tragedy." We now realize that our stewardship of the Philippines might have been conducted on different lines. Cultural patterns are slowly matured. To convert an Asian or African tribe, overnight, to sectarian literalism, jealous nationalism, the party system, the profit motive, might not be an unmixed blessing. We can use these to good purpose, because we have become immune to the evils they contain; others, not so inured, might greatly suffer. American plants brought the phylloxera blight, which killed French vines. Measles, fairly innocuous for Europeans, proved deadly among the native Hawaiians.

Our rule should be: Respect all the forms of life which are not patently harmful. We may even enjoy their quaintness: the native streets of Morocco are charming, and who should want to do away with the British Lion and Unicorn? Anthropology is an admirable guide for tourists, if an unsafe one for statesmen. Above all, do not obtrude your own fetishes. But foster, among other culture groups, and within your own, the dynamic element, the impatience with manifest evils, the desire for a richer life. This was the policy of Lyautey in Morocco: not to crush, but to reawaken, native pride and native energy; so that the many elements in the land, Berbers, Arabs, indigenous Jews, Europeans, without destroying or repudiating their past, might work together for a freer and saner society. This is the doctrine of *converging evolution*: from tribal customs to a world commonwealth. Fanatics may wreck such an ideal: let us see to it that they are not aided and abetted, as the Nazis were, by pseudo anthropology.

CHAPTER III

Civilization and Culture

No one has the right to alter the accepted meaning of a word. But many usurp that right, and get away with it. Thus, as we have seen, anthropologists use *culture* to denote the exact reverse of culture. Atrocities have been deliberately perpetrated by "civilized" people in the name of civilization. Language is a lawless jungle, and we are waiting in vain for the return of that semantic Angel who, according to Mallarmé, "once imparted a purer sense to the words of the tribe." [1]

For the purposes of my teaching and of my books, I had to adopt definitions of *civilization* and *culture* that would offer a modicum of consistency. I did my utmost to shun originality. My interpretations, if not literally borrowed from a popular dictionary, at least are not in conflict with the general acceptations. I do not profess to know what civilization and culture mean in the Absolute and the Eternal. I suspect that in such a Platonic realm they have no meaning whatsoever: they are of the earth earthly. At any rate, I trust the reader will have no hesitation about what *I* mean by these terms.

Civilization, to me, stands for organized society. Etymology, in which as a rule I have no great faith, happens to be on my side. An individual living from birth in complete isolation could hardly be civilized. A chance congregation of men without common purposes, without institutions to further these purposes, is not a civilization. Organization implies consciousness: were it only the obscure, nonlogical consciousness found in

---

[1] Stéphane Mallarmé, *Le Tombeau d'Edgar Poë*:
  "*Eux, comme un vil sursaut d'hydre oyant jadis l'Ange
  Donner un sens plus pur aux mots de la tribu. . .* "
Two of the most pregnant and most beautiful lines in the French language. I fervently hope they mean something.

mores, customs, taboos, folkways. These collective norms are not instinctive, although they may be the result of instincts. They are transmitted and enforced. But they do not inevitably demand a written code and a political philosophy. At this point, there is only a difference in degree between cultures and civilizations.

Primo vivere: man's primary concern is now and was from the beginning his daily fight for survival. All other interests lose their urgency before the necessity of securing food and shelter. Hunger and cold were our first taskmasters; and the blessèd desire to ward them off with the minimum of painful exertion remains our greatest teacher. In his struggle for life, man made, unconsciously at first, two tremendous discoveries. The first was that he could work to better effect in collaboration with his fellow man: he is by nature, and he has grown increasingly, *sociable*; the permanent family, the tribe, the state, have become his necessary environment. The second discovery was that he need not be resigned to the brutish state of automatic adaptation which poets call the Earthly Paradise. By taking thought, he could add to the gifts of nature. He could, within incredibly elastic limits, select his surroundings and even alter them. He could lengthen his arm with a club, borrow furs from creatures better provided than himself, create at will a small circle of summer warmth with a few sticks of burning wood. From the earliest stone implement to the wireless, the airplane, or atomic power, from the first concerted hunt to the elaborate insurance machinery of a modern state, we can trace the progress of this collective and masterful collaboration of man with nature. Society and the useful arts are the essential instruments of civilization.

At this point, there are two misconceptions that must be challenged. The first is that, since civilization is organization, the more complex the organization the higher the civilization. Nothing of the sort: it is quite possible for a civilization to hamper itself through excessive organization, and there is a kind of sophistication which is a sure sign of decay. The end of the middle ages is a case in point. Then scholastic theology, feudal law, the rules of heraldry, the study of genealogy, the minute regulations of guilds and crafts, all suffered from the same blight: they had become fantastically intricate.

In many cases, progress is simplification: from the serried steely prescriptions of Leviticus and Deuteronomy to the two commandments which Christ declared to be all-sufficient. A less controversial example: by 1800, there was in France an incredible mass of legislation: custom law was still widespread and potent (it had left traces in the Paris of my youth), the memories of Roman law and canon law lingered, the edicts accumulated by the kings survived, and for ten years, the Revolutionary assemblies had been pouring forth a stream of chaotic statutes. Under the Consulate, a committee of jurists, prodded by the young head of the State, Napoleon Bonaparte, turned that rank jungle into a classical French garden, the *Civil Code*, a triumph of civilization. Mr. Herbert Hoover long nursed the hope that he might simplify the exuberance of our public administration: the efficiency of a service is not measured by the number of its Assistant Vice-Directors. The same rule obtains in the arts. I am not averse to the ornate, if it be disciplined, and functionalism to me is but a mangled truth: still, the very fine Alexander III Bridge in Paris would be greatly improved if it were stripped of every adventitious ornament. Therefore it is possible to seek simplicity without advocating a return to the primitive. As a matter of fact, it may happen that the primitive is complex: civilization introduces order, which is the pruning off of useless complications. Otto Jespersen has shown that a highly developed language could be simpler in structure than the speech of certain primitive tribes. English accidence and syntax are marvels of economy. The full grammar of Esperanto can be printed on a postcard, while a compendious grammar of French or Latin would fill a hundred pages. Giuseppe Peano, the mathematical logician, came to the startling conclusion: "The best grammar is the simplest; the simplest is no grammar at all."

The second fallacy is that civilization is purely material. This has been exposed times out of number; but it will probably be reasserted on the very morning of Judgment Day. It is no paradox to say that civilization is essentially *moral*, in the literal sense of the term: it is identical with morality. Civilization is the quest for security, decency, comfort, which, if not ethical in themselves, are primary conditions of all ethical values. Civilization consists in curbing the brutal, antisocial instincts, greed and violence: in their obvious forms, theft and murder, but also in their less virulent manifestations, self-seeking, self-assertion, bullying. A civilized community is a company of gentlemen: the man who grabs and jostles, the man who "gets tough," is not civilized. The vulgarian may be farther from the goal than the barbarian. And the code by which the vulgarian (man or nation), conducts his life is: "Myself, first, last, and all the time." Perhaps the first commandment of civilization is: "*Après vous.*" Now large elements of Roman society under the Antonines had reached a very high degree of civilization without any of our modern gadgets. A well-ordered summer camp in the wilds, on a very primitive material level, is a fine product of civilization, whilst a gangster is not, even though he should make use of a jet airplane, and of the latest model of machine guns. Men who resort to war, with atomic weapons instead of stone axes, are reverting to barbarism.

The aim of civilization is to liberate us from worldly cares. A man threatened with violent death at every crossroad is not free: security is the first condition of freedom. A man reduced to starvation is not free; a man brutalized by exhausting labor is not free; neither is the man whose thought is absorbed by financial worries, from the clerk compelled to pawn his watch to the magnate whom a depression drives to suicide. Every state strives to be a welfare state: try to find the sturdy individualist who will dare to profess that his ideal commonwealth is dedicated to the danger and discomfort of its members! Therefore, every society is by definition *social* and socialistic. Through organization, it seeks to lighten our common burden. I have often professed myself a philosophical anarchist. But there is a plane on which anarchism means the destruction of civilization. On that plane, which is the political and economic, a liberal seeks for a more enlightened government, not for the sweeping away of all government.

The reward of such a civilization is leisure. If insecurity and waste are reduced, man will have free time, that is to say time to be free. He may make the most outrageous use of that free time. He may manufacture silly gadgets or play silly games. He may spend his spare hours destroying what he has saved, through conspicuous waste or through war. But down the ages, leisure has also given him time to reflect and to dream. Literature, arts, philosophy, religion, are the fruit of such liberation. The slave who works until he drops dead with sleep is debarred from that higher realm: no matter whether the force that drives him be the lash or the profit motive.

These activities beyond the decent maintenance of physical life are what I call *culture*; and I repeat that I have on my side etymology, Goethe, and Matthew Arnold — an impressive trinity. Culture is made possible by civilization, if by civilization we understand the concerted efforts which create security and leisure. But — here is the paradox, the challenge to Taine, Karl Marx, and all economic interpreters of history — culture does not depend upon any particular kind of civilization. Whether the "system" be patriarchal, tribal, feudal; theocratic, autocratic, plutocratic; pastoral, agricultural, commercial, industrial: provided it creates leisure — time to be human — it will serve. It will not serve equally well: I believe there are degrees in civilization. That civilization is best which produces, not the largest possible amount of goods, but the largest amount of freedom, i.e., leisure, and distributes that precious commodity most equitably. But it is not civilization that determines the quality of our leisure. Again, we may use it to get drunk, to fight, or, less harmfully, to whittle sticks. We may also use it to sing, to ponder, and to wonder.

Culture, made possible by civilization, leaves civilization behind: it is bad manners to talk shop in polite society. This is why a humanistic brotherhood exists, across weary miles and dim centuries, among all minds liberated for culture. The men who in the remote past have reached that realm of freedom are our fellow citizens today; our next-door neighbor is not, if he is totally engrossed in material cares. So we can enjoy *Job* and *Antigone*, even though their civilizations and ours have practically nothing in common. It is not the mission of the humanities to teach contempt for civilization: the good servant deserves respect and gratitude, Martha should be honored, even though Mary has chosen the better part. But we should bear in mind that the sole purpose of civilization is to increase our opportunities for culture.

Without such a guiding principle, civilization would fall into decay: striving to be self-sufficient, it would become self-devouring. To insure security through the protection of arms is, at times, a legitimate form of civilization; but, if all-absorbing, as it was with the fighting caste in early feudal times, it turns into a peril. To produce more efficiently is the very basis of civilization; but if we think first of all of stimulating consumption in order to increase production, culture will be stifled. For the sake of mere living, we shall forfeit the real values of life. Next to "My country, right or wrong!" the most deadly heresy in the world is: "America's (or Russia's) business is Business." It is not wrong that the soldier and the businessman should be at the head of affairs, provided they are never allowed to forget that they are the servants, not the masters and not even the guides, of the community; provided they keep their steely fingers off the delicate processes of culture. I am not proposing a Platonic republic ruled by philosophers. I have been working for a democracy in which *the individual*, in the sanctity of his leisure hours, will be ruled by philosophy, the love of wisdom. Such a citizen will accept all necessary material labor and discipline: but he will never allow his officials to cramp his soul. My Utopia — a very definite goal — is a highly organized community of philosophical anarchists.

In the half-century of my academic career, I have been a student and teacher of civilization *and* culture. In two companion volumes, *Literature and Society, Art for Art's Sake*, I have attempted to trace the elusive line between the two, and their very active, very beneficial interactions across that line.

I am not a Manichean: the *business* of life cannot be wholly evil, if life itself is not rejected. Indeed, the business of life has certain delightful aspects: like my master Voltaire,[2] I am not ashamed of worldly pleasures. But if living is turned into an art, it is menaced by frivolousness or perversity.

Almost every activity is capable of being either *pure* or *applied*, and both branches are legitimate. Practical men had no call to despise Einstein because, for decades, he ventured into strange seas of thought alone; devotees of *culture* have no cause to cast him into outer darkness, because his theories are now linked with a tremendous release of energy and because the most obvious application of that energy is murderous: applied — and misapplied — higher physics. The most disinterested of the sciences, astronomy, serves as an aid to navigation, and is the basis of chronometry. Biology is a pure science; medicine a useful art, a social function; yet we do not consider the practicing physician as inferior to the research worker. Philosophy is the quintessence of thought: but philosophical hypotheses, philosophical processes, philosophical training, can and should be made available to education, psychology, history, government, law. Love belongs to the realm of the ideal: it is indeed the one adumbration we have of that realm. Marriage is an institution which offers definite worldly advantages, and entails definite responsibilities, legal as well as moral. But love need not be frightened away by matrimony, and the purest love match is heading for disaster if it is not also, to an acceptable degree, a *mariage de convenance* and a *mariage de raison.* The core of religion is mystic faith, the direct communication between the individual soul and the Mystery which is the ultimate reality. But this does not condemn institutional churches, rites, ministrations, teaching, charities, and even the providing of innocent social pleasures.

Civilization is collective well-being; culture is the striving for individual perfection. When the difference is recognized and accepted, the essential point is to keep the two distinct, yet not separate. My *Delenda Carthago* is what I called elsewhere the

[2] Cf. his sprightly poem *Le Mondain*, an apology for refined luxury.

Excelsior! fallacy: to do lip service to the ideal, and banish it altogether from the practical world.

Here the problem becomes extremely delicate. It is evident that, on the plane of purely material applications, ideal considerations have no place. When you want to buy the best article for your money, you are *Homo Œconomicus* in his stark simplicity. When you are solving an equation or performing a chemical experiment, you are steering clear of all theological hypotheses. But there is a level on which it is important for you to decide whether it would be right to buy an object, irrespective of its cheapness. You may have scruples, because it was made by sweated labor, or because its sale would help a power which you consider inimical. You may rule that it would be sinful to indulge in idle luxury when your family, or your neighbors, or some of your fellow citizens, or even certain remote human beings, are suffering from want. It may be futile, at given moments, to spend your time on some forms of scientific research. It may even be criminal: the death-factories at Buchenwald and Dachau had well-equipped laboratories. In his practical life, the devotee of culture, poet, artist, or priest, is subject to the law of civilization: decency and efficiency.[3] But the servant of civilization, on his part, is subject to the philosophy of culture. Both should strive to do well that which is well worth doing.

We are living in a world, not of sharp irreconcilable antitheses, but of dissolving pictures. (This, incidentally, might be stated in Hegelian terms, and thus receive a warrant of profundity.) Philistine civilization considers culture not as an enemy, but as the flower of human life: with the qualification that flowers are not very substantial food, and that, in profusion, they might clutter up the work bench or the counter. The Philistines even strive to produce culture by factory methods:

---

[3] Courtesy, a social virtue, is part of civilization (politeness, urbanity). It has nothing to do with gadgets, and especially with the machine. In the realm of culture, which is that of freedom, the rules of courtesy are irrelevant. No poet or prophet will be curbed by the fear that he may seem rude to the well-bred. But the highest culture — charity — carries with it inner courtesy.

I have heard universities described as *refining plants*. More: there is a gleam of culture within the darkest Philistinism. The perfect Philistine is a pure artist in his own line: he turns the sale of shoe polish or bubble gum into a method of self-realization.[4] Great administrators, captains of industry, are virtuosi whose instruments are railroads, canned foods, plastics. Napoleon said: "Power is my violin." The Fords, Rockefellers, Du Ponts de Nemours are composing the great symphony, writing the mighty epic, of American life. Certainly we have no work of culture in the traditional sense that can match their achievements in scale or quality.

Conversely, the mystic, philosopher, artist, has to be a Philistine for nine parts out of ten of his waking life. Even his religious or artistic activities cannot be kept on a strictly "cultural" plane. If the mystic ceases to be an anchorite, in rapt communion with the Ineffable, he becomes an apostle, a preacher, the founder or director of an order: St. Bernard complained that he was constantly wrenched away from solitude, his only happiness, and St. Teresa was a vigorously practical woman. The poet's motive is not purely the silent joy of self-realization. He is not satisfied with the part of a mute inglorious Milton. He craves for recognition: else he would not attempt to publish, he would not even write. Now recognition is a *social* fact. It is part of civilization. It posits certain economic conditions, a common education, at least a common language. It depends to a marked degree on "race, environment and time." It translates itself into material rewards: privileges, honors, and in coarsest form, money. Before we cast a stone at the artist who is "in the business," let us remember that Shakespeare, Molière, and Ibsen, no less than Scribe or Sardou, Jacinto Benavente, Sacha Guitry, or Noel Coward, had an eye on the box office. Walter Scott, Balzac, Dickens, Zola ran, single-handed, efficient and profitable novel-factories; Dumas was the head of a whole organization. Again, *pure* and *applied* are terms which have no aesthetic or moral connotation: I en-

---

[4] Cf. Sinclair Lewis: *Work of Art*: Hotel management as a form of aesthetics.

joy the *applied* art of Shakespeare better than the *pure* art of many poets.

It takes some reflection to realize how large a proportion of artistic creation is really of a *social* nature. Any manifestation of the spirit, in art, thought, or religion, that is intended for the public ceases to be purely individual, becomes collectivistic, takes its place in civilization. There is a finely graded hierarchy from *pure* business [5] to *The Divine Comedy* or *Faust*. Nearest to the business level, we find the arts of *reproduction*: printing, engraving, casting, photography, recording. They are secondary or ancillary no doubt, arts only in the sense of crafts or techniques; but they deal with artistic material, they appeal to the aesthetic sense, they demand of their practitioners a fair degree of artistic sensitivity. Then we find the arts of *documentation*: a great deal of painting and statuary, the whole of historical writing and travel descriptions, journalism, and, according to the avowed intention of their authors, the bulk of realistic art. Next we shall place the arts of *decoration*, painting and sculpture again, architecture even in our functional days, landscaping, interior decoration, jewelry, costume, and cosmetics. Men of culture are not indifferent to such arts, which are the utmost refinement of civilization. Finally, there are the arts of *suasion*: salesmanship, advertising (the most prolific and the best rewarded), education, propaganda: with the three mighty branches of eloquence: political, forensic, and religious. The purpose of all these arts is not to probe the Mystery, but to make this world a pleasanter place. Lest this should sound too cruelly Philistine, let us reword it negatively, with Baudelaire: "to make the universe less hideous and the moments less heavy." If we were to sweep all these from the temple of art, it would appear bare and deserted, with only, according to the old ballad,

> Dada chirping in the rafters,
> Gertrude crooning in the crypt. . .

The distinction we are attempting to draw between civiliza-

[5] *Pure* business? If chemically pure, business becomes a racket. For the racket is based on the profit motive unashamed, without any pious nonsense of uplift or social service.

tion and culture cannot therefore be of a material nature. The key is *the predominant intention*. We sell hosiery, or we twist wires "abstractedly," for a variety of motives. These motives, so long as they are not probed too closely, do not create a palpably absurd situation, causing intolerable discomfort. But a moment may come — if we actually think, it must come — when we have to choose: good housekeeping, or the pursuit of our total perfection. Then fellow travelers come to the parting of the ways.

We should prepare ourselves for such an emergency. Civilization is of this world, and seeks to gain the whole world: the taming of nature, the organization of society for the greater comfort of mankind. And it is a most laudable ambition. But if that conquest should obliterate, or even imperil, or even blur, the chief end of man, that Quest which theology calls salvation, then it is the duty of man to turn his back upon mere civilization. It can be done without seeking a material Walden. Twentieth-century man should be able to make use of all the gadgets, from the splendid (creaking) machinery of the United Nations to the humblest "Atomic Shoe Polish," with a nod of grateful acknowledgment, and yet remain at heart an anchorite. "What shall it profit a man, if he shall gain the whole world, and lose his own soul?"

It is the purpose of this *Testament* to discuss exclusively "the things that are Caesar's," organized society, material progress, in a word civilization. "The things that are God's" are examined in the concluding volume of this inquiry, *Bottle in the Sea*. In the following chapters, I shall deal with practical problems in a practical spirit. As a citizen of this country and of the world, I do not believe that I have done my full duty by dropping a ballot in the box every second year: I am under obligation to contribute my share of experience; after all, the teacher should have learned something in half a century. I even plan to offer suggestions so definite that they could be translated into legislative language, and voted upon. This *Testament* is also a program. But, as Joan of Arc said, *Dieu premier servi*: never forgetting man's first right and greatest responsibility, which is to call his soul his own.

PART II

Political Freedom

CHAPTER IV

The Coming Victory of Liberty

I. THE MANIFESTO

J am not and cannot be a Communist, and first of all for the same reason that I am not and cannot be a Democrat or a Republican. Like the Founders, who denounced parties as "factions," I abhor the party line, the party machine, the party spirit. They warp judgment and deaden the moral sense. I know that there are degrees: certain parties are more perfectly partisan, that is to say more objectionable, than others, because they have a more definite ideology and a more rigorous discipline. But looseness in principles and organization is no excuse: it makes a party inefficient, not harmless.

Most of all I dread that monstrous absurdity, the One-Party System, such as it prevails in our own South, and such as, under the plea of loyalty, blind forces are attempting to create throughout the land. Partisanship per se is the enemy. If consistent, it must be fanatical, and every fanatic is resolved to "drive the rascals out." Not out of power merely, but out of life: there is a Robespierre lurking in every good party man. ¡*Mueran los salvajes inmundos Unitarios!* Purge to the right of you, purge to the left of you, until the Pure alone survive. No party man can be thoroughly honest with himself; no scientific, judicial, or rational investigator can be a party man.

I am not and cannot be a Marxist for the same reason that I cannot be a Fundamentalist in any other domain. It is impossible for me to believe in the literal inerrancy of any book written by human hands, in human words, and about human affairs. No blind believer in *Das Kapital* is fit to teach; and this is true of all blind believers. I have no desire to debar all orthodox Jews, Mohammedans, or Mormons from their constitutional rights.

Still, it is obvious that, on many capital questions, they are committed beyond the reach of free inquiry. There is an escape clause: they remain free insofar as they are not consistent, free through the saving grace of muddleheadedness. Or they may seek refuge in total darkness: all contradictions absorbed, not resolved, into an impenetrable mystery, the inscrutable will of God, the ineluctable dialectic process. But this is a mask for agnosticism rather than a positive faith.

I am not and cannot be a Totalitarian, White, Black, or Red, for the same reason that I cannot accept hundred-percentism in any form. There is no single Way of Life among free men. The essence of Americanism, it must be constantly reaffirmed, is the right to dissent in peace, and if possible in amity. America *was*, according to David Starr Jordan, the Land where Hatred Expired, because we had made it "safe for differences." Every culture worthy of the name is pluralistic, not monolithic. The age of Louis XIV was truly great so long as it enabled many conflicting tendencies, pagan and Christian, traditional and rational, local and national, to live and work together, with only a "grand style" in common. When the aging king attempted to impose actual uniformity — the T. S. Eliot orthodoxy — swiftly the glory departed. The thirteenth was indeed the greatest of Christian centuries, not because of its unity, but because of its incredible and dramatic diversity: Frederick II, *Stupor Mundi*, and the saintly Louis IX breathed the same air. Even in the crudest cultures, unity is but a matter of superficial patterns. No anthropologist is able to measure with what degree of enthusiasm, assent, resignation, irony, or secret revolt the taboos are obeyed. Patterns are akin to the rules and traditions of a language: they may hamper and twist, they never completely stifle the activity of the individual mind. That culture is greatest which promotes the highest degree of diversity. Chaos is not the result of liberty: it arises from the clash of rival tyrannies.

All this is, I trust, orthodox to the point of triteness. This, we all know, is the land of liberty, and it is liberty, ours and the world's, that we are defending. Here enters the Tempter, chief of the Realists: liberty is so precious, and at the same time so ineffectual, that it must be defended by illiberal means. We might as well say — and how often has it been said! — that truth can best be served through effective lies, and Christian mansuetude through the torture and massacre of heretics. "O Liberty! How many crimes are committed in thy name!" Manon Roland said in the shadow of the scaffold.

The one essential liberty is the liberty of thought. Take from a man his earthly treasures, and he is not degraded. Frighten him out of voicing his honest opinion, and he will be either stupefied, or wounded to his very soul. In a free society, material hardships can be allayed through the coöperation of the citizens and the amendment of the laws. In a slave society, however successful it may be on the material plane, the loss of dignity is irremediable. And with the decline of independence, even if the barbarians from without and the barbarians from within did not swoop upon the hoard, these boasted riches would inevitably melt away.

The core of the problem then is how to preserve our freedom to think, not our freedom to grab. And not our own freedom merely: freedom is indivisible, and we must grant it equally to all men. It is tempting to impose our own opinion, when it seems to us the merest, the most obvious common sense, when dissent appears as madness or perversity. But that common sense is but a complex, precarious, ever-changing consensus, not an absolute and eternal verity: read in Montaigne the vagaries of common opinion throughout the ages. Tomorrow we may be outlawed in our turn. We may even be outlawed in the name of liberty, for not being sturdy individualists in the official pattern. Even if we remained in miraculous agreement with the all-powerful majority, our thought, unchallenged, would lose its vigor. "It is meet that there should be heretics," said a Father of the Church. Thinking is a process, not a state; it is combat, not repose.

Here we reach another hoary platitude, if we dare call a platitude something which is so high beyond our present grasp. It is the declaration ascribed to Voltaire, and true at any rate to the Voltairian spirit: "I hate your ideas, but I'll fight to the death for your right of voicing them." This is the crux: when thought, even crazy and obnoxious thought, is silenced by material force, liberty is dead. Not even "two and two are four" should be imposed as a dogma.

I am not suggesting a universal tolerance born of skepticism or indifference. Ideas do matter: even if they do not actually create trends in human history, they check, divert or favor them. It is not totally indifferent, as materialists would have it, that certain groups among us should be striving for world empire, race supremacy, theocracy, social justice, political democracy, Christian charity, scientific investigation. I have faith in the conscious will of men — another term for thought — even if only within narrow historical limits. I believe earnestly in defending and promoting our ideals, and our material interests as well. But I maintain that the clash of ideas should remain on the intellectual plane, and be fought out solely with intellectual weapons. To burn a dissenter, or, more cruelly, to starve him into hypocrisy, is a shameful abuse of brutal power. If we have the least confidence in our own ideal, we should be ready to meet all comers in debate, on equal terms, without fear or favor. A theory in chemistry cannot be disproved by clapping its proponents into jail. And this is true in all fields, religious, moral, political, social, as well as scientific. It is time we should grasp at last the meaning of Galileo's muttered protest: "And yet it turns!"

I am aware that thought can easily pass into action, just as unreasoning action can easily be rationalized into the semblance of thought: ideas are incipient deeds. They may be *subversive* and lead to material destruction. The problem is delicate, and cannot be solved by a single crude formula, either libertarian or authoritarian. By some, this appeal to fine distinctions may be called casuistry; by others, the judicial spirit.

Let us note that all ideas are to some extent inevitably subversive. Thought is the formulation of a problem, that is to say of a conflict; and the solution we adopt is the denial of other solutions. Every affirmation implies a negation. The theistic hypothesis rules out the atheistic; Christianity was subversive of paganism; American independence was subversive of English rule; the republic was subversive of monarchy; self-determination (the right to secede) was subversive of an indissoluble union. In a more general way, the philosophical anarchism of Herbert Spencer, Albert Jay Nock and Herbert Hoover is subversive of all government, just as any government, armed to enforce the collective will, is subversive of absolute individualism. Every reform is subversive of some established wrong. Every progress is subversive of some vested interest. You cannot advocate civil rights for all men, irrespective of color, without threatening the deep-rooted belief in white supremacy. You cannot plead for enlarging the share of labor in the management of business without challenging the age-old distinction between *masters* and *men*, and the principle inherited from Rome that a man can do what he pleases with his own. You cannot urge peace through justice under international law (i.e., a world government) without sapping the foundations of our cherished absolute independence.

Subversiveness is relative: nothing could have been more subversive than the principles professed by the late Senator Robert Taft, or by former Governor Thomas Dewey, if these very sound statesmen had attempted to smuggle their ideas into the Hungary of Admiral Horthy, the Greece of Metaxas, or the Spain of Caudillo Franco. Secretary Dulles, doughty champion of the Free World, would be a subversive if he had to live under military rule in Guatemala. Nothing could be more subversive of our secular, libertarian democracy than the theocracy implied in the faith of Roman Catholics, Covenanters, and Jehovah's Witnesses. Thinking is a subversive activity; and we must never be weary of repeating that thinking is the whole dignity of man.

It is the right and the duty of the secular arm — material power, or Caesar — to catch thought at the very moment it passes into action, but not a moment before. No doubt such fine timing requires eternal vigilance: but this with us is a familiar thought. And by action, I mean lawless, violent action, not lawful activity. Men have a perfect right to advocate the *sub-version*, i.e., the repeal, of any law. It was ruled by the Supreme Court that an income tax proposal was subversive of the Constitution, until the Constitution yielded, and was amended by constitutional means. It would be legitimate for believers in private initiative to propose that the armed forces, the judiciary, public works, the schools, now communistic, should be returned to free enterprise, and run strictly for individual profit, as they were in ages past. It would be no less legitimate, and perhaps a little less paradoxical, to assert that all "public" utilities should be in public hands. One might even propose doing away with the Constitution altogether, provided it be by peaceful and legal methods. One ultimate suicidal amendment: "The Constitution is hereby abolished," would create among us the conditions which have prevailed in England for centuries. And all such proposals, whether they be cautious or radical, sensible or preposterous, may properly be supported by active leagues, with publications, meetings, and, if they believe in that foolish argument, parades.

On the other hand, one should be liable to prosecution for urging even the most harmless kind of action — the destruction of an eye-sore, for instance — by forcible means and in defiance of the law. Radicalism in thought (radicalism of the right as well as of the left) should be met by a counterattack in thought. Appeal to force should be checked by force, even before the threat has taken material form.

But at this point, great caution is necessary, if liberty is not to perish. It would be too easy for a majority party to outlaw the minority, and then declare any activity of the minority to be subversive, a threat to law and order, since such a party exists in defiance of the law. Such an act would obviously be a form of tyranny, worthy of the dictators at their worst; it would be Jacobinism, or the Single Party System, in its most dangerous form. First of all, we must prove — not before an assembly of politicians, but before a body of respected judges — that the accused actually advocate violence. If this be proved, repression should follow: no mere "registration" of criminals, but the jail.

Until it be proved, the group under accusation must be held innocent.

Now there is a distinction, which I admit is subtle at times, between advocacy and prophecy. Revolutionists in thought, including the founders of great religions, desire and announce the downfall of the existing order. It is an essential part of their creed: Armageddon heralds the Millennium, which the early Christians believed to be at hand. The existing order can best answer them by remaining vigorous and healthy: "News of my death greatly exaggerated." But those who crave for the Millennium may also prophesy that the vested interests will not yield without a violent struggle; that the classes in power will not calmly envisage the destruction of their privileges through the free play of democratic institutions; that they will juggle with elections, as Bülow under William II gerrymandered the constituencies in order to stop (in appearance) the growth of Social Democracy, or as the Third Force in France did in 1951 alter the electoral laws, so as to keep a majority against Gaullists and Communists. If free institutions are thus tampered with, if a reign of terror, brutal or insidious, is inaugurated, then resistance to oppression becomes once more the right and duty of every citizen. We have no hesitation on this point when other countries are concerned. We are in sympathy with those elements that are preparing, or actually waging, physical resistance, because they are denied legal methods of redress. As a matter of fact, we are ready to help them, not with platonic good wishes, but with hundreds of millions of hard money.

Now every measure that we take against a "subversive" group confirms the members of that group in their belief that the existing order is resolved not to play fair; that it will become increasingly tyrannical; that it will punish not acts merely, not velleities, but words, but thoughts, and even the most indefinite sympathies or aspirations. It is for us, as believers in liberty, to prove the falsity of their prophecy. Democracy must remain true to its own principle; it must welcome every challenge; it must refuse to load the dice against any ideology. Let liberty prevail, and let the existing order take its chances. That order may endure indefinitely, growing actually stronger through the criticism which compels it to correct its flaws. It may dissolve into a new order by almost imperceptible degrees, as is now the case in Sweden and England. It might even change overnight by a peaceful twist of the kaleidoscope, as Japan changed in the Meiji era, or Turkey under Mustapha Kemal. The one thing essential is that there should be no insuperable obstacle to a peaceful evolution. Every act of violence under the French Revolution was caused, not by a sudden explosion of demented radicalism, but by an effort on the part of the Ancient Regime to counter the will of the people with the force of bayonets. The royal bayonets stood for anarchy, and the mob that stormed the Bastille stood for the very foundation of order, the only legitimate order, order through the consent of free men.

If we are to remain true to our tradition of liberty, every law against any ideology as such, and against any party professing that ideology, must be declared unconstitutional. Individuals and groups should be prosecuted, relentlessly, under the long established laws, for such clearly defined offenses as conspiracy, espionage, sabotage; but never for heresy or prohpecy. And so long as individuals or groups have not been proved guilty of treason, their rights as citizens should not be abridged in any way. They should not be denied positions on the staff of universities, among government officials, among officers in the armed forces.

This policy implies no capitulation to the powers of evil: it is the reaffirmation and defense of our one essential principle. It does not leave us disarmed: far the reverse. If the money and energy we are squandering in a nation-wide witch-hunt were devoted to tracking criminal activities, we should be considerably safer. And if we waged a spirited campaign, on the intellectual plane, on behalf of our own beliefs, trusting to the full in the liberty we are preaching, then we could easily disprove all misstatements, refute all fallacies, dispel all ambiguities. It is possible for a cause to thrive under repression; but any cause that relies upon repression has forfeited its spiritual claims, and will lose even its material power.

I entitled these reflections "The Coming Victory of Liberty," frankly borrowing the phrase from Thomas Mann's *The Coming Victory of Democracy*. As in the case of Mann's spirited address, *coming* expresses passionate desire rather than scientific certitude. We are reasonably sure that Halley's comet will keep its appointment with the astronomers: we cannot assert that truth, justice, liberty, and least of all charity, shall inevitably prevail in human affairs. My affirmation is sheer wishful thinking: which is legitimate enough when the wish, father to the thought, inspires and guides us to action. We shall never save freedom by ceasing from mental strife. Freedom is not found in nature: it results from the unceasing efforts of man.

It may be that we are striving in vain. There is little doubt that, in the last two hundred years, the Enlightenment has paled. Mankind's yearning for Obscurantism, voiced by poets and theologians as well as by dictators, might well herald a new age of darkness. Perhaps we, defenders of human freedom, fossils of the liberal age, stand half-engulfed, like the last philosophers of antiquity, or like the last free spirits in Islam, soon to be crushed by inexorable orthodoxy. One voice after the other is stilled. This feeble cry of mine may be stifled too, and find no echo. The *coming victory*, or the last obscure skirmish of a lost cause? Perhaps faith is noblest when unsullied by hope.

II. POST MORTEM

The foregoing pages, with a few excisions, appeared in the fall number, 1951, of the *Southwest Review*. They called forth spirited responses from many friends known and unknown. Even those who most vehemently disagreed with me refrained from cursing: they only deplored that, meaning so well, I could be so utterly wrong. They confirmed me in the belief that the American Way of Life is freedom to differ, not in peace merely, but in amity. If I had dreamed that I was striking a Hugolian attitude:

> *Et s'il n'en reste qu'un, je serai celui-là,*

"and if but one remains, I shall be that one!" — my claims to heroic defiance would have been gently smiled away. I found myself a very modest witness encompassed about with a great cloud of witnesses. Within a few months, such "citizens of distinction" as Justices William O. Douglas and Hugo L. Black, Francis Biddle, James Landis, Gerald Johnson, Robert Sherwood, Corliss Lamont, Monroe Deutsch, Howard Mumford Jones, Raymond Swing, Edward R. Murrow, Elmer Davis, Carey McWilliams, Mark Van Doren, Owen Lattimore, Ralph Barton Perry, Archibald MacLeish, Paul H. Hoffmann, Robert Redfield, Lewis Mumford, Dorothy Canfield Fisher, Thomas Mann, had expressed themselves in defence of liberty with an authority that a lonely retired scholar could never command. I am as rugged an individualist as any man, to the point of solipsism and anarchism. But I was delighted to find myself a mere private in such a mighty host.

In the active correspondence initiated by my essay, three or four points came out that I had not sufficiently emphasized.

I had dealt with the problem of *subversiveness*, which seemed to me the essential point. I had neglected two other terms, which are constantly hurled at the defenders of liberty. One is the accusation of *fellow traveling*. The other is that of *disloyalty*.

"And whoever shall compel thee to go a mile, go with him twain." In the extra mile, you may persuade him of the error of his way, or you may discover that he has chosen the right path. Voltairian irony consists in agreeing with your opponent better than he agrees with himself: to achieve this, you have to start as a fellow traveler. And you may find the company both profitable and pleasant. I have told Canon Ernest Dimnet and Jacques Maritain that I should like to remain their fellow traveler unto the very end *in this world*: about the world to come, I have no reliable information. In questions of science or technology, we find it difficult not to be fellow travelers with our worst enemies: microbes and atoms are indifferent to Hammer and Sickle, Stars and Stripes. The Soviets must have created great embarrassment, a while ago, when they opened a crusade against moral laxity; and the religious orders have not

abjured their communism in a desperate effort never to agree
with Marx, Lenin, and Stalin. It happens that on the problem
of colonialism, the bulk of American opinion and Soviet propaganda follow exactly the same line: I have elected a slightly
different path. There are two essential ideas for a liberal: the
infinite variety of human opinions, and the wastefulness of
strife. So I am glad when I can discover some point of agreement with any sincere thinker. I know we shall inevitably come
to the parting of the ways: many, alas! are the former friends,
and many the former selves, that I have left behind. But in the
meantime, let us profit by companionship and coöperation. And
once the time comes, let us part with a courteous word, and the
hope to meet again.

Disloyal, as Bagehot said of *un-English*, is a perfect fallacy
compressed into a single word. There can be no *open* disloyalty,
only differences. What we have to combat is *deceit*. If you pre-
tend to agree with a group, and secretly work against its aims,
you are a scoundrel. If you candidly differ, you may be mistaken,
but no moral stigma attaches to your thought or action. I have
repeatedly stated — it is a crucial point — that "My country,
right or wrong!" is blasphemy. It means: "Thou shalt have no
other god beside America: *not even God.*" War, which perverts
everything, does not release us from our obligation to think
honestly and fearlessly. It was the glory of England that the
Liberal Party, during the Boer War, dared to condemn the
government's policy and its "methods of barbarism." We admired those few courageous Germans who, like Thomas Mann
and Friedrich Wilhelm Foerster, dared to be disloyal to Hitler.
It would have been a victory for enlightened patriotism if a
vigorous opposition could have stopped Mussolini in the initial
stage of his Ethiopian adventure, or if public conscience, in
North Korea, had stood guard on the Thirty-eighth Parallel,
and prevented the crime and the blunder of aggression. Repeatedly, in the crisis of the last few years, public sanity has
balked the warmongers.

Who can speak in the name of "My country"? Is it: "My
Government"? But we welcome with open arms the transfuges

who are "traitors" to Russia their native land, foes of a regime which has been established for nearly four decades. And what shall we say of those men who for twenty years opposed every move of our Presidents? What shall we think of a raucous Senator who impugned the loyalty of that great military organizer who was also a great Secretary of State? Our sole loyalty is due, not to the party in precarious power, but to essential Americanism, the principles and traditions which are the very backbone of this country.

The first principle that we profess, as a "self-evident truth," is that men are created equal; let us add, cautiously: in the eyes of the law. Every attempt to establish a caste system, to create discriminations based upon race, must be considered as rank disloyalty to the American spirit. Yet how many patriotic Americans have been, and are to the present day, guilty of such an offense! [1] The hoariest of our traditions in foreign policy, so hoary that it had practically attained the dignity of a principle, was never to become entangled in special alliances. Temporary association for a definite purpose is another thing; universal agreements, covenants open to all and openly arrived at, are the fulfillment, not the destruction, of our democratic ideal. But long-range commitments to particular nations against other nations are absolutely contrary to the wise counsel of Washington and Jefferson. Yet we are at present, without a qualm, *disloyal* to the reasoned conviction of the Founders. There is only one essential Americanism to which our loyalty should be pledged: liberty under the law. And that principle is not tribal: like Roosevelt's four freedoms, it is valid and deserves our support "everywhere in the world."

I had stated that "no blind believer in *Das Kapital* is fit to teach, and this is true of all blind believers." Admittedly this is a hard saying. Agreement will be easier, however, if we lay the emphasis on *blind*, not on *believers*. No blind man is fit to teach

---

[1] To be sure, the men who are working against discrimination are "echoing the attacks of our enemies" and "following the Communist line." But the fear of agreeing with the Communists should not lead us to persevere in evil.

about colors; but all thinkers have to be believers. They believe at least in a general trend, in a method, and, provisionally, in a working hypothesis. This book of mine is an act of faith.

"Believers" in the narrower sense, those who profess a definite orthodoxy accepted once for all, have their place in an institution of learning, but under three conditions. First of all, they must be *honest* believers: not retained advocates, propagandists, seekers after notoriety, candidates for power. Then they must measure up to the academic standard of competence: they must never resort to glaring fallacies or garbled information. Finally, they must be willing to discuss all problems, even the problems of their faith, with their colleagues and students, according to the rules of evidence which are accepted equally in philosophy, scholarship, science, and the law. A man whose orthodoxy is firm can afford to be open-minded: he is ready to "prove," i.e., to test, all things. It is only the half-believer, the "would-be," the uneasy dweller in the mist, who is afraid of his own thought. The very essence of Thomism, which Jacques Maritain expounds, is that revelation is not contrary to human reason, although it could not have been discovered by human reason alone. I feel confident that Maritain meets all three of these tests. The problem is a little different with Ludwig Lewisohn, who, after many wanderings, has worked himself into a position of extreme Hebraic fundamentalism. He is so candid about it that his students are duly warned: "Believe it or not, I believe." And the power of his intellect, the richness of his culture, the appeal of his character, are assets too precious to be rejected. There can be no personality without a personal equation. A university which has on its staff a majority of independent seekers after truth can be thankful to have also a few *blind* believers, blind as Dante was blind, if they are of outstanding merit. This would apply equally to Catholics like Gilson and Maritain, to Jews like Lewisohn, to Calvinists like Clarence Macartney, to the delightful Latter Day Saints with whom I was associated at Logan, Utah, to materialists, to agnostics, to Communists. Leon Trotsky, more radical than Stalin, should have been offered a chair in Los Angeles, there to conduct a debate with a far more dangerous revolutionist, Bertrand Russell.

Great thought, even biased, remains great thought; it heals the wounds that it inflicts; whereas mediocrity is innocuous but debilitating. The risk, at any rate, is worth taking. But great thought is rare, and for biased mediocrity there is no excuse. When it comes to oaths, my rule is: "Swear not at all." But if the teaching profession had a set of rules similar to those of Æsculapius, the first one should be: "Seek fearlessly for the truth; let no orthodoxy stand in the way."

Another point was raised with vociferous cordiality by Burton Rascoe, with subtler modulation by Peter Viereck: if I am a defender of liberty, why do I not concentrate my fire on the most obvious enemy of liberty, the Soviet Union?

A casual answer, not wholly irrelevant, but of minor significance, is that I see no reason why I should carry coals to Newcastle. Admitting that the first duty of man is to hate Russia and all her works, there is a large body of experts who are most efficiently attending to the task. I have never been tempted to become a Communist: therefore I lack the aura of infallibility which magnifies and dignifies all converts from Communism.

A second reason is that I know practically nothing about Russia; and this is true of the vast majority of my fellow citizens. For years, we have been denied access to a fair presentation of the Communist case. We have a packed jury, and one-sided evidence. Certain *liberal* magazines and associations, which have enrolled men whom I greatly respect, are fine examples in point. All thoughts and facts are welcome, and the freest possible discussion: are we not liberals? — provided the unequivocal result be to damn Russia. We used to have more dispassionate information, particularly from British sources. *A Scientist among the Soviets*, by Julian Huxley; *Russia in Flux*, by Sir John Maynard (with a foreword by a man who had made a lifelong study of Russia, Sir Bernard Pares), not to mention the ponderous tomes of the Webbs, gave us pictures which, if blurred, at least were not solidly black. In this country, there was a time when the books of Maurice Hindus were among the best sellers, when Joseph Davies' *Mission to Moscow* swept the book trade, both at full price and in pocket reprint, and was popular as a movie. At present, no book of that kind is easily available; and it would be accounted treason even to reread the old ones. Some handsome propaganda still reaches us from Russia, and is accessible in those few universities which remain citadels of freedom. But they have to be discounted: I cannot believe that the two hundred millions who live under the Red Star invariably wear such happy smiles. Some learned institutes are publishing studies which, I take it, are truly scientific in spirit: but they presuppose just the kind of elementary knowledge about Russia that John Doe most obviously lacks. I refuse to condemn the Albigensians offhand, because I do not have their own side of the case. I shall not consider the Argentine *Unitarios* of a hundred years ago as "obscene" and "nauseating," on the authority of Dictator Rosas. My duty as a student of history is plain: until the conditions of free inquiry are fully restored, I must refrain from judging.[2]

In the third place, I am powerless to do anything about Russia. I am living in America, under American conditions; I might, in however limited a measure, hope to influence the American Way of Life. My interests and my duty coincide; I have information and the possibility of action; and this entails a responsibility. Even if we took it for granted that Russia is the inferno described by American orthodoxy, and that Khrushchev has inherited from Stalin the fateful number 666, still that would not excuse any dereliction of duty on the home front. We must see to it that, when 1984 comes, it shall not resemble the nightmare evoked by Orwell. And to avert that peril, not a moment should be wasted, not an effort should be spared.

It is too easy to complain that I see the mote in our eye, not

---

[2] In the days when Samuel Gompers was a greater offense to all right-thinking Americans than Mr. Harry Bridges is today, a lady asserted: "Certainly, Gompers ought to be suppressed!" and *sotto voce* to her neighbor: "What *are* gompers, anyway?" She had the saving grace of asking a question, although it was not the right question and not at the right time. In our days, her spirit of inquiry would seem suspicious: not for us to ask what gompers are.

the beam in Comrade Ivan's. It is his beam, and if he likes it, he is welcome to it. But let me take care of our mote at once: I find it exceedingly annoying, and it might easily become dangerous.

A surgeon, in a perfectly equipped hospital, complains that some aseptic precaution in the operating room has been neglected. The assistant at fault retorts: "Why fuss about such a little thing? Are you not aware that there are hundreds of millions in all parts of the world who live in total disregard of elementary sanitation? Why do you not get after *them*?" Whatever may be taking place in Spain or Formosa, in Moscow or Peking, I am resisting any abridgment of American liberty, because I have the right to judge America by America's exacting standards.

I have been for many decades a student of language, a man of words if not a man of letters; and I am keenly conscious of what Stuart Chase called the *tyranny of words*. Beyond the purely technical domain, words stand for complex, many-shaded, often conflicting realities. No word is to be accepted at its face value without diligent inquiry. A man is not necessarily a fiend because he is called, or calls himself, a communist, a royalist, or an agnostic. He is not an angel of light, because he professes belief in the flag, capitalism, the party system, or the Athanasian creed. First of all, let us ascertain what we actually mean: not grossly, but as definitely, as delicately, as we can. This is impossible without searching criticism, without a permanent challenge to all taboos, shibboleths, and slogans. The most effective instrument of liberty is a command of accurate language.

CHAPTER V

Politics and Government

𝒯his book is dedicated to the proposition that government is not necessarily evil. To the anarchist, this is heresy; to the realist, it is abysmal naïveté. I might salvage my respectability by affirming that all things and all men are evil in this evil world, but that some are worse. If there are degrees, there is a choice.

The confusion between "realism" and pessimism is among the worse fallacies that befuddle our thinking. It can be found even in such a clear-minded and generous spirit as Crane Brinton. He closes his admirable book *Ideas and Men* with the rejection of an idealistic democracy and the praise of a realistic pessimistic democracy, one in which the citizen will approach morals and politics with "the willingness to cope with imperfection that characterizes the good farmer and the good physician." But we "cope with imperfection" only with the purpose of making it less imperfect. The farmer is an optimist: aware of bad weather and blights, he works in the hope of a crop. The doctor — of the body, of the mind, of the spirit — is an optimist: he strives to restore health. I am a thorough pessimist about our present political conditions: I could quote with hearty approval two lovely lines from *God Save the Queen!*:

> Confound their politics!
> Frustrate their knavish tricks!

But I consider such pessimism as a challenge, not as an acknowledgment of permanent defeat. Perhaps God alone can "frustrate their knavish tricks": but to God nothing is impossible. The only irremediable pessimism is the one Dr. Pangloss learnt from Leibniz: "All is for the best in the best possible world."

From another pole of thought, Dr. Clarence E. Macartney, doughtiest of Fundamentalist Boanerges, thunders his anathema at "international literati and international dreamers and treaty-makers." "The sooner [they] recognize the fact of sin, the better it will be for mankind." [1] This is an amusing travesty of the facts. We may not agree with their hopes and methods, but all "dreamers" are keenly conscious of sin. Their dream is to face sin and force it back: they are fully as orthodox as Calvin Coolidge's minister. Hypocrisy is sin; cowardice is sin; violence is sin; pride and greed are sins; and according to the gospel, wealth is sin. But there are two kinds or degrees of sin, simple and compound. The first was aptly defined by Baudelaire as *consciousness in evil*. The second is evil rationalized into good, through a complacent ideology: I surmise its proper name is "the sin against the Holy Ghost." The only issue between Dr. Macartney and myself is the historical point whether apple stealing was the original sin. He may be right: but the fact is not established beyond reasonable doubt.

We have repeatedly conceded that from the theological, metaphysical and scientific points of view, liberty is an illusion. Predestination, fatalism, and determinism alone make sense — and kill sense. Liberty must be assumed as a datum, just as we assume motion to exist, even though Zeno irrefutably demonstrated that the arrow could not fly. On the practical plane, the true realization of liberty is a negative: *freedom from* rather than *freedom of*. Liberty is freedom from compulsion.

Now justice, in the heart of man or in the hand of the state, implies compulsion. We are restrained, by inner or outer checks, from acting unjustly. If we have been convicted of injustice, we are forced to make amends. We are placed under restrictions, even to the abridgment, not of liberty merely and the pursuit of happiness, but of life itself. And what is justice? Not merely "truth in action," or "the will that truth shall pre-

[1] Literary Review of the *New York Evening Post*, November 21, 1925, p. 4.

vail." It sounds well to say: *Magna est Veritas et praevalebit*: but everything that is, is true, which does not mean that it is rational, and even less that it is right. Again, there are noxious truths: the microbe is as true as the germicide.

Justice therefore is relative to the human race, and purposive. It consists in maintaining and fostering those conditions that will promote security and comfort among men: justice and civilization are one. A limited sphere, no doubt: joy, love, and righteousness soar beyond *human* justice.

Every state exists for the purpose of helping the individual by curbing undesirable individual activities. This is the eternal problem of man in society: freedom is essential, but cannot be absolute. In a healthy community, restrictions and compulsions should, on the whole, make you freer: freer from bodily harm, freer from that anticipation of harm which is called fear. You are made to pay taxes for the support of the police, and you are made to obey the officers of the law: all this is not tyranny, but nation-wide insurance. Experience has taught us that these restrictions to our liberty are better, by and large, than being held up or murdered. There is nothing abstract in all this. Every state is by definition a police state and a welfare state: no community can survive on the basis of anarchy and *ill-fare*. Therefore government is not by its very nature evil: it is the pooling of good. It is a constant striving to attain Utopia, that is to say, security and comfort. Those things which lie beyond security and comfort cannot be forced upon us by the state. The moment the state starts meddling with them marks the beginning of oppression.

Here we reach an apparent absurdity: government is in itself a good thing, politics manifestly evil, and in the minds of most people the two, if not identical, are at any rate inseparable: politics being both the science of government and the practical methods of carrying out government. We constantly come across such contradictions: religion, for instance, covers both a universal aspiration and the practices of particular sects, both the purest mysticism and the crassest superstition. My old dictionary is careful to distinguish between *politics* (*a*) and *politics* (*b*).

Politics (*a*) is "political science; a branch of ethics; the administration of public affairs in the interest of the peace, prosperity and safety of the state." *Politics* (*b*) is "the administration of public affairs so as to carry elections and secure public offices; party intrigues; wire-pulling; trickery." For *Politics* (*a*) I should prefer statecraft and statesmanship; for *Politics* (*b*), let us keep the word politics, as commonly understood.

For politics and politicians have become words of ill-repute throughout the world; most of all perhaps in the "sister republics" America and France. Hence the extraordinary confusion of our thinking about the common weal. We assert that politics, which we identify with the party system, is fundamentally and incurably evil. In the same breath, we affirm that it is the best conceivable method of managing the affairs of the state. This is part of our hoary, cherished, and dishonored *realism*.

It need not be so. To take an active part in government should be and might be the highest of professions. As a matter of fact, so it is, for the very few who deserve to be called statesmen. There are many callings in which evil is but an accident. Although there are bad judges, bad teachers, bad engineers, bad physicians — bad in the sense of incompetent, lazy or corrupt — still it is taken for granted that the practice of justice, teaching, engineering, medicine should be, and normally is, good. There are more dubious cases: the lawyer, the soldier, the financier, the merchant, the journalist are exposed to professional risks. Their codes may tolerate, and even recommend, actions which are not in rigorous agreement with standard morality: *noblesse oblige* in reverse. Still, on the whole, they are expected to serve worthy ends by decent means. In politics, worthy ends are derided as naïve (the dreams of the *do-gooders*), and decent means as unrealistic (*starry-eyed*). We had a few years ago, for instance, a conservative leader, a man of education, standing, and substance, with a great name to uphold, universally respected for his personal integrity. Yet in crucial instances — the Korean War, and an alliance with the Dixiecrats — he played fast and loose with his principles; he sought, not truth and justice first of all, but the position from which he could do most damage to his opponents. He may have had in him the possibilities of statesmanship: he did play the orthodox game of politics. And this was true also of a man who was undoubtedly a statesman on the grand scale, Franklin Roosevelt. It was rightly said, early in his career, that he had an appointment with destiny, but stopped on the way to talk it over with Jim Farley. At present, there are courtesies among politicians, although they seem to be wearing rather thin, just as there is a modicum of honor among thieves and of chivalry among gangsters. But on the whole, politics is a stench. No concern, church, school, army, factory, store, would consent to be run by "political" methods. When these do appear, they are felt to be, not the basis of sound management, but a scandal and a peril. The chief objection to turning certain activities over to the state is that they might fall into the hands of the politicians.

It is evident that no sweeping, immediate, and permanent cure is conceivable, since, barring a revolution, politics could be cured only through a political campaign. My blessing on all reformers: as a result of their efforts, individual malefactors may be denounced and punished, particular abuses may be corrected. But the fundamental evil remains untouched. A boss is exposed: but it is possible for his loyal henchman to reach the White House. Women were brought in with the hope that they would clear up the mess: but they have conspicuously failed to do so. Popular primaries were intended to wrest politics from the clutches of politicians: but it is the politicians who manipulate the primaries. "Barring a revolution," I said: but a violent change that would sweep the politicians away and give us a dictator as incorruptible as Robespierre, as efficient as Napoleon, would only concentrate in one person and his clique all the evils now diluted among thousands. There is at least a particle of truth in the adage: Nations have the governments they deserve. It works both ways. We have bad politics, because we spurn the idea that politics and morality should be one. And our national life is tolerably healthy, because, in spite of politics, we as a people have "a good constitution": enterprise, hard work, decency, friendliness, humor. The finest tribute to America's vitality is that we are able to survive our politics. It was aptly said that politics with us is a skin disease: annoying, disfiguring, but not fatal.

I am using as instances the governments of America and France, the only ones I know at first hand. There is reason to surmise that the evils all of us are denouncing are not limited to those two senior democracies. A generation ago, Marcel Pagnol wrote a satirical farce, *Topaze*, against municipal corruption. It dealt with a topical French problem: it was triumphantly performed in all countries, because it was of universal application. So far as I can judge, the "politics" of certain Latin American states, of the late Russian and Chinese empires, of the Spanish monarchy, of Chiang Kai-shek's regime at the height of its power, of Egypt under King Farouk, did not exhale a delicate fragrance. Unsavory politics is by no means the unhappy privilege of democracies. On the contrary, it might well be, like the concept of a national honor to be upheld by the sword, a tradition inherited from the absolute monarchies. Montesquieu has a chapter [2] to demonstrate that virtue is not the principle of a monarchical government. "Ambition coupled with sloth," he says, "servility under the mask of pride, the desire to gain wealth without working for it, aversion for truth; flattery, treachery, perfidy; the spurning of all promises; contempt for the duties of a citizen; fear lest the Prince should be upright; ridicule constantly poured on virtue: all these, I believe, constitute the character of most courtiers, manifest everywhere and at all times." The sovereign no longer is Louis the Well-Beloved, but King Demos. With this difference, the description admirably fits the "courtiers" of today.

On the other hand, there was a long period in the Victorian Age during which English politics preserved an aura of gentlemanliness. The cynical "jobbing" that prevailed in the eighteenth century, inseparable from the memory of Sir Robert Walpole, was curbed, or at any rate veiled. Both conservatives and liberals were men of education: a false quantity in a

[2] *De L'Esprit des lois*, Livre III, chap. 5.

classical tag would endanger a political career. In each party, there were men who could ride to hounds, shoot grouse, and drink port with the best. The House ranked among the most distinguished clubs. That era passed with Lloyd George, perhaps the first Premier who was not recognized as a gentleman. But even today, an M.P. is still presumed to be honorable, as a judge to be learned, a prelate to be venerable, an admiral to be gallant. It is a pity that England is "not a precedent but a miracle."

I have defined government as the pooling of efforts toward the *common* good: the damning fault of politics is to stand for the defence of *particular*, i.e., selfish, interests: regional, class, or personal. This would be acceptable if *politics* were merely a check on *government*. Government should be warned at what point its activities prove harmful to individuals, so that proper adjustment be made. But if politics usurp the function of government, the result is disastrous. While lip-service is paid to virtue in the form of well-sounding phrases, selfish greed is enthroned. The lobbies and pressure groups are inextricably interwoven with politics. This is corruption, even when no direct bribe is involved.

I have no instrument wherewith to compare the results of such a blight in America and in France. The tone of the press is no guide: the French grumble more than we, but they do even less about it. I am inclined to think that the case of France is worse than ours. French Parliamentarians are not openly for sale: they simply have a very natural desire to be reëlected. There exists an ubiquitous pork-barrel system, for dividing the bounties of the state; and its defensive equivalent, for the protection of vested interests. This is achieved through tacit deals, and irrespective of party lines. Big Business is by no means the worst of the lobbies, even though the Comité des Forges once achieved a rather sinister eminence. Far more dangerous is the universal, amorphous, unnamed, irresistible coalition of the *little fellows*, the small farmers, the home distillers, the corner tradesmen, the saloon keepers, down to the squatters in the sordid "Zone," the No Man's Land which encircles the former fortifications of Paris. It was hoped that proportional representation, by fostering parties on a truly national scale, would check the greed of the *petits bourgeois*; or, in the words of Aristide Briand, that it would "drain the stagnant marshes." But the Communist Party, devoted to a clear-cut ideology, supranational in its scope, is just as ready as the old-fashioned Radicals to barter special promises for votes.

The evil is not special to politics: it lies deeper than politics. It is the gospel of self-seeking, if need be at the expense of others, which we glorify as sturdy individualism. There is barely a step between "seeking advantage" and "taking advantage": the temptation to pass from one to the other is almost irresistible. So contest, with the least possible admixture of scruples, becomes the rule of life; and success is measured, not so much by your own peace and comfort as by the defeat of your opponent. The key word is not to earn, but to win. To win a debate, even through claptrap; to win an election, even by smearing or gerrymandering; to snatch a customer from a competitor; to win a case, if only on a technicality; to score a diplomatic point: in every field, the guiding thought is, "There is no substitute for victory." This is war, and in war, we are told, all means are fair. Force and deceit are right, if they are the keys to desired ends. Great nations have erected monuments, and almost altars, to Napoleon and Bismarck; politicians and businessmen dream in their hearts to be Napoleons and Bismarcks in their chosen domain.

The problem is to restrain — we cannot hope to destroy it altogether — this spirit of selfish greed; more accurately, to confine it within its proper channel. This is the last step in *civilization*, and it is not easy. If you are afraid of copybook morality, let us reword it in this way: selfish greed in human relations ought to be curbed, not because it is evil, but because it is wasteful. It means friction and useless heat: the efficiency engineer knows that there are better ways of adjusting differences than through mutual destruction. The world manages to exist in spite of the "knavish tricks" of politicians, hucksters, shysters, diplomats, and war lords. These men do not actually

create the activities they seem to control: they only "muscle in."
From day to day, they impress us as the strong, the successful,
the practical men: in the long record of civilization, these misleaders appear merely as parasites. Europe has survived Napoleon, Bismarck, and Hitler, as it has survived many a pestilence:
the world will survive the annoyance of party politics and
profiteering. The great delusion is to believe that these hin-
drances are necessary; the unforgivable sin is to proclaim that
they are right.

"Again," saith the Realist in his heart, "what is the use? To
alter the very nature of politics is not practical politics." Furthermore, I might well be asked: "Have you not been safe and
happy under what you call the dull and corrupt tyranny of the
politicians?" I am ready to concur. My life in America has been
full and pleasant. No thanks, however, to politics. For half a
century, I have been living under a regime I despised, and
against which I was completely disarmed. In the political field,
my situation was akin to that of a freethinker in sixeeenth-
century Spain, of a liberal under Tsar or Soviet. As Siéyès said
after the Terror, "I have survived." Better men, or less obscure,
have been crushed. I did not rebel, but I did not submit. I know
the remedy, and I know it is hard to take. It is not a nostrum,
not a sudden conversion, least of all a violent revolution: it is a
rigorous program of self-education, for the individual and for
the community. A slow process, no doubt: but when started, its
rate of acceleration might confound the pessimist. Mankind
dreamed of aviation for thousands of years, and made fumbling
attempts for centuries. Nothing can be effected overnight, except catastrophe. But there is no desirable change in thought
and practice that cannot be achieved in a single generation.

There is, however, one domain in which the problem is immediate: the international field. We are rightly proud of our
achievements, material, social, cultural, and on that account,
we are ready to assume leadership of the Free World, which
ought to be the whole world. Because we do not properly dis-
criminate between what is right and what is wrong in our Way
of Life, we are offering our political pattern as a model to man-

kind: whoso rejects it is hopelessly benighted or perverse. Now it is a fact that the vast majority of mankind have never practiced our methods, and are not in the least tempted by them. In their eyes, there is no aura of sanctity about our precedents. Their own solutions, actual or in the making, are very probably worse: at any rate, they provide alternatives which are worthy of consideration.

I am not speaking merely of countries which we might dismiss as engulfed in barbarism or tyranny. Nations of commanding cultural importance, Germany, France, are by no means committed to our ways. Their deepest tradition is not one of party politics. In Germany, the conception of a government above parties was fundamental until 1918, and again — a loathsome caricature — after 1933. In the fifteen hundred years of her history, France has played the political game, according to Anglo-American rules, only under the Directory, Louis-Philippe, and the Third Republic, with its feeble ghost the Fourth. None of these regimes commanded much love or respect: they were *bourgeois* in the worst sense of the term. Throughout Europe and throughout the world, the very structure of the state is not a foregone conclusion, one of the Eternal Verities: it is a live issue, and therefore it is practical politics. No one today could prophesy with assurance whether any country will adopt, amend, or reject our system.

Their headache? Ours too. If we want to win them over to our way of thinking, we shall have to do some thinking ourselves, besides the perennial spring-cleaning which is required by the neatest household. We are engaged in a tremendous debate, in which we are upholding, pell mell, liberty, democracy, the dignity of man, the profit motive, party politics, Machiavellian diplomacy; with long credits or outward gifts as rewards, and the atom bomb as ultimate deterrent. It is not a very orderly package; and it does not prove universally attractive. Call it the American Way of Life if you please; but we should not be shocked if in many cases the response is: "Then America had better mend her way."

A country's Way of Life is the sum total of its aspirations, not of its prejudices and abuses. This sounds lamentably ideal-istic: but we are caught in the web of our own virtuous pro-fessions, and our ideal is being forced upon us. Leadership works both ways: if it is not to degenerate into sheer tyranny, it compels the leader to respect his own principles. A particularly striking instance is the race problem. Isolated, we were unchal-lenged; we could manage in our own pragmatic way to jog along with practices at variance with our essential doctrines and with the plain letter of our Constitution. When we as-sumed preëminence, these contradictions struck the rest of the world as hypocrisies or absurdities. It was hard for us to deny the charge. So the American Way of Life was forced by global opinion — friends as well as neutrals and enemies — upon a reluctant America. We have made tremendous strides in Ameri-canism since the Cold War was declared by President Truman, and we may yet see a Jewish negress as President of the United States. Let us hope that the other great American tenet, liberty under law, will likewise echo back to us, and compel us to give up witch-hunting and enforced conformity. We should face such possibilities with confidence. If this be the land of liberty, away with smugness, which paralyzes thought like a gluey sub-stance. If this be the home of the brave, away with the craven "realism" which denies that evils can be faced and checked.

CHAPTER VI

Democracy and Its Rivals

I believe in democracy, although I am no Democrat. The words of the Apostle apply admirably to my political faith: "the substance of things hoped for, the evidence of things not seen." There this inquiry ought to stop: if a faith is to be kept pure, it had better remain undefined. But above purity, which cannot be attained short of Nirvana, there is life, which is "fluctuating and diverse." In practical terms, what do I mean when I affirm that I believe in democracy?

I have been told many times that the word does not figure in our Constitution. This is mere quibbling. The Preamble opens with a clear profession of democracy: "We, the people. . ." The meaning is not lost when a term is translated from Greek into English; it becomes even plainer without the classic veil. By this simple and solemn declaration, America brought down to earth Rousseau's shadowy Social Contract.

Democracy is the denial of every authority that does not originate with the people: absolute monarchy, military despotism, the caste system (hereditary aristocracy), the class system (plutocracy). Democracy can be restated as "government by consent of the governed." The rule of the most enlightened despot — saint or philosopher — is illegitimate if it is imposed upon reluctant subjects.

It is by no means self-evident that "we, the people" are fit to govern ourselves. It is even less evident that we are fit to govern others. So democracy is not necessarily the best government. Theocracy, technocracy (the rule of experts), anarchism, all three have theoretical and practical claims to excellence. It might be argued that all three do qualify as "governments by consent." The Jews, the Roman Catholics, and the more logical

Protestant sects such as the Covenanters and Jehovah's Witnesses, are persuaded that they possess the very Law of the Lord: to such a law no sane man would deny his assent. In a technocratic utopia, no body of men, however expert, should hold arbitrary power. They must be ready to explain their courses whenever these are challenged. Under such a regime, a demonstration would be the warrant of a political law, as it is at present the warrant of a physical law: no scientific truth is established except through the assent of competent judges. It need hardly be emphasized that anarchism ("sturdy individualism") is the perfection of government by consent: under its dispensation, no man can be forced to do another man's bidding. Anarchism is a cluster of sovereignties: if these are in harmony, we have reached the millennium; if they clash, we lapse from anarchism, Spencerian or Tolstoian, into anarchy, which is sheer chaos.

Democracy implies the rejection of every political privilege, that is to say of every right which cannot be shared by all the people. The law must be universal: democracy, in this respect, is strictly in accord with Kant. So democracy is inseparable from the concept of equality. If I were to indulge in formulae *à la* Montesquieu, I might say that the foundation of theocracy is righteousness: conformity with the will of God. The foundation of technocracy is scientific truth: conformity with the laws of nature. The foundation of anarchism is liberty. The foundation of democracy is equality. And, to be sure, in the Holy Writ of our nation, equality is affirmed as the first of those truths which we hold to be self-evident.

This, however, is a matter of emphasis, not of conflict. Equality is implicit in the rival systems. A demo-theocrat could argue that all men are equal in the sight of God, and that their souls, to Him, are all equally precious (Jews and Calvinists, with their diverse doctrines of *election*, might demur). Demo-technocrats will say that the laws of nature apply equally to all human beings, irrespective of birth or station. Demo-anarchists assert the inalienable equality of sovereign individuals: inequality is destructive of liberty, for every privilege abridges the freedom of the nonprivileged. Thus all doctrines meet and merge in the ideal.

In the practical world, the emphasis does make a difference. When stated crudely, the fundamental assertion that all men are equal is a self-evident fallacy. No one will persuade me that I am the equal of Einstein in the scientific field, of Marciano in the prize ring, of John D. Rockefeller, Jr., in the financial world. Because it is an absurdity, absolute democracy, the complete equality of all human beings, has never been practiced, attempted or even preached. Like all absolutes, it is a myth. We, who are the vanguard of democracy, do not give votes to babes and sucklings. What we call universal suffrage is adult suffrage; a short while ago, it was manhood suffrage. Age is accepted as a rough guarantee of maturity, education, and economic independence. The same rule which justifies our denying the vote to a college freshman might, and perhaps should, lead us to debar a moron of forty. If age be the criterion, let us at any rate substitute Lewis Terman's "mental age" for the merely chronological. Perhaps voters should be retired for senility at sixty-five, as professors are, and given the emeritus rank of Elder Citizens.

Equality, therefore, has to be more carefully defined. As is so frequently the case, the safest definition is negative: equality is the condemnation of all unjustified inequalities. Natural inequalities cannot be denied; sociological inequalities (a hierarchy of functions) are inevitable as soon as we emerge from anarchy. By removing senseless barriers, democracy makes it possible for the best to rise. Its aim is to permit the selection of a genuine aristocracy; it is identical, not with leveling, but with justice.

The first rule of democracy is that no superiority should be taken for granted, and that none should be accepted as permanent. In this it agrees with technocracy: in modern science, no authority — Aristotle, Hippocrates, Newton, Einstein — is above challenge. But democracy is at odds with the caste system, hereditary aristocracy, which does not permit its own crude criterion, "birth" or "breed," to be questioned. It is likewise antagonistic to theocracy: no true believer will submit the Law of God to a man-devised critical test.

In broad terms, free and equal competition is the democratic method: elections, examinations, the rough-and-tumble of business. A true democracy holds nothing sacred. It must be free to *prove*, that is to say, to probe, to try, to test, to examine, all things. The most hallowed truths must consent to be so questioned; the most outrageous paradoxes are entitled to fair discussion. As soon as we pass an edict: "Beyond this point thou shalt not think," a privilege is created, a right is denied, and democracy is maimed.

The second rule is that no *collective* inequalities should be considered: each individual case must be examined on its own merit. I am perfectly aware that there are group superiorities: adults versus children, the educated versus the illiterate, our own Heaven-descended race versus the lesser breeds, perhaps even men versus women. But these, if they be truths, are statistical truths, and do not infallibly apply to individuals. Statistics will tell us that Scandinavians are taller than Italians; but if you want a big man for the police force, you will not reject a Primo Carnera in favor of a Norwegian midget. Even literacy is not an infallible standard. An illiterate (perhaps Homer was one?) may have more native wit and wisdom than a polished dullard stuffed with erudition. The illiterate masses of India and China managed to evolve and to follow such leaders as Gandhi and Sun Yat-sen, while the most learned country in the world groveled at the feet of Adolf Hitler.

The third rule is that any individual superiority, when established by a fair test, is special, not general; it confers no authority in a different field. Physical strength, learning, business capacity, are by no means interchangeable. If they had chosen, Einstein might have been a captain of finance, and J. Pierpont Morgan a supreme scientist: but we do not know, for it did not happen. There are no valid general intelligence tests. Among the great men whose achievements I have studied and could gauge — a motley company including Jean-Jacques Rousseau, Napoleon I, Napoleon III, Raymond Poincaré, Marshal Joffre, Franklin Roosevelt — any one might rate an Intelligence Quotient of 160 and over for some of his acts, and one of 80 or less for others. Even aptitude tests of a pragmatic nature have very little scientific value. They prove that a man can do a standardized job according to the accepted method; they do not prove that he could not find a short cut by methods of his own. I am convinced that Beaux-Arts architects, forty years ago, would have turned their thumbs down on the "aptitudes" of Le Corbusier, and high school teachers of English on the style of Gertrude Stein. As a matter of fact, they still do.

Every test in a democracy is therefore individual, special, pragmatic: "approximately," this man seems the better qualified for this definite task; but in the end, the loser may prove to be the genius. Even in technical fields, no judgment is irreformable and absolute. Between the pragmatic superiorities in different domains — and this is our fourth rule — there is no common measure. Neither the price they would command in a competitive market, nor a vote in a popularity contest, is to be accepted as a final criterion. The athlete, the hero, the poet, the scientist, the organizer, may each be supreme, but they are not comparable. According to the Elders in Troy, to Baudelaire and to Renan, beauty outranks them all. And in the eyes of God, saintliness in humble guise is more precious than wealth, power, beauty, or genius.

This doctrine of "incommensurability" closely approximates the doctrine of equality. It leads to that equality in social intercourse — freedom from snobbishness — which is the concrete manifestation of democracy. Never take your superiority for granted: the most modest artisan may be able to do certain things better than you. The beggar, even the idiot, may have sparks in his soul which, with all your breeding and success, you will never possess or perhaps comprehend.[1] There are definite occasions when it is not your privilege but your duty to assert the authority conferred upon you. Authority means responsibility, which you have no right to shirk. The police

[1] I had that feeling with certain Arab beggars; but then I had it even more when looking into the eyes of certain cats.

officer would be reprimanded if, in an emergency, he showed himself too discreet and self-effacing. Except when such an emergency arises, however, it is vulgar to pull one's rank. I, as a temporary lieutenant, met Marshal Foch off duty, and he behaved like a gentleman. But at that time the American army still frowned on any social relations between officers and enlisted men; among the crusaders for democracy, snobbishness, which is virulent anti-democracy, was rigidly enforced.

Democracy is government by consent. But there are many degrees of consent. On the threshold of consciousness, there is the force of custom and tradition. Chinese women "consented" to have their feet bound, and Mohammedan women to wear the veil. For certain anthropologists, as we have seen, such "government by unspoken consent" is the only one that is natural, and, therefore, legitimate. Polygamy, slavery, cannibalism, human sacrifices, ought not to be interfered with: if you encourage people to challenge and subvert their taboos, you will destroy the delicate equilibrium of their *culture*. This is what Burke called, proudly, the wisdom of prejudice, and Voltaire, indignantly, the tyranny of superstition. Although we might call it "preserving the American-Way-of-Life," it is not in full harmony with our questing, dynamic modern democracy.

Consent may be lethargy, sullen acquiescence, despair, the mere absence of rebellion. It can be achieved, for a time, through the relentless weeding out of subversive elements. If the French were able to jail enough Moroccan nationalists, the Moroccan people would "consent" to French rule: I am glad to say that at least one French Premier thought of a less drastic method, and applied it in Tunisia. I "consent" to be ruled by party politicians: what else can I do? But to stifle protest and to secure consent are not equivalent.

The only way to be sure of the people's active consent is through an explicit consultation. So voting is inseparable in our minds from democracy. But the machinery of voting, although not irrelevant, is not sufficient to make democracy live. De Gaulle was the legitimate ruler of the Free French before elections could be held; and the elaborate elections in totalitarian countries impress us not at all. To be valid, the voting must be free in every sense.

First of all, it must be free from pressure. If men are herded to the polls in terror, the result is an unconvincing farce. But there are more insidious and more effective forms of intimidation than the force of bayonets: and they are no less destructive of the democratic spirit. In a world of utopian liberalism, every man should feel free to proclaim his opinions from the housetops. This day has not dawned, and, realistically, the most advanced democracies take elaborate precaution to protect the secrecy of the vote. But what by law is secret must remain secret, if the spirit of the law is to be preserved. It is preposterous that an investigating committee should be permitted to ask you how you voted, or — the same question in different words — what your party affiliation is; and, to reach the *ultima Thule* of the absurd, what the affiliation of your friends was ten or fifteen years ago. For a citizen of the free world, the only answer is contemptuous silence.

There must also be a real freedom of choice, in the form of genuine alternatives. In December 1848, Louis-Napoleon reached power through a perfectly legitimate election: there were at least five candidates, and the cards seemed stacked in favor of the incumbent, General Cavaignac. But later, on two different occasions, Louis-Napoleon asked the people: "Do you want to confirm my power, or do you want civil war and anarchy?" The inevitable answer was given in 1851 and again in 1870. In neither case could it be considered as an unequivocal expression of the people's will. Of course, the single-party system, whether in our own South or in the totalitarian states, can never be democratic. Voting is meaningless, if the opposition is outlawed, as in Franco Spain or Soviet Russia.

But we, the guardians of democracy, are coming perilously near a similar situation. We too have for all practical purposes outlawed the opposition. Our plea is that the opposition is "subversive": need we repeat that every opposition that is not a sham is subversive of entrenched interests? We have the right to prevent, and therefore to guard against, *acts* of treason and violence: laws of long standing, and the police force, should be adequate to cope with such perils. But we cannot remain a democracy and suppress the lawful expression of opinion. If there are Americans who prefer Communism, they have an in- alienable right to do so. Our own right, and our duty, will be to meet their arguments with arguments, not with repressive legislation. I myself have argued all my life against Marxism, totalitarianism, police methods, and military aggression.

At present, there are two parties in the United States: the Communist Party, which is being driven underground, and the loose conglomeration of factions, six or more, which, although they flaunt two rival banners, are firmly united against Com- munism. The Communists may be an infinitesimal minority: I do not believe that there is a Communist hiding under every bed. But minority parties are entitled to the full protection of the law. Shall we plead that no man should be left free to choose evil? God Himself conferred that right upon us, some six thousand years ago, with corresponding responsibilities. What democratic pontiff has the right to define evil? In the totalitarian state, evil is liberty. In the theocratic state, evil is free thought. In the Communist state, evil is private prop- erty. In the liberal state, evil is coercion. Nothing could be more antagonistic to our principles than attempting to terrorize citizens into apparent conformity.

Voting is a cheap and humane substitute for civil war: in the good old phrases, it means ballots rather than bullets, and counting heads rather than breaking them. But voting — homeopathic war — carries with it the peril which is inherent in war itself: the belief that might is right, that the aim of total victory is the unconditional surrender of the defeated. This degradation of the democratic dogma may be defined as "the divine right of the majority." Once a vote has established which are the "ins" and which the "outs," the losers are identi- fied as "the rascals," and should be treated as rascals. However competent in their special jobs, they should as a matter of course be deprived of all positions under the state: the spoils system which prevailed so long in America, without any protest except from cracked idealists. They should even be prosecuted for having guessed wrong: the Fourth Republic in France purged the Collaborationists, yet Pétain and Laval might have been the Marshal Smuts, the Emperor Hirohito, of their country. Not a few experts, by 1946, were of the opinion that it was not safe to back the Chiang Kai-shek regime to the full; when we chose to declare undeclared war on the conquerors of Chiang Kai-shek, the men whose advice had been rejected were retrospectively branded as traitors.

The majority is in sole and absolute possession of the right: this is strictly in accordance with the gospel (one of several conflicting gospels) of Jean-Jacques Rousseau, father of democracy. Robespierre, who was the *Social Contract* incarnate, relied on the will of the majority, which was identical with virtue, which was identical with himself. He controlled the Committee of Public Safety, which controlled the Mountain, which controlled the Convention, which controlled the strategic points in France. As a result of the democratic process carried to its logical consequences, one dictator could purge everyone to the right and everyone to the left of him. This is not democracy, but Jacobinism run mad. A tragic caricature: but it emphasizes a manifest danger.

It happens that at the moment when these lines are written (January 1955), there is no decisive majority in any of the great democracies. In America, the Executive is still Republican, the Senate is poised on a needle point, and on almost every issue, each of the several factions in the House is of several minds. In England, the party which is "carrying on Her Majesty's Government" has a majority in the House, but not in the country. In Italy, France, and Germany, the loose coalitions in control are exceedingly precarious. This should be welcome as a protection against tyranny. But it also constitutes an infallible recipe to foster muddleheadedness.

Yes, the divine right of majorities means, not the government of the people by the people, but a tyranny in which the defeated lose their rights. The condition of normal activity is peace, and peace, among nations and between parties, should be attained, not through the brutal argument of numbers, but through intelligent and sympathetic adjustment. It is not "Winner take all," but "How much can the winner afford to take, without damaging vitally the loser's interests and even his pride?" Because this principle did not guide our Congress after the Civil War, Reconstruction was a failure, and the Southern wound is festering still. Because it affected the form of a *Diktat,* the Versailles settlement bred a second world war.

Three examples, two actual, the other hypothetical, will illustrate the limitations of majority rights. In the Czechoslovakia of Masaryk, a model democracy, the German minority was treated with scrupulous fairness. The Germans were fully represented according to their numbers. But, in the national parliament, they were hopelessly in a minority. Their sole right was to be defeated, automatically, by the Czechoslovak element. It did not work. Masaryk himself, a scholar and a statesman, had favored a federation of the Swiss pattern, in which every canton or district would have been practically independent in local affairs, and in which the foreign policy of the country as a whole would have been based on strict neutrality. Suppose a large country should desire to annex a small neighbor. Hitler, for instance, could have offered a referendum *in Germany as well as Belgium,* on the issue of a Belgo-German union. Belgian voters would have been given exactly the same rights as German voters: equality is the foundation of democracy. The defenders of Belgian independence would have been snowed under. According to good democratic theory, they should have bowed to the will of the majority. This may sound absurd: many among us pin their hopes on "national elections" exactly of that kind for the re-unification of Korea and Germany. In the United Nations, we command, whenever we choose to exert our influence, a steady majority of at least forty to six. Even if the neutralists should cast their votes solidly against us, we still would have a safe margin. So we proceed from victory to victory, well satisfied with our righteousness, never making the slightest attempt to see how much we could concede without detriment to our vital principles and interests. We call it democracy, and we are indignant with the Soviet group for not offering its unconditional surrender. But this is not democracy: it is a campaign in the cold war, and the United Nations never will function satisfactorily in such an atmosphere. In so far as democracy is akin to war, it will remain, like war, a wasteful and incompetent method of conducting human affairs. The true key to democracy is not strife, but free and friendly discussion, with a genuine desire to arrive at a workable agreement. Perhaps England has come nearer such an ideal than any other great country; and the result is that for nearly three hundred years, England has escaped civil wars and revolutions.

Voting is therefore a rough-and-ready method, but not a panacea. There is no aura of mysticism about the democratic principle. The voice of the people is emphatically not the voice of God: for there is no voice of the people. Demos, "a herd confused, a miscellaneous rabble," is inarticulate: he can only grunt discontent or delight. His moods, which are neither ideas nor policies, have to be interpreted, directed, and to a large extent created, by leaders — not single individuals as a rule, but teams, small conscious organized minorities. These leaders would be powerless if they were not followed; but the mass would be aimless, not even conscious of its bewilderment, if it were not guided — or goaded. "America is grimly determined . . .": pure figure of rhetoric; the determination and the grimness are provided by a few. Democracy, which is very real, is the opportunity of choosing between rival groups.

I must constantly reaffirm that, except in the domain of pure science, the choice never is unanimous. There is no universal and irresistible verdict of taste, morality, or religion: dissent is the rule. And perhaps dissent is salvation: no man has a chance of developing *taste* unless he rejects the thrall of *good taste*. The one deadly heresy is orthodoxy. So it is in political affairs. There were Tories or Loyalists at the time of the Revolution. In the secession crisis, there were high-minded

Northerners who urged that the erring sisters be allowed to depart in peace. Some of our best fellow citizens opposed World War I and World War II. Unanimity is bluff: "Be unanimous, or face the firing squad." Who was ever fooled by the ninety-nine per cent majorities of the dictators? If they were not faked, the case would be even worse. I am fond of quoting the phrase: "Unanimity is the *rigor mortis* of a nation's thought."

A spontaneous single thought, arising from the depths of the masses, is but a beautiful myth: the realities of collective life are at one end cliques and cabals, at the other devoted bands of apostles. The masses never rebel: but the direction of their stampede may be altered. In American life, these "small, conscious, organized minorities" or pressure groups, lobbies, educational associations are innumerable, from the churches to the Anti-Margarine League. In pure(?) politics, a very small number of fairly permanent and fairly general bodies have emerged. These — perhaps half a dozen — are known as parties; and only two of them effectively count. As this is the garment which our democracy assumed, most of us take it for granted that the party system is identical with democracy. Nothing could be more palpably false. In this I take my stand with the Founders, who considered the rise of parties as a peril for the Republic, and called them by their proper name *factions*. Parties are the perfect example of what my dictionary calls *Politics (b)*: they have long ceased to be groups seeking support for a distinctive policy in which they believe; they are gangs athirst for power and spoils, seeking "with both ears on the ground," the policy most likely to catch votes. It is parties that turn politics into war, brutal even when it is bloodless. Parties are based on the fiction that all right-minded men, on our side, think exactly alike on all questions and are in sole possession of the truth; whereas the dupes and knaves on the other side likewise think alike on all questions, but are infallibly wrong. The rabid hostility between Communists and anti-Communists is simply a global extension of the party spirit.

The incompetence and corruption of party politics are basic

facts in our experience. We cannot open our daily papers without being choked with the pungent stench. No man can reach the heights of statesmanship except by transcending party politics. But even men of intelligence and integrity give up, *consenting* to the present muddle out of weariness, helplessness, and despair. The students of political science, rigorously objective, virtuously scorning Utopia, simply chronicle the episodes of the fray. Thus they eliminate from their researches what is truly science. For science is more than a mere inventory: science is foresight and power.

I propose to examine later the means by which the evils of politics could be mitigated. The means I have in mind, so far as America is concerned, are very simple: but *simple* and *easy* are not synonymous. My proposals are surprisingly conservative: the recapture of forgotten values rather than a dash into the radical unknown. But, at this point, I should like to indicate, in a more general manner, the ways in which the rival systems — theocracy, technocracy, anarchism — could provide safeguards against the dangers inherent in democracy.

Theocracy denies that spiritual truth can ever be determined by taking a vote, although such was the method of the œcumenical councils down to 1870. Wisely recognizing its own limitations, democracy gives up the right to legislate in religious matters. It will place no obstacle in the path of religious beliefs and observances. On the other hand, in spite of the efforts of the Covenanters, it cannot put a dogma on the statute book. Jules Simon once boasted that he had the French Senate vote the existence of God by a handsome majority: the news must have been received in Heaven with a courteous smile. Theocracy legitimately warns democracy: "Thus far and no farther."

Technocracy denies that a scientific truth can depend on the returns of an election. Kipling's village voted that the earth was flat, Tennessee that Darwin was wrong, and the American Congress, through a Nordic slant in our immigration laws, that Gobineau, Houston Stewart Chamberlain, and Hitler were right. The only answer is Galileo's: *"E pur si muove!"* Democracy should put no barrier against the quest for truth: the Lysenko affair seemed to us a horrible example.

Finally anarchism, or sturdy individualism, is also a useful monitor. Government inevitably is coercion, and coercion is evil. So there is an evil in the very nature of government, an evil which cannot be eliminated but which must be restrained. The state is at the same time our servant and our enemy, the promoter of the common good and the master threatening our freedom. Our response should be ambivalent: loyal support combined with eternal distrust.

Democracy, yes; but democracy severely limited by Theocracy in those things which are not Caesar's; served, but also warned by Technocracy; challenged by Anarchism whenever it is tempted to disregard the interests and the self-respect of the individual: a complex formula, no doubt, and very different from the holy simplicity of *Vox Populi Vox Dei*. But the conception of checks and balances, i.e., of complexities, is not unfamiliar to students of the American Constitution. The chief instrument in *Politics (b)* is claptrap. The key to *Politics (a)*, statesmanship, which may be identified with the service of civilization, is accuracy. "Let us strive to think accurately," Pascal said; "such is the foundation of moral life."

CHAPTER VII

What Can Be Done?

I

I believe that we are not disarmed before manifest evils, however deep-rooted. This is radicalism naked and unashamed; but I hope I shall make it clear that I have no thought of offering a panacea. I have little faith in systems and in paper organizations: the only good constitutions are those which would lose none of their power if, like the British, they were left unwritten. If I took part in the Committee to Frame a World Constitution, it was not in the hope that we were to bring down the eternal Tables of the Law from our Chicago Sinai: it was simply to provide an incentive and a guide to further thought. A constitution, to use the French phrase, should "go without saying." But I beg to offer the very French amendment: "It goes even better if you do say it." We should have no fanatical belief in the inerrancy of dumbness.

The one thing needful is to bear in mind that government offers a constant succession of ever-changing problems, and that to face them from day to day requires a constant mental effort. There are many possible ways to perdition; but the only one that is infallible is standpattism; for the world moves, and the standpatters are stranded in 1688, 1776, or 1789. I feel certain that many countries with different traditions should try different approaches. I should consider it healthy if one country — our own — should feel free to conduct many experiments, provided they be at the same time cautious in method and bold in spirit.

I urge caution as well as boldness. But in a liberal, i.e., a tolerant or pluralistic, state, caution is almost automatic. Any reform, limited to a definite object, permits the survival of other

institutions and customs, provided they are not palpably harmful. It is only the monolithic, totalitarian state that needs to
be afraid of total subversion. But caution does not commit us
to gradualism as a rigid dogma. There are new departures in
history: the release of atomic energy was one. Arguing the
point with Edward M. Sait many years ago, and recently with
that lovable High Tory Max Lerner, I used as an illustration
the San Francisco Bay Bridge. The defenders of slow, organic,
unconscious development tell us that a sane practical bridge
must evolve by haphazard installments in the course of untold
generations: trestles extended a few yards at a time, a sunken
ship used as an improvised pier. To start by "dreaming" of a
bridge, drawing the blueprints of an unrealistic structure which
is not there at all, is sheer Utopianism. We must take things
as they are, not pull them out of our teeming brains. All this
is irrefutable good sense, and palpably in contradiction with the
facts. The bridge was first dreamt of, by no less a personage
than the Emperor Norton; it was then definitely conceived,
blueprinted, constructed in as short a time as possible according
to plans and specifications. It was opened, not piecemeal, but
through its whole length and on one particular day. To the
great scandal of the Burke-de Maistre-Sait school of historians,
the *planned* American Constitution works, the *planned* city of
Washington lives, the *planned* San Francisco Bay Bridge carries
tremendous traffic.

Gradualism, often a fallacy when we are thinking of construction, is more patently a fallacy when destruction is concerned. It would be ideal if old men, old landmarks, old
institutions, were to age gracefully. Even for the worst of them,
"innocuous desuetude" might be a better solution than instant
death. Kings, armies, theologies, like feudal castles and Roman
temples, will outlive their usefulness by decades or centuries,
achieving slowly the pure beauty that transcends any earthly
purpose. They will have — they already have in my eyes —
their respected place in the vast museum or Antique Shoppe
of mankind. They are the living monuments of a storied past;
and when they die at last, as heroes and gods must die, I shall

not grudge them their purple shroud. But men and institutions often refuse thus to fade gently into the impalpable esthetic realm. They fight for life, and they fight hard. In such cases, it may be a cruel duty to remind them that they are ghosts.

This is called a revolution: inevitably a painful, an ugly, a wasteful process. Louis XVI in 1789, a kindly man, slow-witted but not stupid, could have become either the true leader of his people, or at least a respected figurehead. He rejected both possibilities, and chose instead to champion, against the plain realities of the time, antiquated privileges, abuses, and super-stitions. He had to be restrained by drastic means. We may sigh: "The pity of it." But Louis XVI had failed to understand that *gradually,* through half a millennium of growth, the Third Estate had become the very armature of the kingdom. So the Ancient Regime collapsed, as the Campanile crashed down in Venice early in this century, as the Tower of Pisa, we are in-formed, will topple over in the year 2043. Death and birth are revolutions, and as such they are fraught with pain and peril. But the realist must acknowledge that they were not invented by radicals. My one hope is to see the elasticity of our political thinking so developed as to avoid a catastrophe. I am "subversive" only of doctrinaire rigidity. I cannot admit that arteriosclerosis is a blessing.

The problem is to secure the benefits of *government* — the pooling of efforts for the common good — without the curse of *politics* — the clash of narrow, unscrupulous interests. Here I am conscious of an apparent contradiction: what business have I to write about the problems of government, when I have constantly spurned practical politics? Have I not been a fugitive from social duty, a thin-skinned, tender-minded recluse, leaving to others the indispensable back-breaking, dusty, sweaty labor?

I plead not guilty. This testament of mine is not an apology, but a confession, first of all for the cleansing of my own con-science; and, on this point, I feel no remorse. I have no word of blame for my friends and colleagues who engage in practical politics: they saw their duty and did it. As a thoroughgoing individualist, I had the right to take a different view. No one is morally obliged to join in activities which seem to him wrong, futile, or simply irrelevant. No free spirit could take part in politics under the Fascist, Nazi, Bolshevik or Franco dispensations: he could only withdraw into solitude or exile. There always is some Ivory Tower, science or art, as a last resort the cloister or the jail, to serve as a citadel of integrity.

Yet I am not committed to anarchism. I firmly believe in government, as the promotion of the common good, the management of the common wealth. I could easily have conquered my squeamishness, and handled a greasy tool, if I had thought that it could serve a worthy end. But I am a democrat, not a ritualist of democracy. I believe in the government of the people by the people and for the people, not in the grabbing of power by rival gangs of profiteers. So long as we have freedom of thought and speech guaranteed by an independent judiciary (both the freedom and the guarantee are seriously threatened as I write these words), there will be other lines of action: not merely cleaner, but more effective.

The truth as I see it, speaking as a lifelong student of history, is the infinitesimal part played by *Politics* (*b*) in human affairs. O the momentary momentousness and abysmal futility of men and parties, great in their own conceit! Who cares today for the various ministers who tripped one another so cleverly under clever King Louis-Philippe? Laffitte, Casimir Périer, Molé, Soult, Thiers, Guizot, where are they? A dismal puppet show, like the whirligig of cabinets under the Third Republic — and the Fourth. Politics and politicians are but the scum — for the sake of courtesy, let us call it the foam — on a mighty stream.

A full-grown man with a serious turn of mind has something better to do than work strenuously for Harding or for Cox — with a Coolidge as the ultimate prize. It is by performing his own work honestly that he does his best for the common good. But his duty does not stop there. To accept such a limitation was the fallacy that paralyzed so many admirable Germans under the Bismarckian Empire, or the Hitlerian: out of modesty, or out of contempt, they allowed the political powers to have full sway. I see no virtue in such resignation: had I been a German, I hope I should have been against Kaiser and Führer, even though they had captured the machinery of the state and claimed to speak in the name of the nation. In America and France, I stand against the politicians. "Vote them out of office, then!" What! Turn the rascals out, and bring in others with slightly different labels, but belonging to the same system? What I can do is to thwart their power, and first of all by refusing to acknowledge their authority over my thought. Even if they were to jail me — and they have prosecuted others far less "subversive" than I — I should still be a free man. Enslavement begins with the admission that a Coolidge counts.

But my attitude is far from negative. Let me reaffirm my faith that government can be made the instrument of the common will for the common good: the problem is to enlighten public opinion, not to take part in the shadow-boxing of machine politicians. To enlighten public opinion does not involve offering ready-made solutions: it means fostering honest and intelligent discussion. To govern is to educate, not to indoctrinate.

I am convinced that politicians are noxious; but I am convinced also of their comparative insignificance. They "muscle in," play their dreary antics, draw their paltry profits: all this does no earthly good, but it is not the cause of our deepest evils. The worst that it can effect is to divert our attention from the real problems of community life. It is the people as a whole who must bear the responsibility; and most of all the intellectual leaders whose task it should be to enlighten the people. One of the direct causes of World War II was our refusing to join the Court of International Justice. It was a declaration of isolationism, the blunt rejection of an organized world conscience. Now the Senate vote, which apparently clinched the matter, was a mere episode. The deeper fact was the vast informal influence of men like Will Rogers and Father Coughlin: thanks to them the Senate was deluged with menacing telegrams. The deepest fact was the pusillanimity of those who should have thought the problem out, and who shirked the hard work of informing their fellow citizens. A *thinking* America would have compelled the Senators to vote for peace through justice, irrespective of party lines.

The disaster that made World War III all but inevitable was the proclamation of the Truman Doctrine: "getting tough" (i.e., deliberately ceasing to be intelligent); "containment" (i.e., encirclement); "rearmament" (i.e., a mad race in mutual provocation, until a shooting war seems a relief). Now this doctrine was given out, of his own authority, by the Official Supreme Politician, and tacitly ratified by the professional politicians. But every one knew at the time how much and how little that august personage counted in our national life. It was aptly said of him that "he held the whole world in the hollow of his head." The decisive factor was the unreasoning acceptance of the doctrine, without any realization of its ineluctable and tragic consequences. The masses of the American people were passive at first: the doctrine offered an easy vent for a vague irritation in which righteousness, pride, and fear were oddly blended. The alternative: a firm, intelligent, generous discussion, was not even considered. The public had not been educated by the press, and by those whose business it should have been to substitute clear thinking for nervous reflexes. We, not President Truman, were to blame; and not merely for the venial sin of electing him. Had Tweedledum been President instead of Tweedledee, the result would hardly have been different. If America had learnt, and not merely bought, *The Art of Thinking,* and realized *The Power of Positive Thinking,* even bad politicians could not have wallowed in bad politics. And such an America would not long tolerate bad politicians.

Wilson, almost alone among official leaders, sought to *educate* America and the world; and his teaching was not wholly in vain. Unfortunately, he was also a politician: else he would never have reached political heights. He played the orthodox game: machine against machine. He fancied himself as "the shrewd realistic diplomat," another Talleyrand, a Bismarck *pour le bon motif,* a less flashy Disraeli. He probably prided himself upon having so neatly tricked poor old Clemenceau into giving up the Rhineland. Had he gone to Paris as an American Gandhi, the moral leader of a crusade for peace through justice, the world might have been spared a heart-breaking frustration; for the common man was readier for Wilsonism than Wilson himself. Even defeat would not have lacked greatness: a cause unsullied never is irretrievably lost. But how could a man rise above politics, if he believes in politics? Wilson asked for a partisan victory, and failed. So he went to Paris as the defeated leader of a bankrupt party. Wilson, Root, Lowell, Taft, and Hughes ought to have constituted themselves into a Faculty of International Law, to teach the American people their new opportunity and their new responsibility. And the people were eager to learn.

Franklin Roosevelt, who had a good heart and a good mind, was at least nine-tenths politician, and rejoiced in his ungodly skill. He maneuvered America into world responsibility: maneuvered, but failed to educate. As a result, we were to jump stiffly from isolationism into imperialism (renamed, for the sake of decency, *leadership*), and of the two, imperialism is the worse. He had started maneuvering — not educating — his allies into decent conditions of peace, but through an inextricable tangle of cleverness; and he died leaving poor Mr. Truman bewildered in the darkest twist of the maze.

Teaching means looking beyond immediate interests: it is the immediate interest of the boy to play truant, so as to have a good time, or earn a few nickels. And looking beyond immediate interests is the reverse of practical politics. My life has been dedicated to teaching: not selling subjects at retail, but training minds. This was done not through the classroom alone, but through addresses, essays, and books intended for the general public; and it was done with no expectation of a reward in the form of position, cash, or fame. In so doing, I have attempted to follow my *political* duty. I have been a *regular* all my life, for I have sought to live my law. With politics as understood by the boss and the ward heeler, I never had anything to do.

II

There is a very practical approach which leaves political problems untouched while rigorously limiting their field: it is Civil Service extension and reform. By this means, it is possible to do away with the spoils system, nepotism, favoritism, and a great deal of corruption.[1] The aim is to secure the best qualified men, technically and morally, for every post; to offer them the adequate rewards, and above all the security and freedom, that will attract and retain their services. We need efficient management, whereas *Politics* (*b*) was excellently defined by Emile Faguet, two generations ago, as "the cult of incompetence and the fear of responsibilities." I am ready to grant that efficiency is not all; but honesty and professional ability go a very long way. On this point, Mr. Herbert Hoover, the great engineer and organizer, never fully at home in the political world, is well qualified to speak. "The right man in the right place," and that place clearly defined, so as to avoid duplications, gaps and conflicts: surely a sensible and conservative ideal. But it means the end of pull and patronage; it implies that *Politics* (*b*) is a virus that must be held in check.

We must bear in mind, however, that securing good technicians will not suffice. Two essential problems remain unsolved. First, if the technicians are mere instruments, who is going to use them, and for what ends? The old Prussian administrator, well trained and rigorously honest, was a perfect cog in the machine — with a neurotic William II at the controls. There was marvelous efficiency in the Third Reich, even in its death-factories: but the ruler was Hitler. I rely on technocracy to limit the area of party politics; but the central evil is not eliminated.

[1] The spoils system, universally condemned, is still rife with us, although not under that dishonored name. It is logical enough, in partisan politics, for the winners to declare that the losers, from President and Secretary of State to dog catchers, are traitors. (Rosas, as we have seen, with Latin ebullience, used a whole string of picturesque adjectives.) They must be ousted, not officially as members of a party, but as suspect of disloyalty, and a risk to the security of the nation. Of course, they are replaced by "safe" men.

Unless the technocrats themselves assume power: but this poses our second problem. The misrule of politicians would be superseded by the enlightened despotism of experts. For most of my life, I have been resolutely opposed to such a dispensation. The technocrats would become a privileged body, serenely proof against the criticism of the uninitiated, impregnable in their own infallibility. Power would corrupt them, as it corrupts every man and every group. It would soon turn technocracy into bureaucracy, all the worse for the prestige of its expert knowledge. (A theocracy, by the way, is such a technocracy: the rulers are the men versed in the doctrines and practices of their church.) I am particularly averse to mandarin government, the rule of scholars, selected for their familiarity with the classics. I have lived among scholars and given examinations all my life: I know the limitations of my class and of its methods. The system was used in China for ages, and the world is not tempted to borrow the pattern.

A new condition was created, however, by the sudden revelation of atomic power. Hitherto, scientists could work calmly for science's sake: the use made of their discoveries was no concern of theirs. This aloofness was justified, or at any rate it could be condoned, because the contributions of pure science to practical life were not revolutionary. They were overshadowed by the enormous mass of traditions, by practical business, by an industry still largely in the empirical stage: I remember with what pride an English friend told me, about 1900: "Watt and Stephenson knew nothing about thermodynamics." The dramatic achievements of nuclear physics have altered the situation. A revolution has occurred. Within the range of human history, nature, unaided, had not split the atom in any way recognizable by man; and that fantastic development started in pure research. It was a victory of science alone, not of agelong ubiquitous fumbling.

And the released power is stupendous. Thus the scientist is abruptly made aware of his responsibility. Should he turn over those formidable weapons to men whose minds linger in the Dark Ages, and perhaps in the Paleolithic? For a Dr. Oppenheimer, a Senator Knowland can hardly be considered a good security risk. Georges Duhamel proposed to meet the danger by declaring a moratorium on all further discoveries, until the world had fully adapted itself to the recent ones. I do not believe that the political mind is adjusted to aviation, or even to gun powder. We cannot unlearn what we know; we cannot cease learning more. Duhamel's suggestion is sheer *petit bourgeois* defeatism: *"Reprenons nos bonnes petites habitudes!"* — let us return to the good old days of Napoleon, Genghis Khan, and Attila, who were innocent of any nuclear taint. As there should be no power without responsibility, so there should be no responsibility without power: and the responsibility of the scientist is appalling. Instead of attempting to educate our political and economic masters to the facts of contemporary life — I grant it looks like a hopeless task — why not turn our allegiance to the men who already know?

The autocracy of the scientist: Ernest Renan had toyed with such an idea in his *Dialogues et Fragments Philosophiques* as early as 1876. Profoundly shaken by the apocalyptic events of the "Terrible Year" (1870–71), and particularly by the Commune, he thought of the people as Caliban, to be sternly disciplined, through torture if necessary, by the magician-scientist Prospero. He envisaged the ruthless dictatorship of the Academy of Sciences. It was confessedly a nightmare: soon his marvelously complex and resilient nature recovered its balance, and in a later drama, Prospero actually became reconciled with Caliban-Demos, not such an outrageous monster after all.

Aldous Huxley offered us a sinister Utopia, or Swiftian satire, *Brave New World*. There autocracy is exercized in the name of eugenics. I interpret the book rather as a denunciation of my *bête noire,* enforced conformity: Huxley's biologists have evolved a perfect *culture.* Both Renan and Huxley are right in warning us against any kind of autocracy, whether it be in the name of God, or Science, or the People. Perhaps both insisted overmuch on the mechanistic aspect of scientific thought, as do the Marxians. Men who propound eternal laws will believe in their own infallibility; but the essence of the scientific spirit is discovery, the basic method in science is experiment: both imply that our present knowledge is imperfect. This changes the perspective: a dynamic science could not lead us into a static Utopia. But it must be granted that power is a peril unless it is directed to some worthy purpose; and that the conception of *worthy purpose* is humanistic, not scientific. As ruler of this world, science was bankrupt from the very first.

I feel certain that scientists as a group do not crave power: it is too messy a job for their meticulous minds. I doubt whether they are trained for power: the governance of men is an art, and eludes the rigorous methods of the laboratory. But their share in the direction of human affairs should increase, at the expense of mere tradition, and above all of selfish interests. Scientists have the right and the duty to demand from those who wield authority some at least of the qualities that science requires. Among these are intellectual honesty first of all, freedom from prejudice, the courage to consider new and startling hypotheses, the rejection of all fakes and all claptrap, contempt for the desire of scoring small points. The scientists should tell us, in no ambiguous terms, that the neglect of these qualities leads to catastrophe, a catastrophe enormously amplified by the very victories of science. In the horse-and-buggy days, one could afford to smile when the driver happened to be a drunk or a moron: the horse had sense, at any rate. You cannot show the same indulgence with the man in charge of a supersonic plane and a hydrogen bomb.

The scientists do have responsibility: I know it weighs heavily upon some of them. A Brain Trust with advisory powers should be a recognized institution. Such a Brain Trust should not be *at the service* of the politicians, as were the *científicos* under Porfirio Díaz, or the haphazard group of well-meaning men under Franklin Roosevelt: it should remain at least as independent as the Supreme Court. Inevitably, it would be non-national in its outlook. Theologians like Reinhold Niebuhr may deny that mankind is one; they cannot deny that science ignores political boundaries. Nothing could be more cosmopolitan than the team of scientists who evolved the atom bomb.

In any country, the Scientific Council would consider itself as the local branch of the Universal Research Association.[2]

III

At Versailles, on the fourth of August 1789, the holders of privileges acknowledged the victory of the Enlightenment and abandoned their feudal rights as incompatible with modern conditions: I cannot imagine politicians rising to such a height of self-sacrifice. There are times when the politicians, who are men, and shrewd men, must be nauseated by their own performances. It came nearly to that on the eighteenth of Brumaire (November 9, 1799): the *prattlers,* as Napoleon called them, were ready for suicide. It was definitely the case in 1940, when the Parliament of the Third Republic admitted bankruptcy, and appointed Marshal Pétain as receiver. Politicians, however, are rarely stunned or panicked into such a meek surrender: even on the nineteenth of Brumaire, the grenadiers had to march in. As a rule, a regime has to be openly murdered, not gently put to sleep. This, whether in the form of insurrection, Putsch, pronuciamiento, or coup d'état, has become one of the commonest phenomena in our era. As I was writing the first version of these lines, on March 11, 1952, I heard that General Bautista had seized power again in Cuba, "almost without bloodshed." At the present stage of my work (winter 1954–55), the latest coups have taken place in Brazil, Guatemala, Egypt, Pakistan. There will be many more before this book appears in print.

But, in revolution or a coup d'état, the people do not resume power and responsibility: they, as well as the discredited politicians, abdicate. Even if they approve of the change, it simply means that in their opinion, a new set of masters, and even one man in absolute control, might be less annoying and more efficient than the old Five Hundred. Dictatorial politics is politics. It has obvious virtues of its own, and they offer a

---

[2] This is in harmony with President Eisenhower's proposal for a world council on atomic research.

temptation which we should not minimize. But it has also vices which are invariably fatal. For the dictator, although he claims to be national and nonpartisan, like the two Napoleons, like Díaz, like Mussolini, like Stalin, like Hitler, like Franco, like de Gaulle, must, in the name of national unity, fight against "traitors, rebels, separatists," all those who cannot see in him the pure and complete incarnation of the national ideal. The result is, as in old Turkey and in old Russia, a despotism which can be tempered only by assassination.

It is utopian to decree the end of crime, and to believe that crime will meekly accept its outlawry; it is highly practical to have a police force and curb crime. It is idle to proclaim health as a national ideal: it is realistic for doctors to circumscribe and alleviate disease. The bubonic plague, cholera, yellow fever, typhoid, are no longer the scourges our ancestors knew. More modestly still: I understand that diabetes cannot be cured, but can be held in check. The problem is to find the equivalent of insulin for the dread *morbus politicus*.

The oddity is that the palliatives I have to offer are so modest and so conservative. They mark a return to orthodoxy rather than a venture into the dim uncharted unknown. What could be sounder, for instance, than reviving the *representative system*? We take it for granted that, wherever there are elections, there is representation. This is not quite the case. The true representative system implies that the average citizen has neither the leisure nor the knowledge properly to attend to the affairs of the state. He picks out a good man, whom he entrusts with the task of studying these problems for him, and deciding upon the solution. The citizen's sole responsibility is to choose the best man available: quite possibly one who does not push himself forward. The duty of the representative is to report to his constituents, and explain how he arrived at a decision: a highly educative process.

This means a single member for each constituency, offering himself on his own personal merits. No "voting for the best man, provided his name be on the Democratic ticket." Dr. David Starr Jordan, true to the original representative idea, claimed that he always voted a straight ticket by scratching out all the crooks. The candidate should commit himself to nothing, except to voting according to his conscience: his intelligence and his integrity are the sole guarantees offered to the elector. This used to be the theory, and even the practice, in France at the end of the nineteenth century: men were returned on their personal record as men, not as politicians. I have a faint recollection of my father's voting for Denys Cochin, a Royalist of unblemished character, because his Republican opponent had a dubious personal reputation. The *mandat impératif,* the strict obligation for the representative to vote exactly as he was told, was considered a dangerous heresy. If the representatives are not men with a mind and a conscience of their own, but automatic organs of transmission, they are a waste and could be eliminated: it would be simpler to vote, *en bloc,* for a party and its program.

I must admit that the representative system, both in England and in France, served the wealthy men who could, as the saying was, "nurse" a constituency. Daniel Wilson, whose dubious activities caused the downfall of his father-in-law President Grévy, preserved his seat for many years after the scandal. Pierre Laval was a perfect illustration of that danger. He belonged to no party (he vaguely called himself an Independent Socialist), but he was the most expert and diligent of *fixers. Politics (b)* can be a scourge even in the absence of party lines.

If the representative system, as intended by the Founders, is no panacea, it can at least be used to check the worst evils of party politics. The balance of power, in America, is held by the voters who are not committed. They cannot destroy the existing machines, and the repeated attempts to create a third machine have failed; but they can assign a limit to their nefarious power. The politicians can "get away" with a great deal: they cannot get away with everything. Even in the single-party states, the voters who take their responsibility seriously can "break the slate," and write in on the ballot the name of an independent candidate. It requires no change in the Constitution to make the average man realize that *regularity* is not a virtue, but an evil; that there may be men labeled Democrats who are not rabble-rousers and men dubbed Republicans who are not the tools of Wall Street. Every true American should issue his own Declaration of Independence.

The second palliative would be to give at least some semblance of reality to the brilliant abstraction evolved by Locke and Montesquieu: the separation of the three powers. Neither in England nor in France, and least of all in America, has it ever corresponded with the facts. But it remains the official theory, just as meekness, nonresistance and the scorn of riches remain the official doctrine of the Christian nations: man has a marvelous capacity for evolving and keeping alive incredible monsters, centaurs, sphinxes, and chimaeras dire. Mr. Herbert Hoover, who had painful reasons to know better, still affirms in his *Memoirs* that our system provides for an independent executive. Perhaps the letter of the Constitution does: the plain facts of political life tell a different story. In an absolute monarchy, whether by right divine, or in the form of democratic Caesarism, the executive is all-powerful: the legislators are but technicians who work out into formal texts the directives of the master. In England, on the other hand, the House of Commons is sovereign: the executive is the Cabinet, which for all practical purposes is a committee of the House. In America, the original confusion has never been cleared. We shift unconsciously from the Presidential form of government, when the man in power is strong and personally supported by the people, to the Congressional, when through his own weakness or through the circumstances of the time, the Chief Executive has lost his grip. This does not mean that there is constant conflict between the two powers: as a rule, there is a *modus vivendi*, uneasy at times, but frequently amicable.

Now the Executive is the substance of government: the Legislative can only talk about it. Vast countries have lived for ages without a separate legislature: none could survive without an executive. It is much easier for a good executive, even if he is the elect of a party, to rise above partisanship and become truly national than it is for a divided assembly. Except when it follows a strong executive — a Clemenceau, a Churchill, a Roosevelt — an assembly is in danger of stumbling helplessly. The irreconcilable conflicts of minds which are the norm in any free assembly would be exposed as schizophrenia if they occurred in an individual. Clear-cut decisions can hardly be expected of a hydra, half of whose five hundred heads are snarling at the other half.

The Legislative would have an honored and useful place in the state, if it limited itself to its proper functions: after careful investigation and debate, to place permanent laws, not emergency measures, on the statute book. It should give up any thought of interfering with the Executive or the Judiciary. This was General de Gaulle's ideal, and it remains attractive: the French people ratified it twenty to one, when they voted to do away with the Constitution of 1875; but the politicians managed to crawl back into power. Naturally, any one who proposes to check the usurpations of the *prattlers*, to use again Napoleon's term, will be accused of strangling democracy.

Candidates for the position of chief executive are now picked out by the parties, and are inevitably enmeshed in the system. Even Messrs. Hoover and Eisenhower, who were not politicians, and were elected largely on their personal merits, had to act as the *regular* heads of a party. How could we pick out an executive wholly independent of such commitments?

One method would be to revitalize a now vestigial organ in the Constitution, the College of Electors. It was intended to have a function: now it is barely a form.[3] If the Electors were given substance, if they were true representatives, not mere cogs, if they actually met to choose a President, the evils of the party system would be greatly mitigated. Such a change would be less of a departure from the spirit of the Constitution than our present practice is.

But the Electoral College is more likely to be swept aside as a mere shadow. It would be possible to call together a *single*

---

[3] One wonders what would happen if the candidate of the leading party were to die between the general elections in November and the casting of the votes by the Electors.

National Convention for the sole purpose of nominating two or more candidates. The people would then decide by preferential ballot. As originally intended, the man standing second in the people's estimation would, irrespective of party, become Vice President. Perhaps we could have the great interests — Labor, Agriculture, Industry, Commerce, Education — through their national associations, nominate a candidate each, *not out of their own numbers*. Several of these nominations might coincide. Indeed, a single name might conceivably emerge. Again, the final choice would rest with the people. I am not offering any such solution as an infallible nostrum. The one important point is that we should be released from the blind and weary acceptance of manifest evils.

An independent national executive might easily lead to Caesarism. As a matter of fact, it is closely akin to Caesarism. The dangers of monarchy (for this, not the pleasing harmless pageantry of hereditary throne and crown, is truly monarchy) are patent; so are its advantages, which make it such a temptation even for highly cultured countries. I admit that against the perils of autocratic leadership (Duce, Führer, Caudillo) the ultra-legislative powers of the Legislative are an effective check; but the check may prove clumsy and wasteful as well as effective. We need brakes; but we want the kind of brakes that will not be applied too jerkily — or too constantly.

It would be better to preserve and strengthen what other checks we have — or ought to have, for they show signs of weakening: a free press and a free judiciary. I shall discuss them in other sections of this book: let us be satisfied for the present with the barest indications. The eighteenth century, the most "enlightened" of all, evolved two rival Utopias. The first is summed up in the famous phrase: "There are judges in Berlin." The autocracy even of a Frederick II can do no irreparable harm, so long as the king himself submits to the law. The windmill at Sans-Souci commemorates that tradition: alas! unfounded. The Frederick who respected windmills also stole provinces. The other Utopia, strikingly French, was: "I do not care who writes the laws, so long as I write the songs." Among civilized people, mockery is an effective curb. In France, in particular, ridicule is deadly. The age of Beaumarchais was freer than ours.

In many countries, particularly those in the Spanish tradition, pretorianism is an ever-present danger. Spain under Franco, Guatemala under a military junta, are recent examples in point. The armed forces, like the Pretorian Guards, the Janissaries, the Mamelukes, could easily be tempted to seize power, instead of being merely the instruments of power. There were traces of that virus in militaristic empires like Hohenzollern Germany and pre-war Japan. The two Napoleons used the army to attain power, yet under their rule the army was not dictating policy. Although America has had many generals among her Presidents, the danger with us is remote. We emphatically do not want to be governed by "old soldiers" who believe that "there is no substitute for victory." But the threat might be very real with the European army tomorrow, and, within a foreseeable future, with the World Police Force, if they grew faster than the spirit they are supposed to serve: nothing could be more dangerous for a weak Europe than a strong European army. The new weapons create a radical disparity between the organized military and the unarmed masses. The days will not return when it was possible for embattled farmers to defy tyranny. Those who control the instruments of wholesale destruction could rule for a while by methods of sheer terrorism. A nobility of the Atom Bomb might result in a new feudalism.

Against this very real peril, I can think of two remedies. The first is the most rigid intellectual and moral selection for the Army (this would rule out selection by and for the politicians): only the best can be trusted with irresistible force. All officers, and all enlisted men also, should be gentlemen in spirit and in truth. The second is a constant rotation, both in the ranks and among the officers, between military and civilian duties. A man would serve for a number of years in command of a unit, then be for a period an educator, an administrator, an engineer. There are many examples of such alternations in our history, including Washington, Grant, and Eisenhower. Here the scientific character of modern warfare is a help. Soldiers of the old type, dashing cavaliers like Murat, beefy heroes like Sir Redvers Buller, are no longer adequate. The army leader needs the same qualities of character, the same degree of technical training as the great industrial or academic executive. In such a way, the growth of a purely military spirit and of a close-knit military caste would be prevented.

The idea of a plural or collegiate executive should not be lightly dismissed. In France it still suffers from the dismal failure of the Directory, one hundred and sixty years ago. But it works well in Switzerland, oldest and purest of democracies; and it has recently been adopted in Uruguay, a remarkably sane country in a frequently distracted continent.[4] Divided authority is no authority at all: that is why I am so averse to the Parliamentary system of the French type. But an executive commission need not be divided. The great services might be left in charge of single managers, with no lack of power and responsibility. The Board of Directors would be mostly an instrument of coördination. At any rate, I hope this system will be tried in several other places, including some of our own states. This is One World, but a pluralistic one; and experiment is the key to orderly progress.

In the third place, we can get away from purely partisan politics through more democracy, direct democracy: the *initiative* and *referendum*, which exists in several of our states as well as in Switzerland. Of this, the *plebiscite* cherished by dictators is not even a caricature. It occurs only after the event, and offers no choice but acquiescence or chaos. A general election is no substitute. Woodrow Wilson suggested "a solemn referendum" in 1920; what happened was totally different. The result was, not a definite consultation, but a confused fight. America voted, pell mell, on the record and promises of the parties, on the character and performances of individual men, on a vast array of local and national issues. Many Republicans, in answer to a definite question, would have voted for a League of Nations;

[4] In theory, the executive in the Soviet system is collective, a *Presidium*.

even their Presidential candidate was hazily in favor of it; and
World War II might have been averted. The Gallup and other
polls, even if further refined and made official, would be an
uncertain substitute for a direct consultation of the whole
people. We overlook the fact that modern technique would
make such a referendum easy. If we had the machinery constantly in readiness for such an emergency, a vote could be
ordered on Monday, taken on Tuesday, and the result known
on Wednesday morning. The telegraph is well over a hundred
years old: it would enable us to restore on a continental scale
the Greek agora or the New England town meeting.

Again this is no panacea; again I must deny that "the voice
of the people" is unmistakably "the voice of God"; again I must
urge that pure democracy, if democracy be majority rule, should
be checked by theocracy, technocracy, and anarchism. But when
groups are clamoring that "America is grimly determined" one
way or the other, the most honest method is to consult America.

Precautions are needed. We hope for a plain answer to a
plain question. But a plain question may be crude, and a subtle
question is likely to prove bewildering. There is no substitute
for education: the people must learn to think carefully about
political problems. Under present conditions, it would be quite
possible for the people as a whole to be as confused as their
elected representatives, and to register contradictory votes, in
quick succession or even at the same time. We all want greater
expenditure for our pet schemes or interests, and a sweeping
reduction of taxes. We all want the utmost freedom, and the
curbing of objectionable elements. I could well imagine "America" giving a thundering majority in favor of peace, and a still
more thundering one in favor of a tough policy which must
lead to war. The questions must be worded beyond all ambiguities. If you will not be a "warmonger," you should realize that
peace implies a sincere desire to agree, a willingness to hear the
other side, a readiness to grant reasonable demands: a Christian
and judicial attitude which might easily be branded as "appeasement."

Even when the issue is clear-cut, we must guard against

tricky wording. In California, a well-intended social security measure had to be repealed, because in the copious fine print that nobody read, odd stipulations had been smuggled, including even the names of the persons to be placed in charge. The proponents of a measure should discuss the text with a non-political committee of experts: technicians in the particular problem at hand, jurists, and even semanticists; so that the final text would represent clearly, honestly, and succinctly what the people will have to decide upon.

The three methods discussed in this section: the representative system in its original purity, a more independent executive, and direct democracy through a referendum, if they were applied singly or in combination, would save the essential of popular rule, while reducing the evils of professional politics. Lobbies great and small would survive: lobbies are not simply instruments for achieving selfish ends, they may also serve general purposes. But parties would gradually fade away.

IV

The above considerations were based almost entirely on American experience. They urge a self-education of the voter within the framework of our Constitution. In this section, I have chiefly French experience in mind. That experience has been dismal enough: our first reaction is that it can be of use only as a warning. But in a complex situation, a crude and hasty diagnosis might be deceptive. Critics are still debating whether Carlyle's preternatural grumpiness was due to the Scottish climate, Calvinism, dyspepsia, or Mrs. Carlyle. France, for historical and geographical reasons, has to encounter difficulties from which we are blissfully free. If in this particular field, France has failed — but are we certain we have succeeded? — it may not necessarily be on account of her chief contribution to political practice, the multiplicity of parties. No doubt her failure creates a prejudice, just as the failure of the Directory is still urged as an argument against a plural executive. But closer examination is needed before we arrive at a final verdict.

In spite of long custom, it is unnatural and harmful for men to array themselves into two antagonistic camps: the "regular" parties. It is natural for men to combine their efforts for definite purposes: world government, states' rights, religious education, socialized medicine, free trade or protection, the single tax. These are lobbies or pressure groups in the higher sense of the term: circles may be virtuous as well as vicious. They are the substance of American politics, under the vain and vulgar squabbling of the machine politicians. It would not involve a revolution in thought to give the name of *parties* to these associations for a common aim. They present a more finely shaded picture of the nation's mind than the rude dichotomy between two allegedly "monolithic" gangs, Democrats and Republicans. It cannot even be said that these machines represent two fundamental tendencies, conservation and progress. Every one knows that many Republicans are far more progressive than certain nominal Democrats. A man may be an ultra-conservative in religion and a liberal in politics, as were Gladstone and Bryan; he may be a Tory with a modern sense of social responsibility, like Disraeli; if a radical, he may also be an aggressive imperialist like Joseph Chamberlain, or attached to peace and reform like John Morley. For that reason, a nimble mind like that of Sir Winston Churchill had to leap repeatedly over the fence of parties.

If we want a true mirror of a complex reality, we need, not two parties, but a dozen or more, so that no important shade will be sacrificed. And if Parliament is to be in practice as well as in theory a genuine epitome of public opinion, this would demand proportional representation: else the minor parties would be sacrificed, and the results distorted. We need hardly say that, if we have proportional representation at all, it should be thoroughly honest. Nothing could be so shameful, or so ominous for democracy, as the action of the Fourth Republic in 1951, deliberately "fixing" the electoral law, so as to "gyp" both Gaullists and Communists out of a number of seats in the Assembly. As a swift punishment, this ill-gotten majority proved incapable of concerted action.

The consequence of a multiplicity of parties is government by coalitions. To some theorists, this is abomination: it is indeed destructive of the old-fashioned conception of "regular" parties. There again, doctrines and facts fail to coincide. Although not formally acknowledged, government by coalitions is the rule in England and in America, as it openly is in France. We have already gone over this ground, but it might profitably be traversed again: after the tenth repetition, people will keep repeating slogans rather than face realities. The old Conservatives, in the days of Salisbury and Balfour, under the name of Unionists, included high Tories, moderates averse to sweeping change, imperialists flirting with protection, and even those Radicals who were opposed to Irish Home Rule. In the Liberal camp were old Whigs like Harcourt, imperialists like Lord Rosebery, Radicals like John Morley, Labor men like John Burns, and Irish Nationalists in uneasy alliance with British Non-Conformists. What is our Democratic Party, which remained in power for twenty years, but the oddest association of the once-solid South, the demagogic machines of the big Northern cities, some Labor men, some farmers distrusting Wall Street, and a sprinkling of progressives throughout the land?

Since 1871, France has had but two homogeneous cabinets: the brief administration of Léon Bourgeois, nominally Radical; and the more substantial conservative one of Jules Méline, both in the nineties. With these two exceptions, France has had none but coalition governments for over eighty years. The most frankly "partisan" government in recent years, Léon Blum's Front Populaire, was an alliance between the Communists (as friendly outsiders), the Socialists, orthodox and independent, the Radical-Socialists, an unstable hybrid, and the old-fashioned *petits bourgeois* Radicals.

French practice corresponded closely with what is called party government in England and in America. The differences were obvious because they were superficial. In France, the necessary adjustment to the changing political situation was done by means of frequent partial substitutions rather than by

sending in a whole new team.[5] Under the disagreeable whirligig of cabinets, French political life was, not capricious, but if
anything too steady and even too sluggish. The same names
constantly reappeared in the reshuffled ministries; and the
bureaucracy was such a ponderous balance wheel that a little
jolt at the Palais Bourbon was hardly felt at all. The evil from
which France was, and is, suffering is not constant change, but
excessive reluctance to change. The result is best stated in the
weary phrase that Ecclesiastes ought to have coined: *"Plus ça
change, plus c'est la même chose."*

An alternation of "more conservative" and "more radical"
coalitions would be orthodox enough. But repeatedly, the
French gave examples of coalitions of a different pattern:
ignoring party lines, these were formed for a limited, extremely
definite purpose. Strangely enough, these combinations, frankly
temporary in character, proved more durable as well as more
efficient than those which followed the traditional lines. The
most striking example was the Waldeck-Rousseau administration, born of the Dreyfus Case. Radical in its general trend, it
was presided over by a great conservative. It comprised Miller-
and, at that time a Socialist in good standing, and the first of
his party to attain cabinet rank in any of the larger nations. It
was graced by the presence of General de Galliffet, the *beau
sabreur,* a picturesque old aristocrat who had taken such a
ruthless part in the repression of the Commune. And it counted
the enigmatic Caillaux, conservative in his origins and training,
erratic in his political views, highly competent in finances. Of
the same type was Poincaré's last administration, devoted to
"saving the franc": it included Herriot, Poincaré's constant
opponent.

More striking still are the truly "National" governments, like
the Sacred Union formed by René Viviani at the beginning of
the First World War, and the one headed by General de Gaulle

[5] When the joint policy of Messrs. Dulles and Bidault failed, M. Bidault went out of office, Mr. Dulles remained "in power." But he had
to alter his line: it must have been an agonizing reappraisal. In both
cases, there had to be *resignation*: but in two widely different meanings.

at the close of the second. In the latter, Communists, Socialists and the Catholics of the MRP (Popular Republican Movement) worked together with excellent results. This, of course, is familiar to us. Franklin Roosevelt's war administration, very different from Woodrow Wilson's, represented such a union; so did the war cabinets of Lloyd George and Winston Churchill.

This, I believe, points the right direction to the French and to ourselves as well, if it be desired to preserve a parliamentary form of government; this, and not a hankering for the shadowy fights between Whigs and Tories in the eighteenth century, between *Resistance* and *Movement* under Louis-Philippe. Why should the solution which is obviously right when the greatest issues are at stake, when efficiency is most desperately required, lose all its virtue as soon as the peak of the peril is past? "A desperate remedy reserved for a desperate crisis"? But is the crisis over? We live in a critical age, in every sense of the term. In the present crisis, which has already lasted several decades, party government of the familiar type is so inadequate as to be criminal. And "normalcy," when presumably people will again feel free to indulge in the paltry game of party politics, is not just around the corner. What we call crisis may simply be a permanent acceleration of political life, to match the formidable acceleration in the progress of science. No one knows how much longer we shall be shooting the rapids. In such an emergency, we cannot afford a divided crew.

So I propose that we adopt as the rule that which so far was only the exception, with Viviani, Churchill, de Gaulle, Roosevent himself: *let all parties be represented in every administration.* This might lead us to the still higher conception: let every administration be formed of the most competent men, irrespective of party lines. Would this make confusion worse confounded? The confusion is in the conditions of modern life and in the mind of the country itself: it can be cured only by accurate *nonpartisan* thinking. It should be easier to work some kind of order out of that confusion if a dozen men of good will, representing all shades of opinion, got together for that very purpose. No administration should be either vindictive or utopian. It should strive to find out what measures are imperiously needed — national security, the quest for peace, the end of colonial adventure, balancing the budget, saving the currency; which may be undertaken in a cautious experimental spirit; which may safely be postponed.

This means using the methods of science and industry instead of those of the free-for-all fight. It means substituting the idea of coöperation — the very foundation of government — for the idea of strife, which is anarchy. It means national health and sanity instead of national schizophrenia. This is no glimpse of Cloudcuckooland. It has been tried, and it has worked, whenever tragic events have shaken men out of their petty delusions and into their sober senses. The question if whether we can learn wisdom on the eve, not on the morrow, of catastrophe.

CHAPTER VIII

Justice: Virtue, Art, and Technique

In complete isolation, a man could be *free*: he would be subject to no man, only to the laws of nature. But man is a sociable animal; freedom, in society, is necssarily limited by the liberty of others. Justice, the adjustment of these conflicting claims, is the essential function of government. We can easily imagine a state indifferent to cultural values: those things are not Caesar's. We could conceive also a community in which the whole economic field would be left to private initiative, free contract, and self-adjustment: a laissez-faire Utopia. But a land without justice would cease to be an ordered common-wealth. Of the three powers, the judiciary is central and su-preme: the law is enacted for the guidance of the judges, the Executive exists in order to enforce their decision. Either under primitive conditions, or as the distant goal of a very refined civilization, a society could be ruled by *Judges* alone, if the authority of the judges rested upon the people's craving for justice. The world has survived bad executives and worse legis-lators: but when the judges are craven or corrupt, the nations perish.

History and folklore offer many instances of man's persistent dream, justice on the throne: King Solomon in his wisdom, St. Louis under the oak tree at Vincennes, and even Sancho Panza in Barataria: native shrewdness exposing the vanity of smart tricks. The growth of the French monarchy for eight centuries was founded on the development of royal justice: the people trusted the king's tribunals more than the courts of the feudal lords. Of the two inseparable components in the prestige of the dynasty, material power (force), and moral power (justice), the second was capable of steady growth, the first was exposed to perilous fluctuations, and even to sudden collapses. Ultimately, in spite of the shortsighted perversity of men, *Right is Might*: the reverse leads from Bismarck to Hitler, that is to say, to destruction. Nothing is settled that is not settled justly: there is no substitute for the victory of wisdom. Mankind could have enjoyed peace for the last half-century, if nations had been willing to subordinate selfish interests and pride to their desire for justice. We need not point out again that the immortal words: "My country, right or wrong!" imply the rejection of justice as a national policy.

Justice is first of all a process of clarification: we must establish the facts, and we must also probe the motives. Oddly, and lamentably, when we approach this realm of lucid dispassionate investigation, we first encounter a host of ambiguities. *Justice*, like *religion*, like *politics*, should be analyzed into (*a*), (*b*), (*c*), etc.; and there are sharp conflicts between concepts which bear the same name. This is true even in Latin and in French, languages which take pride in their logic and precision. Latin did acknowledge the confusion, and Cicero could quote as a well-worn proverb: *Summum jus, summa injuria*. A praiseworthy French association advocated *La Paix par le Droit*. But *droit* means the text and the practices of the law, as well as the will to righteousness; and the two may be in conflict. Strictly, we can conceive of justice without formal law, justice as an art serving justice as a virtue, and spurning the justice that is merely an intricate apparatus.

It is obvious that chicanery can defeat justice; it should be more obvious still that passionate prejudice and serene justice are wholly incompatible. In all civilized countries, political trials are now conducted with scrupulous respect for the letter of the law and the approved forms of procedure. But if the law itself is only the embodiment of blind partisanship, if judges and juries are irresistibly biased from the start, then every trial, however meticulous in details, becomes a Night of St. Bartholomew, a massacre of the Albigensians, on a minute scale. Legalistic pharisaism is but a mask for the brutal fact: "Crush those whom you hate and dread!" The very first condition of justice is to be liberated from rancor and fear. But if this simple rule were urged, the men of holy wrath, in the twentieth century as well as in the sixteenth or the thirteenth, would exclaim: "Are you attempting to protect these enemies of the state and of God?"

May I allude once more to a cardinal fact in my personal experience, the Dreyfus Affair? It started in 1894, not as a conspiracy, but as a mere error; it ended, lamentably, as a political squabble, vindictive and unscrupulous. But at its height, in 1897–1899, it clearly posed before the people the problem of *justice*. Protestants and Catholics, as well as Freethinkers, rallied to the defense of an orthodox Jew. Proletarians fought for a capitalist, pacifists for a professional soldier. It marked a summit in the long spiritual history of France: the whole country was passionately concerned with a question of pure justice, transcending classes and parties; and the Supreme Court (*Cour de Cassation*) proved an impregnable rock.

There is in French history a curious institution, the *Parlements,* or High Courts of Justice, among which the Parlement of Paris was by long odds the chief. In their own conceit, they claimed to be *sovereign*: as ancient as the monarchy, older than the dynasty, they were the heirs of the *Curia Regis,* itself a vestige of the Frankish assemblies of free men, which had once elected the kings. Whatever we may think of these lofty assertions, it was a fact that the Parlements never assumed direct legislative power: between them and the English Parliament, there was little more than a name in common. They did not deny that the king was the fount and origin of all law, the Living Law. But they had evolved a conception of kingship as something higher than the frail individual of flesh, who might be a child or a dotard, infirm of purpose, swayed by favorites: the true king was the *eternal* king, ruler of eternal France: a principle embodied in one man, but enduring from generation to generation. It was to this ideal king that the Parlements appealed against the caprices of the individual monarch. They had assumed the right of *remonstrance*: that is to say, they were privileged to point out the discrepancies between a new edict and some previous one, or even the contradiction between a fresh decision and the whole spirit of French tradition. In this wise, they had appointed themselves the guardians of the collective conscience. This permanent check on tyranny might have served as the center of a constitution liberal enough to satisfy La Fayette, historical and organic enough to win the praise of Edmund Burke.

History is full of bitter ironies: the best and the worst blend to the despair of theorists and puritans. The key to the power of the Parlements was their independence from the crown; and that independence, in the seventeenth and eighteenth centuries, was the result of an indefensible abuse. Seats on the bench were actually sold. The judges had a proprietary right to their positions; they generally managed to keep these sources of honor and profit within their families. So there arose mighty dynasties of jurists, almost a new feudal order, a nobility of the robe which in wealth, culture, and influence more than matched the nobility of the sword. In this manner, the Parlements acquired a prestige which even Louis XIV could not wholly destroy. If the judiciary is to serve as a check on the other powers, it must be independent from them. But the method evolved by the Ancient Regime had obvious faults, and could not serve as a model for our own days. Even in a plutocratic Utopia — a world whose business is Business, ruled by businessmen and by business methods, for the sole benefit of Business — it would seem incongruous for a judgeship to be openly bought.

So the judiciary became a class, almost a caste, eager to defend its own privileges, with scant regard for the long-range interests of the country. It defended not *liberty* but *liberties,* i.e., vested interests. It claimed to check despotism: but what it chiefly checked in the eighteenth century was *enlightened* despotism. Had it not been for the opposition of the Parlements, the monarchy of Louis XV and Louis XVI might have been able to carry out reforms which would have spared France a revolution. The *Philosophes* themselves were bewildered by this conflict. Voltaire saw clearly that the Parlements were a reactionary force; Diderot deplored the arbitrary act by which

Chancellor Maupeou superseded the Parlements with new courts appointed by the king.

The Parlements, restored by Louis XVI the Well-Meaning, made a great flourish on the eve of the Revolution, but swiftly disappeared in the storm, leaving no regret and barely a memory. If I discussed at some length this confused instance, it is as an illustration, not as an argument. Two things we may learn from the aspirations and the blunders of the past. The first is that the courts should be wholly independent both from the Executive and the Legislative, but that their independence should not lead to the formation of a separate, privileged order: *judiciarism* would offer the same kind of danger as *clericalism* or *militarism*.

Perhaps the proper balance would be struck if, in the United States, the President appointed the judges, but only from a list prepared by the judiciary itself. This would constitute a sufficient check on the President's prerogative, and no confirmation by the Senate would be required.[1] I should like to carry the reform one step farther: the list of nominees should not be drawn up exclusively by the judiciary, but also by other great representative bodies, economic and cultural. Justice must know and respect the law, but is greater than the law. In other terms, the ideal *legal* mind should be judicial rather than legalistic. *The letter killeth* is true in all domains. Eminent judges are eminent men, not purely eminent jurists. If a legal training is a good preparation for governors and statesmen like William Howard Taft and Charles Evans Hughes, conversely the qualities of a true statesman would be precious on the bench. Every court needs a body of experts on procedure and precedents. (Ultimately, they might profitably be replaced by masterpieces of cybernetics.) But there is a hierarchy among qualifications. A mastery of technicalities, although indispensable, counts for less than an upright character and a philosophical spirit.

The second and chief point I wanted to illustrate is that the judiciary does not exist merely for the moment's sake. It repre-

---

[1] This was proposed by Roger Potok, in a thought-provoking essay, *The Evolution of the Supreme Court* (New York, 1954).

sents the enduring, the dynamic conscience of the people. It should rise above squabbles, whether in the king's antechamber or in democratic assemblies. It is not the duty of the courts to consider "the present emergency," even when it reaches the point of "imminent danger." The judges should contribute to the stability of the social edifice: but their duty is to warn us that this cannot be done by turning our backs on vital principles, or by arbitrarily suspending essential articles of the law. However dire the perils, they can be met through the existing statutes against definite *acts* of terrorism, conspiracy, espionage, sabotage. The First and Fifth Amendments remain the law of the land. When they are swept away by every wind of panic, the whole fabric of the law is shaken. If they were repealed through the appointed process, the letter of the Constitution would be respected, and we would remain in name a democracy; but we would cease to be a free people.

The burden of my song, as trite as a music-hall ditty, is that the earth turns and that time marches on. The desire of man for security, freedom, comfort, is constant; the ways in which this desire can be satisfied vary from moment to moment. We cannot cling to any system or institution as an eternal verity. These plain remarks apply to the judiciary as well as to the other functions of the state. But the administration of justice is the field in which we are most hopelessly drugged with self-satisfaction. Individual failures and incidental flaws are freely recognized; the machine creaks all the time and breaks down once in a while; but we must not be perfectionists. The system as a whole is beyond challenge. If an isolated scholar chooses to challenge it, it is easy enough to dismiss him as a crank. But a jibe is not an argument.

Perry Mason never takes a case unless he is firmly convinced that his client is innocent. But Perry lives in a pleasant world of realistic fantasy, like the heroes of space and time travel. He is a Don Quixote who, miraculously, is successful as well as right. I wish such a world did exist. In sober fact, lawyers give (or sell) their clients the benefit of the doubt. They will not act against their conscience: but rigorous training and strenuous practice have made their conscience at the same time tough and supple. The most ethical lawyer cannot be what a scholar, a scientist, a doctor, a confessor must be: a man who believes that truth alone has healing in its wings. Even when lawyers are defending the truth, they are compelled to present it in a dramatic or sentimental light; and they must avoid those fine shades which might create an ambiguous impression. In a word, they are out to win: it is their honor, their duty, as well as their profit. This tampering with rigorous truth, however slight, however well-intentioned, is wrong; and on the naïve but indestructible principle that wrong is not right, that wrong cannot permanently masquerade as right, the wrong that is inherent in the lawyer's calling must some day be eliminated.

The present situation in the legal profession offers another abuse, the sign of a deeper and more general evil: in matters of justice, money talks, in a hushed but imperious and decisive voice. There are cheaper lawyers than Perry Mason, but they are not so good. The counsel appointed by the court to defend a pauper seldom is a man who has achieved recognition. In the very choice of a lawyer, there enters an element which is capable of thwarting or defeating justice. Brennus threw his sword into the scale, and exclaimed: "Woe to the defeated!" The rich throw in their money bags, and *think* (shrewder than Brennus, they will not speak aloud): "Woe to the indigent!"

This evil does not operate merely in the choice of a lawyer. Federal Judge Harold Medina said recently: "There are few defendants who can afford to-day's criminal trials. Even though a defendant may be found not guilty, he may be ruined financially by the cost of a trial. And his reputation may be so impaired that he can't retrieve his fortune. The Constitution guarantees every one the right to counsel, but that's not enough without providing transcript for the trial, witness fees, fees for experts, and all other expenses." [2]

[2] Quoted in "If You Were Accused of a Crime, Could You Afford a Fair Trial?" by Allen Murray Myers, in *This Week Magazine*, November 28, 1954, p. 7.

Incidentally, this high cost of justice offers a very easy way of turning prosecution into persecution. If the powerful want to "get" a man who challenges their absolute control, they can afford to bring suit after suit against him. They may know in advance that the Supreme Court will ultimately quash the indictment. In the meantime, they have harassed and ruined their man, at a cost well within their means, especially if it comes out of the taxpayer's money.

Obviously there should be the fullest moral and financial compensation for men unjustly condemned (America has had a number of abortive Dreyfus cases), or even unjustly accused. If the defendant is unable to meet the cost, the state ought to take up the burden: it should be part of the general expenditure for the administration of justice. It may be expensive: but less expensive to a civilized community than brutal injustice. The knowledge that there will be a day of accounting might deter private citizens, and even agencies of the government, from starting futile or vindictive proceedings.

Our endemic disease — and it is not incurable — is the cultural lag. We fail to catch up with our own lights. In mid-twentieth century, we are still in the early middle ages: we believe in judicial combat. The parties — or rather their hired champions — no longer fight with the sword; but they still "fight it out," with the judge as referee. The one essential revolution needed is this: to recognize that in every field, fighting is of dubious validity and is certain to be wasteful. In political, economic, *and judiciary* life, we must attempt to substitute scrupulous investigation for the clash of selfish interests. Adopting such a method might well be what we call *civilization*. I never claimed the path was easy.

Before I offer a remedy for these patent evils, I must consider another essential element in our judiciary organization: the jury system. Here the cultural lag is most evident. Centuries ago, when the lords of the manor administered justice (faint traces of this survived in England until our own days), the common people sought to free themselves from such a bondage by demanding a jury of their peers. In a society founded upon caste, this was an admirable device for the protection of the lowly, and a long step toward democracy. But, full democracy once achieved, this protection is no longer needed; it belonged with the crenellation and machicolation of the feudal castles. The problem now is not to guard against the privileges of an hereditary aristocracy, but to check the prejudices nursed by rich and poor alike. Justice is there not to fight for democracy, but to protect democracy against its own flaws.

My objections to the jury system did not start from a theory. I became aware in early youth of the jury's hopeless incompetence. We entrust the life and honor of a fellow citizen to the wisdom of twelve men whose judgment we would not respect in a plain matter of science, history, or art. The common denominator of twelve men without special training is low. I am not professing contempt for the ordinary man: I believe that there are at all economic levels men who have sounder sense than others. But no effort is made to seek them out. We rely almost entirely on chance. In the Dreyfus Case, one jury after another condemned Zola for attempting to right an injustice. It takes persistent enlightened will power to curb popular prejudices in one's own mind. Of such a victory, few even among educated people are capable: the "officers and gentlemen" of the second Court Martial which condemned Dreyfus were as purblind as a jury of shopkeepers and laborers. Men blinded by the cult of passive obedience, and men picked out almost at random, are not likely to rise to the serene heights of justice.

Can any jury resist the groundswell of prejudice? Jurors show their "patriotism" and their "common sense" by joining the stampede. When public opinion is divided, the jury becomes erratic: its indulgence may be as scandalous as its rigor. In a country like France where dueling has not completely disappeared, political murder is capriciously condoned. The jury acquitted Madame Caillaux, the wife of a very controversial Premier, who had shot the editor of *Le Figaro,* Gaston Calmette. A fanatic killed Jaurès, the most generous-minded of all European statesmen. At the long-deferred trial of his assassin, philosophers, historians, and even political adversaries, brought their tribute to the memory of the great leader. The jury declared the murderer innocent.

In America, I discovered that "the unwritten law" was most effective with juries, and not merely in the chivalrous South. If there be a lady in the case, and if she be comely, justice and sense abdicate. In my long and happy years in the South, I could not be blind to the fact that juries revealed extreme eagerness to condemn a Negro, extreme reluctance to convict a white man.

There is a dangerous aspect of jury trials which is seldom discussed. The decisive contest is the one that takes place in the jury room. There it is possible for assertive personalities to cow into acquiescence the more timid or confused members. This fight goes on in secrecy: the defense is not there to meet new insinuations, a new slant given to the evidence. To correct this glaring and seldom-denounced evil, it would be necessary to have the jury vote in silence and secrecy. If they failed to agree, the trial would be resumed — questions from the jury being submitted to the judge, and transmitted by him to the counsels. This might lead to longer trials, and to more frequent mistrials; but bullying the jury into unanimity is not an ideal solution.

My own suggestion is radical enough: abolish the jury system altogether. This sweeping measure is not quite in keeping with my conservative temperament. I was not converted to it until I read a statement by James Stephen, written a hundred and twenty years ago.[3] "Even in England," he considered trial by jury "except in a few peculiar cases, as a most inapt and inconvenient method of investigating truth." Now James Stephen, son of a great lawyer, himself a Chancery barrister with an extensive practice, Permanent Secretary for the Colonies, made Knight Commander of the Bath on his retirement, later Regius Professor of Modern History at Cambridge, was a highly competent and reputable person. To be sure, he added that he

[3] Report, February 12, 1834, on New South Wales Act No. 12, 1833. In Julian Park, *The Culture of France in Our Time* (Ithaca, 1955). *Trial by Jury*, pp. 262, 263, there is a moderate but very cogent criticism of the jury system.

did not recommend opposition to the jury, "being perfectly aware that the public voice on this subject is guided by prepossessions against which it is vain to argue." If *to argue* is to *offer an argument,* James Stephen was right in expressing his reasoned opinion. He converted me, and may have converted others: who knows but a chain reaction may start at any moment? If enough "private voices" like his speak out the truth as they conceive it, the "prepossessions of the public voice" will inevitably be altered. To expect sudden and sweeping results simply because a problem is clear in your own mind is quixotic and unrealistic. To seek the right solution even though it be remote requires a hard discipline: courting defeat never is an alluring prospect. But it is the path to sanity.

Stephen's criticism of the jury includes a good working definition of the judicial process: "investigating the truth." If we kept that ideal clearly in mind, we could make even the present forms more innocuous and less wasteful. The court would cease to be the lists of judicial combat, and become a research center. There would be no radical difference between judges and lawyers: all would be "Doctors in Human Relations," with a sociological and psychological training. A case would be probed by a committee, with no desire but to get at the facts and understanding the motives. There would be three steps, collecting of data, diagnosis, therapy. I still believe that, *except in political matters,* therapy might include the one great cureall, euthanasia. Why keep obvious misfits alive, as a burden to themselves and to the world?

It must be noted that we are already guided by such principles when we are dealing with the juvenile and the insane. The lingering notion of the judicial duel is swept aside; and so is vindictiveness. Therapy is the goal. We might extend to all ages and to all levels of intelligence the benefit of this more scientific and more humane method. Some men remain juvenile even in their senility: this is particularly true of great poets. And no man, not even Nicholas Murray Butler, Grand Master of Eternal Platitudes, ever was quite sane. On this level of social therapeutics, the technicalities so dear to the legal mind would seem frivolous; the attempt to "retain" experts would be considered bribery; the opinion of twelve good men and true might well appear immaterial, irrelevant, and incompetent.

Call this nonsense, if you please, or, more courteously, paradox. Then, your self-respect preserved and your conservative instincts satisfied, start thinking — if you dare. I doubt very much whether you would reach exactly the same point as I have. I feel confident that your thought, if it starts moving at all, will take you a long way from our present practices.

A Tribune of the People? I must begin this inquiry with an admission which is also a challenge. The thought that there might be such a personage, with a definite official function in the commonwealth, came to me in the discussions of the Chicago Committee to Frame a World Constitution. A congenital taint: for many readers this will suffice to brand the idea as unrealistic and therefore un-American. I refuse to repent. To Robert Maynard Hutchins, then Chancellor of the University of Chicago, Hiroshima brought "the good news of damnation." If Christian charity could not inspire us to live in brotherly peace, the dread of destruction might be more persuasive. Unite we must, or fight: the opponents of world law are warmongers. Mankind — or more accurately its misleaders — chose to defer sanity and good will indefinitely. The realism that leads ineluctably to a third and worse Armageddon might not be so realistic after all. Indeed this way madness lies. I see no reason why we of the Hutchins group should apologize for our reasoned anticipation. If war demands preparedness, so do unity and peace. The most practical engineers do not scorn blueprints. In times of infinite leisure, a path may slowly come into existence through millions of blundering feet; in our urgent peril, it takes thought — *forethought* — to escape from anarchy.

Eight years have gone wearily by. The Chicago project is dust; the thoughts it attempted to focus and formulate are alive, because they dealt not with theories but with conditions. The present section will discuss, not an article in a stillborn constitution, but a function which is real enough, even though in our time and country it is neither organized nor recognized. The Tribunitian Power does exist, but in chaotic dispersion. I thought of it first on the plane of the World Community: today, I should like to offer it as a suggestion for the revised municipal charter of Middletown, Middlestate, U.S.A. Thus helium was discovered in the sun long before it was tapped in Texas; but it had been there for aeons.

Precedents for the Tribune of the People could be found, of course, in the *Tribunus Plebis* of ancient Rome, and also in the Control Yuan of the shadowy Chinese constitution. Too far away, too long ago? Fortunately, it is possible to adduce also the example of modern Sweden. Now Sweden is a miracle of moderation and progressive good sense. If leadership means more than the brutal assertion of force, she should be our leader. I was therefore delighted to find in the Swedish Constitution the *Justitia Ombudsman*: there is dignity in the very name. His appointed task is "to prosecute before the competent courts any official who, in the exercise of his function, by favoritism, partiality or any other motive, may have violated the law or neglected his duties." [4]

The Chicago constitution went farther. Its Article 27 read: "It shall be the office and function of the Tribune of the People to defend the natural and civil rights of individuals and groups against violation or neglect by the World Government or any of its component units; to further and demand, as a World Attorney before the World Republic, the observation of the letter and spirit of this Constitution; and to promote thereby, in the spirit of its Preamble and Declaration of Duties and Rights, the attainment of the goals set to the progress of mankind by the efforts of the ages."

There are three distinct elements in this brief paragraph: we shall examine them in reverse order. The third is unimpeachable in spirit; but its nature is not strictly legal. It ex-

[4] Cf. Elizabeth Mann Borgese: "The Tribune of the People: Old and New Functions of the Spokesman for Minorities," *Common Cause* (Chicago), December 1947.

presses a trend and a desire; it is in the same key (recognizable by a note of eloquence,) as the Preamble and the Declaration of Duties and Rights to which it refers. It could be safely added to every other article of the constitution, or else be taken for granted. If there were in that instrument any provision intended to *impede* "the attainment of the goals set to the progress of mankind by the efforts of the ages," such a provision should by all means be deleted.

The second clause, on the contrary, is of a very precise character. All the officials elected or appointed under a constitution are expected to guard and preserve the covenant which created their authority: many of them have to take an oath to that effect. But they may have to be reminded of that sacred duty: *Quis custodiet ipsos custos?* This position of watchdog of the fundamental law has been assumed, in some essential aspects, by our Supreme Court. In France, the court of highest appeal, the Cour de Cassation, does not possess that right, and limits itself to quashing (*casser*) judgments for technical irregularities; but the Conseil d'Etat (Council of State) is competent to deal with accusations of malfeasance against officials in the exercise of their function. The Senate of the Second French Empire was formally the keeper and interpreter of the Fundamental Pact; but that prestigious prerogative turned out to be a verbal flourish: a seat in the Imperial Senate was merely a richly endowed sinecure. It could be maintained that when the Parlements or Courts of Justice of the Ancient Regime "remonstrated" with the king, they acted as Tribunes. As we have seen, they opposed the immemorial traditions and principles of the monarchy to the caprices of the living sovereign; they reminded him that his *raison d'être* was to provide for the common defence and general welfare of the country. Imagine an Attorney General who is not a member of the administration, and who, on the contrary, has the power to initiate proceedings before the Supreme Court aginst any official, including department heads, and the President himself.

The crux of the problem lies in the first clause: "to defend the natural and civil rights of individuals and groups against violation or neglect by the World Government or any of its component units." Here we leave the purely legalistic domain. The wording of that clause reminded me again of the deepest experience in my distant youth, the Dreyfus Case. Then the *Ligue des Droits de l'Homme* sprang into prominence exactly for the purpose stated in Article 27. It did valiant service, and survives, I believe, sedate and subdued, to the present day. We have in America corresponding collective *Tribunes*: the American Civil Liberties Union, the Civil Rights Congress, the Society for the Protection of the Foreign Born, whose activities are naturally annoying to the constituted authorities. Even in this land of liberty under the law, it is necessary — eternal vigilance! — to reaffirm the Eternal Verities. If not, any obnoxious minority could be suppressed for alleged "criminal aims" not established by due judicial process; and there are minds for whom any form of dissent is evidence of disloyalty. Certainly people *guilty* of high treason should be debarred from commissions in the armed forces, functions under government, positions of leadership in education and labor; as a matter of fact, they should be deprived not merely of these prerogatives, but first of all of liberty. But a Tribune, if we had one, would insist that they be considered innocent until proved guilty. And they cannot be made guilty simply by the *Fiat* of Congress: there are essential principles that stand above current legislation, in the letter of the constitution or in the conscience of the people. It would be too easy for the party in power to "outlaw" all opposition, and then virtuously to brand all dissenters as traitors and law-breakers. A short way with subversive: such is the essence of totalitarian tyranny.

The memory of the Ligue des Droits de l'Homme evoked that of the fearless champions who fought at that time for truth and justice: Jaurès, Anatole France, Clemenceau, the so-called *Intellectuels* (*quorum pars parva fui*), and above all Zola. Zola was emphatically the Tribune we have in mind. He was heir to a great tradition: Victor Hugo, advocate of the oppressed, of *les misérables*, of all the Claude Gueux and Fantines everywhere in the world, of John Brown and the defeated Communards; back of Hugo, Voltaire, supreme court of appeal in the days when the world naïvely sought and welcomed enlightenment, the defender of Byng, Sirven, La Barre, Lally-Tollendal, and above all Calas; and back of Voltaire, vivid across the centuries, the somber and ardent figures of the ancient prophets in Israel, who could tell a king: "Thou art the man." But we cannot hope to create a Nathan, an Isaiah, or even a Voltaire, by a constitutional act.

Nor should we overlook the "small change" of the major prophets, the publicists in all countries who have made it their business — at times a thriving business — to expose abuses and denounce injustices: Maximilian Harden, Henry Labouchère and his *Truth*, W. T. Stead, the "muckrakers," Lincoln Steffens. Of the living, the dreaded columnists who tell us every morning which Senators have put their aunts and cousins on their payrolls, which public characters have received *douceurs* from private interests, I find it more discreet to say not a word.

Because this function has been, brilliantly and fitfully, performed by voluntary agencies and individuals, it is tempting to leave it altogether to "free enterprise." I believe myself in a constitution as brief and simple as possible. We should resist the tendency of certain American states which clutter up their constitutions with details that properly belong to current legislation, or perhaps even to the uncodified mores. So whatever we can leave out of the constitution might well be a clear gain. However, the trend toward extreme simplification would ultimately lead us to anarchism and anarchy: the briefest constitution is a total absence of constitution. If we can do without the Tribune, so can we do without any economic and social legislation, without public schools, without public highways: all these can be provided by "direct action," individual enterprise, and voluntary coöperation. At the limit, we might even dismiss the police and the courts: an individualist, if rugged enough, scorns the cowardly ideal of security.[5] The Vigilantes

---

[5] I am not indulging in ironic fantasy. In 1829, the creation of the Metropolitan Police by Sir Robert Peel (*peelers* or *bobbies*) was opposed by doughty City men as "an insidious attempt to enslave the

and Judge Lynch offer methods of coping with crime readier, if rougher, than the cumbrous processes of regular tribunals. Especially, those methods can deal most efficiently with the most heinous crime of all, that of championing unpopular causes.

The voluntary Tribunes — journalists, prophets, agitators — alone or grouped into societies, are admirable at times, but also capricious and irresponsible. The earnestness and the vehemence of a denunciation are no guarantees of its validity. Operating without a legal warrant, these Vigilantes are apt to scorn the judicial temper and ignore judicial methods. In their eagerness to fight evil, to "watch and ward," they might easily turn into *censors* in the worst sense of the term, and attempt to mold the whole community in their own fanatical images. The French Royalist papers claimed to be acting as "Tribunes," or self-appointed State Attorneys when they hounded into suicide the cabinet minister Salengro, on a charge of military desertion that a court of honor had proved false. And it would be all too easy for such "Tribunes" to turn into gangsters from whom an honest man would have to purchase security.

No, the functions assigned to the Tribune are too vital to be left entirely in the hands of private parties. This, however, does not preclude the possibility of nonofficial intervention, individual or collective, which occurs in every domain. Although we have duly elected legislators, any one has the right to suggest legislation; and the Executive has to move, painfully at times, through a constant stream of unsolicited advice. In a democracy, every one should be in spirit a Tribune of the People. But for prompt, competent, responsible action, there should be a special officer, elected or selected by the best possible methods for that very particular purpose.

The Tribunitian Power should not be attached to any of the others, because it is of a different nature and requires different qualities. In a general way, it is obviously part of the judiciary system. But the judges, as such, are not supposed to originate

---

people by arbitrary and tyrannical methods." In their minds, 1829 heralded 1984.

thought or action. The Tribune, on the contrary, must have a degree of initiative, a quickly responsive sympathy, a power of indignation which are poetic and prophetic rather than strictly legal virtues. Remember also that, as a preventer or redresser of wrongs, the Tribune may and at times even must rise above sheer legalism. The judge has to follow rigorously the rules of the game: some of the best legal minds in this country were persuaded that Sacco and Vanzetti, that Mooney and Billings, had suffered through a miscarriage of justice, but they felt impotent. A legal impasse had been reached: *summum jus, summa injuria.* If the forms or even the text of the law be indeed at fault, the Tribune will refuse to be thwarted. His *Veto* might secure at least a suspension of the sentence: when there is any shade of doubt, the death penalty is a crime. And his action would be an argument for reforming the law. Not that the Tribune should be in any sense an antilegal, i.e., an anarchistic, a revolutionary force: he is *conscience with a warrant.* He might be the power that preserves society and averts revolutions through a timely and lawful exposure of legalized wrong.

In cases when the injustice is not capable of full legal remedy, partial or temporary relief could be brought through executive action, i.e., through pardon. This was done at one stage of the Dreyfus Affair for the sake of appeasement: but the French had no rest until the law was finally vindicated, obliterating an injustice. Historically, the Tribunitian Power as we conceive it stands closer to the Executive than to the Judiciary. To watch for flaws in the application of the law is part of the enforcing process. The Sovereign himself is par excellence the Defender of the City and of the People. In ancient days, the oppressed and the defrauded would sigh: "Ah! If the king only knew!" Subjects had the right to address a petition directly to the head of the state: it was at any rate a lottery ticket. Haroun al-Raschid roamed nocturnal Bagdhad in disguise, to be his own Tribune of the People. The Tribune might be called the eyes and ears of the ruler. But as sovereignty can no longer, even by the wildest legal fiction, reside entirely in one man, it must be recognized that administrative and remedial functions are not the same. At times, they might even be healthily antagonistic.

Most dangerous of all would it be to confuse the Tribunitian and the Legislative. Yet this is done, pragmatically, in most countries. Today, a member of Parliament or Congress is not primarily a lawmaker, or the representative of nation-wide ideologies, trends, or interests: he is the Tribune of *his* people, i.e., of his constituents. Pardonably, he defends most efficiently those who have been most active on his behalf. They take their troubles to him; he protects them from injustices, from annoyances, and at times from the consequences of their own indiscretions. He accelerates, retards, or even arrests for their benefit the cumbrous machinery of the law. Services of that kind explained Laval's very real hold on his constituency or "electoral fief," a workingmen's district: he was the most indefatigable, the most efficient of *fixers*. This may be a caricature of the ideal *Tribunus Plebis*: but we must constantly bear in mind that a caricature, as an overemphasized likeness, is a satire and a warning.

In a more general way, assemblies have assumed, collectively, a function which is not properly legislative, but tribunitian. They create para-judiciary commissions of inquiry, intended to throw light upon certain deals, activities, or intentions beyond the ken of blindfolded Themis. A dangerous usurpation: assemblies have a tendency to claim unlimited authority, with results which are ludicrous in normal times, tragic in a crisis. I must repeat that the famous doctrine of the separation of powers, preached by Locke and Montesquieu, has so far remained a Utopia: it might be well to give it at last a chance. If the proper function of the legislator is not to dictate the details of executive action, it is even less to bypass the courts, and arraign, judge, punish citizens; it is not to be a fixer or a muckraker. His first, and perhaps his sole, duty is to *legislate*, i.e., to prepare general and permanent statutes. Under the present dispensation, political assemblies are thoroughly corrupted by the factional or partisan spirit: a disease which all sound Americans diagnose, deplore, and steadfastly refuse to cure. Legislators are sorely tempted to whitewash their friends and smear their opponents. And politicians easily yield to demagogy: they seek prestige and power by hounding dissenters, which is exactly the reverse of what a Tribune should stand for.

This needs to be emphasized. I spoke of the danger that private censors might become gangsters, preying on heretics as well as on wrongdoers. The danger is far greater when the censors have a cloak of legal authority: then the healthy contempt in which they are held becomes a punishable offence. Here we have the worst perversion, or more accurately the most complete destruction, of genuine democracy: government by intimidation, which is but an insidious and extremely effective form of terrorism. If America capitulated to this pseudolegal tyranny, she would no longer be the land of the free, and most certainly not the home of the brave.

Abuses should be detected, denounced, corrected, by all means, but not by every means, *fas aut nefas*. The power which shoulders that great moral responsibility should stand out of politics, above politics. The Tribune of the People, the embodiment of Eternal Vigilance, the watchdog of liberty, must see to it that the Bill of Rights does not become a bundle of pious wishes, but remains an array of living forces. Zola was called "a moment in the conscience of mankind": the Tribune should be the permanent, authorized, articulate voice of that conscience. By expressing it, and even by challenging it, he makes it deeper as well as more explicit. His function is both idealistic and legal: he does not allow the spirit of the law to evaporate, leaving the letter desiccated.

The great objection of the realists will be: "Why worry about a Tribune? We have done well enough without one." The inevitable answer is a counter question: "Have we done *well enough*? Has the promise of America to herself and to the world been fully redeemed?" But this question takes us perilously close to perfectionism; and perfectionism, as all good Christians and honest citizens are aware, is a deadly sin.[6]

[6] Cf. Matthew 5:48.

CHAPTER IX

Politics at Its Worst: International Relations

For half a century, I have been far more interested in international relations than in home politics. This is not the telescopic delusion: watch the stars and stumble into the ditch. I know that my small garden needs tilling. It is not a matter of sentiment either: like Washington and Goethe, I am proud to call myself a world citizen, but my modest home is dearer to me than any cosmic Utopia. World affairs are my first concern for a very practical reason. In the great Western democracies, at any rate, and in my lifetime, home politics have seldom held even a remote threat of violent revolution and civil war: America, France, and England have grown beyond that stage. On the other hand, the menace of international armed conflict has never ceased to be present. All the inefficiency, squabbling, and graft of the worst politicians within the last fifty years were paltry evils, compared with the material and moral havoc wrought by two world wars, and with the waste of competitive armaments.

For the isolationists of yesterday, foreign affairs were merely a fringe of annoyance. This attitude was best expressed by Mr. Herbert Hoover in his *Memoirs*: we do not like the Europeans, we separated from them because of that dislike, and we have been drifting further apart for the last three hundred years. To my mind, this opinion is diametrically contrary to the facts. Many Americans have never ceased liking Europe, particularly England, France, Germany, Italy. Our culture has been constantly interwoven with theirs. Those who most fervently ex-

toll a literature "in the American grain" would rather read
Dostoevsky, Proust, or Kafka than Joel Barlow and Harold Bell
Wright: a palpable truth, even though denied by not a few
learned professors. I am dealing with actual conditions, not
with lofty doctrines reeking with sentiment: in every field, a
good American may be in closer sympathy with some foreigner
than with his next door neighbor.

Isolationism — *Sinn Fein, Deutschland über alles, Sacro
Egoismo, ¡España arriba! France d'abord! America First, Last
and all the time!* — remains a surly attitude rather than a dynamic policy. It is inspired mostly by timidity and inertia:
when bewildered, it seems safer not to move. But this negative
mood has positive results. To choose indecision may involve
immense responsibilities. Had England faced definite commitments before 1914, the First World War would have been
averted: the Germans banked on her neutrality, born of *Splendid Isolation.* Had America not failed to join the League of
Nations, had we not given the Nazis and the Japanese mili-
tarists the fullest assurance that "the Yanks were not coming,"
there would have been no Second World War either. I am not
advocating aggressiveness, and least of all those entangling alliances against which the Founders so wisely warned us. What
is essential is that the world should know that we are not blind
or indifferent to injustice, within the nation or among the
nations; for injustice is a threat to every man's liberty.

Today, isolationism is dead: the most uncompromising isolationists of yesterday are now eager for intervention from pole
to pole. I never thought I should live to regret isolationism, as
the lesser of two evils. For militant imperialism is another form
of the same disease, only more virulent. We have a global policy;
we plant bases six thousand miles from our shores; we have
missions and agencies in the remotest parts of the earth; but in
these outposts, we remain insular Americans, committed to the
the American Way of Life as the sole and eternal verity. Isolationism is the shrinking twin; imperialism is the blatant one.
Both refuse to admit that God fulfills Himself in many ways;
that others too may have their logic, their traditions, their rights,

their pride and their virtues; and that truth in the making transcends every tribal orthodoxy.[1]

The curse of politics is the assumption that conflict is the very law of life: when something needs to be done, we must first array ourselves into parties, and fight. In home affairs, however, this delusion is corrected to a large extent by the experience of our daily life. We may call the other side "the rascals": still, bloody purges have not yet come back into fashion; a Democrat may cheerfully meet a Republican at Church or on the golf course; we have not sunk to the level of Franco's Spain, or Guatemala under a military junta. In the international field, on the contrary, the disease is unchecked: we glory in it, and call it patriotism. All others are our deadly rivals: they want our wealth, our position, our very blood. Even as allies, they cannot be trusted, and must be treated as potential enemies. War is the normal state among nations:[2] England and France, England and Russia, France and Germany lived for generations in a state of cold war. Keep your powder dry and your dagger ready; be sure not to miss your chance: such was the rule that guided Bismarck, Hitler, Mussolini. In such an atmosphere, there is no difference in spirit between diplomacy and war: diplomacy means pressure, with the plain hint of a threat; actual warfare is but a showdown in the everlasting contest. Violence and deceit, the indispensable instruments, are extolled as virtues: the gentle and the candid are lambs. Toughness in thought and deed, so eminently found in the gangster and the goon, is made the ideal of professedly Christian lands. With it goes toughness of speech. There was a time when *diplomatic* and *courteous* were almost synonymous. A modern statesman, even though he be a gentleman born, would be ashamed of his meekness, if he did not insult everyday nations with which we are nominally at peace. I have read pages by cabinet members, learned geopoliticians, realistic historians, that could vie

[1] To preserve our democratic rectitude, we camouflage our imperialism as "leadership of the Free World." This is the snare which will be discussed in its place.

[2] Suggestion for a headline: NORMAL RELATIONS RESUMED: WAR DECLARED.

with the most lurid columns of Mr. Westbrook Pegler. The velvet glove is out of fashion. We prefer the mailed fist, even with a wet rag inside.

War is a contest in brutality; diplomacy a contest in deceit. How often have I been told by sane and upright men: "But diplomacy is a poker game: it would be foolish to tip our hand." I admit that poker is an innocent pastime: it becomes criminal when the chips are human lives. Surely serious men could evolve a less frivolous and more efficient method of protecting their vital interests.

My fundamental thesis is that conflict, far from being the essence of human relations, plays a minor and reducible part in our affairs. There are too many fatal collisions on the highways, not to mention dented fenders, explosive words and angry glares. But we do not start out with the intention of making our trip a brutal joust. We expect to reach our destination without mishap. As a rule, a nation's prosperity does not involve driving another nation into the ditch. England's magnificent expansion in the nineteenth century did not beggar France, Germany, or America.

We are told in contemptuous tones that the defense of principles is but idealistic nonsense: the Atlantic Charter was claptrap, the Four Freedoms a clever trick, the Voice of America manifest hypocrisy. A "Free World" indeed!; the be-all and end-all of national policy is national interest. But what if self-interest were best served by peaceful and friendly intercourse? Legitimate sea trade is more profitable than piracy. When we are told of "national interests," we have the right to ask: "Whose? And for how long?" Is it to the national interest that some of our "nationals" should grab concessions throughout the world? Was it France's national interest to cling so desperately to Indochina? Is it our national interest to boycott that tremendous market, the People's Republic of China? "Principles" are not absolute revealed truths: they are attempts to discover, beyond the welter of immediate and petty greed, the general and permanent interests of the group. "Grab what you can and keep what you hold," is irreproachably tough. "Thou shalt not steal," even when the pickings seem rich and easy, is experience ripening into a principle.

What strikes me most about the "tough realists," geopoliticians like Sir Halford McKinder (*Democratic Ideals and Reality*) and his less learned followers, like John E. Kieffer (*Realities of World Power*) is their hopeless romanticism. They are at heart conquistadores, drunk, as in Heredia's splendid sonnet, with a heroic and brutal dream. They sing Kiplingesque ballads muffled into pedantry:

"Who rules East Europe commands the Heartland.
Who rules the Heartland commands the World Island.
Who rules the World Island commands the world."

Such incantations, in thought and style, are scrupulously on the Nazi level. It is adolescent megalomania. What good will it do a man to "command the world" — vicariously — if by so doing he loses his freedom? The toughest America Firsters are also the most hopeless sentimentalists. They gloat over the old Jingo song: "We've got the men, we've got the ships, and we've got the money too." They quiver with emotion at the sight of Old Glory waved by the Old Soldier. I would be most happy to join in the feast, if I were told definitely what Old Glory stands for: the right to frame your own thought and shape your own life, or enforced 100% conformity? But as soon as you ask such a question, you are departing from that toughness soaked in sentimentality which is today our quasi-official version of patriotism. Shades of our enlightened Founding Fathers!

Let us start with a few warnings. First of all, we must stop making conflict the center of our political thought. If we are anxious to see things as they are, if we refuse to be swayed by subhuman impulses, if we do not crave romantically for the dramatic, then we must recognize that all profitable activity in this world, in every sphere, depends on coöperation. Conflict is but friction, waste, failure. Creaks, squeaks, jerks, and occasional breakdowns may be inevitable in the best constructed machinery; but they never are its essential purpose. It would be foolish to ignore the menace of conflict. But we should en-

deavor to avert it, not to promote it. To spend most of our mer
tal energy and a crushing proportion of our substance in pre
paring *for* instead of *against* conflict on a cosmic scale is hardly
the path to sanity.

Second warning: we should not put our faith in institutions.
They have no miraculous virtue. When the Supreme Court of
the United States, with its long tradition and its majestic authority, bows to the argument of *imminent danger*, what can we
expect of a World Court? What alone counts is a collective
state of mind, made easier and steadier through healthy habits.
In this distrust of machinery, I am at one with well-meaning
realists such as Reinhold Niebuhr or Frederick L. Schuman.
But there is no excuse for spurning institutions when they are
a summing up of experience, a practical tool of reasonable intercourse. No community can be made safe by courts and police
alone. But a country will find it easier to attain and maintain
a decent and orderly existence by means of these well-tried
instruments; and the world as a whole may learn that elementary lesson. Ultimately, the policeman will give up the
murderous pistol for the less lethal bludgeon, and the bludgeon
for the symbolic wand. Institutions should not be divorced from
the mores: else they remain pious platitudes, like the Kellogg
Pact. But principles, laws, means of enforcement, all have their
place in the scheme, provided they remain in close touch with
the sentiments and the interests of the people. They are at any
rate methods of education: and "civilization is a race between
education and catastrophe." If the people nod perfunctory approval while inwardly withholding their consent, the result is
chaos under a diaphanous veil of hypocrisy. Above all, we must
refuse to serve two gods — both ungodly: a shadowy Idealism
of the *Excelsior!* type, to which we do half-ironical lip service;
and the grim idol Realism, a Moloch to which we bring our
human sacrifices.

I do not believe in disarmament per se: it is not wicked guns
that corrupt innocent men. And I have no trust in chivalrous
and humane laws of war. The most righteous countries (all
countries are self-righteous; but only a few — need we name

them? — are truly righteous) have been the worst offenders. England inaugurated the concentration camp method at the time of the Boer War, and, in 1914–18, attempted to torture the Central Powers into submission through the starving of civilians, women, and children. We used the atom bomb without a qualm, and we are spending billions on the hydrogen bomb. War is the refusal to be humane: if men were sensible and generous enough to "civilize" warfare, they would civilize it out of existence. When hell is let loose, the only "law" that has a chance of being respected is the fear of reprisals.

I am not a radical pacifist, if by pacifist we understand a believer in absolute nonresistance. Only the true followers of Christ have attained that spiritual height, and they are very few. The confused mass of traditions which we call our religion is ambiguous at the core: the Prince of Peace and the Lord of Hosts are one God. I have been veering steadily toward the Gandhi gospel; but I remain convinced that evil must be curbed, not simply overcome with good, when it appears in the form of deadly germs, noxious parasites, wild beasts, mad dogs, or degenerates. Evil is not lessened when it becomes collective; a gang is more dangerous than a lone criminal; and a whole country captured or misled by a gang may run amok, and should be placed under restraint.

But the pitfall is obvious. It is too easy to decide that "they" are the demented herd stampeded by fiends-in-human-shape, whereas "we" are the Galahads of all fair causes in distress. This is merely an enormous caricature of the party spirit at home. Remember Rosas: "Death to those obscene *Unitarios!*" I have read with professional care the story of many wars; and I have lived intensely through the two great crises in our century: the Manichean picture is not realistic. Dynastic wars often were criminally futile; religious wars were the worst of blasphemies; but in the modern age no nation, not even Nazi Germany, has actually run amok. The "angels" had their share of guilt; the "fiends" had at least the glimmer of a justification.

Aggression, which I never condone, has often been the result of what seemed intolerable restraint. There would have been no war of conquest by the French Revolution, and therefore no Napoleonic tyranny, if Austria and Prussia, soon followed by the whole of Europe, had not attempted to crush the principles of 1789, and to restore the absolute sway of the king's pleasure. Peace demands not merely a surly defense of the status quo but generous foresight. There would have been no First World War if England and France had not followed a dog-in-the-manger policy. Proud of their empires, they grudged Germany even the crumbs from their table; thwarting the Baghdad Railway was a masterpiece of "containment," but the ultimate cost was nearly a million British lives. A resolute application of Wilsonian principles, without fear or favor, and above all without "dictation," would have prevented Germany from falling a prey to a crude fanatic. Japan could easily have been won to the ways of peace, if for the last sixty years we had treated all Orientals with scrupulous fairness and courtesy, if Woodrow Wilson had not vetoed from the Covenant the principle of racial equality. Had the French freely granted to Ho Chi Minh in 1945 what they were almost thrusting upon Bao Dai a few years later, a free, peaceful, undevastated Indochina would now be a satisfied dominion in the French Commonwealth. It is the stubborn defense of vested interests and privileges that causes outbreaks of violence. Reasonableness has hardly ever been given a chance. There is no reasonableness in getting tough; there is none either in getting soft, when resistance collapses in a panic, as it did at Munich, and when capitulation under threat, with shame and rage in one's heart, is given the holy name of *appeasement.*

The one thing needful, therefore, is to study resolutely the possible causes of conflict, and examine them with strict impartiality. The Manichean delusion, I repeat, is partisanship on a global scale. It is infinitely more dangerous than party strife at home, because it is not tempered by the reluctance to shed blood, and by the sense of humor, which, within a democracy, make political squabbles ludicrous rather than tragic. We should constantly be on the lookout for legitimate grievances; when detected, they should be righted, not crushed into sullen silence. They should not be righted, of course, at the expense of third parties: this is merely shifting, and probably increasing, the burden of injustice. Many Americans, between the two wars, wept over those poor Germans who were denied the right of oppressing the Poles. If we were to turn Morocco over to a band of Pan-Arab fanatics, this would mean oppression, not only for the European and Jewish minorities, but also for the large submerged Berber majority. To place the whole of Bohemia under the Nazi heel was not the right solution for the very real Sudeten problem.

Claims should not automatically be allowed, out of quixotic chivalry, simply because they are against our interests: we have rights too, which should not be lightly sacrificed. But not every privilege is defensible. We should try to secure fair terms for our *concessionaires* abroad, if the local governments want to nationalize their enterprises. But no vital principle is involved; it is not essential to the American Way of Life that a private concern should preserve a stranglehold on some banana republic. On the practical level, a readjustment of special and temporary interests, even if it requires a sacrifice, is not so onerous as the most victorious war. Yielding is an ugly word, for those whose ideal is still that of the duelist, ready to kill or die in defense of his "honor." But in the eyes of the true gentleman, yielding to a sense of fairness entails no humiliation. What injures our good name is to have it linked with the preservation of injustice.

These are warnings; on the positive side, I can think of two methods which have never been employed to the full: *pluralism* and *irony*. I have a strong feeling that they would be more effective than the hydrogen bomb.

Pluralism is the rejection of the territorial fallacy, itself a form of totalitarianism: the belief that in a given area, and on certain all-important issues, all men must act, think and feel alike; and that dissenters should be crushed as traitors. Wilsonism, which was Napoleon III's "doctrine of nationalities" brought up to date, came to terms with that delusion. Wilson took it for granted that, through the process of self-determination, homogeneous nations could be formed. The many Americans today who sympathize uncritically with the various independence movements in the world nurse the same generous but oversimplified dream. They do not realize that in Morocco, Madagascar, Indochina, or Indonesia, there are many groups which resent and resist forcible assimilation by a single element. In most cases, nationalism is imperialism on a smaller scale. But the fanatical few are more lurid and more vocal than the hard-working many. And they are using slogans which, for historical reasons, sound to us like holy truths.

When history, geography, economics, linguistics clash in many-cornered fights, as they often do, several makeshifts have been attempted. One is to make the contested territory independent and neutral: Luxemburg in 1867, Danzig and Fiume after the First World War, Trieste and the Saar after the second: a wise solution, which unfortunately has so far failed three times out of five, with a fourth case, the Saar, still in doubt. There always is the danger of some flamboyant d'Annunzio, blazing the trail of unwisdom. Even without such a lurid leader, the ways of moderation and peace are insecure. We ourselves, as part of a complicated and unscrupulous poker game, undid with our own hands the sensible Trieste settlement.

A so-called "ethnic boundary" may be traced: the partition of Upper Silesia according to the results of a referendum, the proposed Curzon Line in Poland, the secession of the German-speaking parts of Czechoslovakia, the creation of North Ireland and Pakistan. As no partition ever is a neat job, an attempt is made to correct the evident evils through an exchange of populations: a modern, large-scale, and very painful version of the Procrustean bed. The most successful example was the resettlement which followed the last Greco-Turkish war. The vastest, most chaotic, and most tragic was the "folk-wanderings" after the secession of Pakistan from India.

The most modest and sanest method is the legal recognition and protection of minority rights. This was put into practice by

England when the Dominion of Canada was formed. It was imposed upon Poland and Czechoslovakia after the First World War. It has been adopted by Italy in the case of the Trentino and the valley of Aosta. The trouble is that, as a rule, it has to be imposed. As a result, no "great and proud nation" will submit to it. Neither France, nor even defeated Germany, had such an "indignity" forced upon them in 1919. To understand such an attitude, let us suppose that an international body *compelled* us to recognize the cultural rights of the Mexican minorities in our Southwest. The thought causes no indignation because it is too preposterous. The Wilsonian method — to create a mosaic of independent, different, and homogeneous units — leads to unending bitterness. It is because of this territorial nationalism that every frontier is an infected wound.

History points a way out of the territorial fallacy. There was a time when that totalitarian principle applied with particular force to religion. *Une foi, une loi, un roi*: one faith, one law, one king, was a French motto as early as the end of the fifteenth century. *Cujus regio ejus religio*: he who rules the land also controls the faith, became an accepted principle at the time of the religious wars in Germany. Spain followed that policy with the utmost rigor: Jews and Mohammedans were driven out, and Protestantism never was given a chance. It guided Louis XIV when he revoked the Edict of Nantes. In the heyday of the Enlightenment, Louis XVI still had to swear that he would extirpate heresy from his realm — and compromised by mumbling unintelligibly that part of his coronation oath. The same method was adopted even in England. I wonder when the British sovereigns ceased to vow unrelenting war against Popery. Today there still are nationalisms on a religious basis — Israel, Pakistan — and I like them none the better for it. Attempts are still made to commit America to a theology. But the consensus of civilized people is that Catholics, Protestants, Jews, Mohammedans, Buddhists, Bahaists, Freethinkers, may live side by side and work together for their common welfare. This is the triumph of *pluralism*. Why not admit the same solution for the religion named patriotism? Like all religions, it cannot and should not be forced. Like all religions, it is carried within: a man remains a Catholic under every flag, and a loyal British subject in every clime. The boundaries of Poland may be shifted; Poland may even cease to have an official existence; a Pole may be driven by want or persecution from his native land: but a Pole is a Pole for all that. Like all religions, patriotism should have no arms but those of the spirit. A change of allegiance should be the result of free conversion, not of conquest.

This is no vision of Nephelococcygia: I am familiar with many instances of such pluralism. In Paris, in London, in New York, in San Francisco, I have seen different populations living peaceably side by side, each true to its own ancestral ways, yet all willing to coöperate for definite ends. In saner days, I have seen the same friendly coexistence in Tunis, Algiers, Casablanca. I have seen Polish Day and St. Patrick's Day parades on Fifth Avenue, and Bastille Days in San Francisco: the crowds looked with sympathy upon the festival of another friendly family.

The idea of cultural pluralism was focused in my mind through my sympathy with the Jewish community. There you had a people — a *nation* in the original and more rigorous sense of the term — with more strongly marked characteristics than most, with a more tenacious body of traditions than any. Yet the sober minded maintained against Hitler that the Jews were not an alien element, disloyal and disturbing, in the midst of other nations. The Jews could give England and France great Premiers, America notable Justices of the Supreme Court. This thought I expressed in an address for the opening of the Houston Menorah Society, and the response among my Jewish friends was most favorable. Israel as I conceived it was pointing the way to a pluralistic world of freedom, delivered from the shackles of physical frontiers. In some respects, Zionism was a long step backward: the Jews, a unique supernation, humbly aspired to become an ordinary nation. I wish the Israeli State all success: as a land of refuge and as a cultural center, it is serving worthy ends. But my wider conception still holds true for the majority of the Jews: there is no room for them in Israel, and they have no desire to settle there. This applies particularly to the five and a half millions who live, free and respected, in the United States.

I had also thought of pluralism as salvation in the inextricable problems of Central and Eastern Europe, where the simple Napoleon III-Woodrow Wilson formula bogs down altogether, where Germans, Poles, Lithuanians, Byelorussians, Ukrainians, Magyars, Rumanians, Serbs, Croats, Bulgars, Greeks, Albanians, were at each other's throats in the name of nationalism. I discovered later, not without pride, that this pluralism had been formulated by the great Austrian statesman Karl Renner in the days of the Hapsburg dynasty.

When I call the second method *irony*, I am using the term in its Voltairian sense: irony consists in agreeing with your opponent better than he agrees with himself. It is a destructive weapon: there is none better for calling a bluff or exposing an absurdity. But the same method may have a constructive value as well: it approximates "heaping coals of fire" and "overcoming evil with good." To outbid your opponents in evil makes the evil manifest, and absurd: *quod erat demonstrandum*. But to outbid him also "in whatsoever things are good" makes you realize how much you and he really have in common. If you go with him not one mile but twain, you may remain friendly fellow travelers all the rest of the way. If he offers to open a discussion, take him up at once. If some of his friends want to join your UNESCO, open your arms: UNESCO is exactly the place that would improve their education. If he starts a petition for peace, flood it with your signatures. This kind of irony, to be effective, must be sincere: if it were a mere trick, it would be a feeble one. Sincerity, however, can wrest an argument from your adversary, and turn it, not against *him*, but against the evils from which you and he both suffer. In our condemnation of Fascism, Nazism, Falangism, imperialism, color bars, private greed, graft, partisanship; in our quest for liberty, equality, social justice, we must resolutely take the lead; and no less steadfastly follow the lead of others, whenever they are heading the right way. Half-heartedly to support injustices throughout the world, on the plea that this might secure allies for us and provide bases against the enemy, is a short-sighted, self-defeating policy: morally disastrous, materially futile. We can beat the Russians — *ironically* — only by being better "Communists" than they. The Russians can beat us only by being better "libertarians" than we. Then, each having stolen the other's thunder, all will be satisfied.

To sum up: do not set your pride in an "adamant" policy. Seek obstinately the common denominator. Reduce the area of conflict. Welcome every chance of working together, in science, in art, in technical improvements. Be honest and courteous fellow travelers as far as you can possibly go. Accept eagerly every discussion that offers even a faint chance of an amicable arrangement. Never take the responsibility of a showdown and an irreparable breach. This is not capitulation; this is not appeasement of the Chamberlain type; this is not even compromise, for compromise means the willingness to condone a lesser evil. It is *adjustment*, that is to say accurate thinking, as free as possible from passionate bias. It is good Christianity, good science, and good business.

NOTE

In *A Short History of the International Language Movement*, in *Beyond Hatred*, in *Europe Free and United*, in *Education of a Humanist*, I have expressed my conviction that a neutral auxiliary language would be an admirable instrument of world coöperation. I refrain from repeating in full, for the fifth time, the familiar arguments. An Interlingua would first of all embody the spirit of world unity, as opposed to that of irremediable differences and inevitable conflicts. To me, as to I. A. Richards, it means first of all repudiating any thought of cultural imperialism. The advocacy of English as a world-language, even in the form of Basic, simply rests upon the old song: "We've got the men, we've got the ships, and we've got the money too." An Interlingua would save and protect local cultures, now threatened with extinction by the imperialism of seven or eight giants: I believe in diversity and pluralism, not in a ruthless struggle for survival and domination. Incidentally, it would save the intimacy, the raciness, the historical flavor of the major languages themselves: I should hate to see English, French, or German degraded to the indigence of Basic.

CHAPTER X

The Snare of Leadership

"Lest we forget, lest we forget!"

This is the American century. Whoever denies this palpable fact, prophesied by W. T. Stead more than fifty years ago, is feebly attempting to stem the wave of the future. Long before our spectacular ascent, we were fond of grandiloquent and semihumorous claims: they were part of our folklore. From the day it was hatched, the American eagle could shriek with the best. Now American leadership is held to be a self-evident truth, not by Fourth of July orators merely, but by righteous and sober men, of all political shades. Unanimity ceases only when we attempt to find out what we mean. Understanding is the foe of certainty, and the Devil's favorite shape (a crooked one, to be sure) is a question mark.

Yes, leadership is ours; but there are many conceptions of leadership. Some are mere caricatures, and may lightly be dismissed. There is the leadership of the drum major who took the wrong turn while the band went straight ahead. There is the leadership of Ledru-Rollin, the French Radical who, in 1849, was found at the head of a howling mob. "Where are you going?" — "I don't know; but I am their leader, so I have to follow them." There is the leadership of the British sovereign, who is graciously pleased to endorse now a Tory policy, now its reverse. There is the leadership which means a chance to grab, and the leadership which means a chance to serve. The one essential element in leadership as opposed to brute force or tyranny is the consent of the led. The cowboy rounding up a herd is not a leader.

In this country and at this hour, there prevails about this most important problem an ambiguity which it would be well for us to clear up. Our present position of wealth and power makes our full coöperation in world affairs indispensable. Without us, a world free and at peace under the law must fail, as it did fail when we turned against President Wilson's League. With our whole-hearted support, on the contrary, such a world would cease to be a Utopia: it would turn at once into an organic and growing reality. Decide we must, and leadership we cannot escape: but in what spirit?

For some, — and we shall give chapter and verse — leadership is but another word for isolationism sublimated. We cannot abolish the rest of the world; we cannot even ignore it; we can and we must shape it according to our own pattern, and for the promotion of our own advantage. This type of leadership means, more emphatically than ever: "America first, last, and all the time!" It is a Roman ideal: *regere populos . . . parcere subjectis . . . debellare superbos . . .* There is an Old Roman strain in our imperial republic; and our Senate inherits the spirit of the Eternal City. For others, leadership means striving for certain principles, everywhere in the world; in the faith that our own prestige and our own interests can best be advanced by working for the common good. Such leadership looks forward to the ideal of George Washington, "the great republic of humanity at large." Our history points to us as the pioneers of a government dedicated to liberty and equality for all men.

These two lines of thought are not merely divergent: they are antagonistic. One may be summed up: "My country, right or wrong"; the other: "Where the right is, there is my country." It is true that they can easily be reconciled by combining *idealistic* talk with *realistic* aims. With that simple device, we can fool ourselves for a little while; be certain that we cannot deceive anyone else.

It is difficult to discuss such a problem purely in terms of the present. Let us take things as they are, by all means; but the most thorough realists must admit that reality is complex, and that we are compelled to choose between facts: say between the germ and the antiseptic. Our criterion in such a choice is:

things as we want them to be, in other words wishful thinking. We are on somewhat safer ground when we deal with the past: hindsight is proverbially sharper than foresight. If the mirror offered by history is uneven and blurred, it is less confusing than the mirror of current politics.

Be assured that I have no unshakable faith in "the lessons of history." The course of human events cannot be plotted, even backward, by the most elaborate thinking machine; and the shape of things to come eludes our calculus. Spengler and Toynbee taught us — Paul Valéry concurring — that civilizations were mortal: a hoary and weary truth. But this is no proof that the cosmic civilization now in the making is doomed to die. Slavery, the subjection of women, human sacrifices, which had existed from the dawn of time, could reasonably be considered as eternal. They are dying under our eyes, and war, as old as they, may end in its turn. It was a stern lesson of history, confirmed from remote antiquity to 1776, that no sizable republic could hope to survive: but our country fooled historical experience, and set a new precedent. So my historical examples are always offered for purposes of clarification, not of demonstration.

The simple thesis I want to illustrate is that a certain type of leadership has repeatedly headed for disaster, and always for the same reason: namely that it ignored or spurned the self-respect of the led. "Pride goeth before destruction, and a haughty spirit before a fall." The pattern is a familiar one. It has lost some of its virtue because of that very familiarity; but wisdom, if it be wisdom, never becomes trite. Solomon, echoed by Rudyard Kipling, might be a better guide for us than the men who clamor for "supremacy" unhampered by any idealistic nonsense. Again, this is an indication, not an infallible law. We may imitate Napoleon and avoid Napoleon's fate. All I can say is that the odds are against it.

We can hardly hope to achieve a more unquestioned leadership than the one wielded by Louis XIV at the zenith of his course. His word was law, not in France only, but in Europe. He could order the Doge of Venice to Versailles, and exact an apology from the Holy Father himself. Germany, after the Thirty Years' War and before the rise of Prussia, was wallowing in impotence and chaos: when a French court decreed the annexation of Strasbourg, Germany could only mourn and submit. In England, Charles II was in the pay of the French crown. The prestige of Bourbon France was not due purely, or perhaps even chiefly, to the power of her armies; it was the whole French way of life that Europe admired and sought to emulate. Every prince built for himself a Versailles, and his courtiers strove to speak French. The Elector of Brandenburg appointed an official Favorite, because without such a glamorous personage his imitation of the Grand Monarch would have been incomplete. History records the tragic sunset of that magnificent reign.

A century later, the Revolution and Napoleon made another bid for European hegemony. There again, victories in the field, dazzling as they were, were only one of the factors. The fame of the Philosophes, the charm of the Paris salons, the delicate luxury that found its perfection under Louis the Well-Beloved, prepared the way for the triumphs of the Republican and imperial armies. The French conquered, without any unnecessary gentleness; but they also swept away medieval cobwebs, and offered a more rational design of living. Western and southern Germany rallied gladly to the French system. Goethe himself was impressed, and even in our own days, such free spirits as Heinrich and Thomas Mann could admire Napoleon as a good European and the creator of a New Order. Many Italians accepted the French pattern. There were *Afrancesados* in Spain, Gallophiles in Russia. The Revolution and Napoleon did not succumb before the reactionary forces that they had challenged: the Dynasts merely muscled in at the very end, and claimed the fruit of victory. The curse of French leadership, enlightened and effective though it appeared, and, by modern standards, marvelously humane, was its being French through and through. The Directory created satellite republics, and drained them of their substance. Napoleon turned them into vassal kingdoms, exclusively to the greater glory of his own imperial majesty. What if Holland was ruined by the Continental Blockade? It was but a minor incident in the great plan of the conqueror. When King Louis began listening to the complaints of his Batavian subjects, he was summarily dismissed. Napoleon had a short way with recalcitrant satellites, even if they wore crowns and were of his own blood.

It is no paradox to assert that Hitler's conquests were swifter, more extensive, more spectacular than Napoleon's. At one time, directly or through allies like Mussolini and Franco, the New Order prevailed from the Strait of Gibraltar to the Caucasus, from Sicily and Crete to beyond the Arctic Circle. There again, material power does not tell the whole story. In most countries, Hitler had his choice of Quislings. The French Right had vowed before the war: "Rather Hitler than Blum!" There is a tendency now to throw a merciful veil over the extent of the Collaborationist spirit; but independent witnesses like Gertrude Stein and André Gide testify to the popularity of Marshal Pétain; and the Pétain who met Hitler at Montoire, the Pétain who said: "M. Laval and I are one," had accepted his place in the New Order. Laval worked with and for Hitler, not out of cowardice, not out of self-interest, but out of conviction. He sincerely believed that a better-organized Europe, free from eternal wars of revenge, ready to use boldly the resources of modern technique, had a chance of arising under Nazi leadership. We are unjust to the protagonists of history when we ignore what might have been. Laval's bet was not absurd: he narrowly missed passing to posterity as the Marshal Smuts, the Emperor Hirohito, of his country.

But, like Louis XIV, like Napoleon, Hitler was solely guided by the immediate and apparent interests of his own people. He led the Germans to leadership, and they worshipped themselves in his omnipotence. He had made Germany *la grande nation,* and he did not want any satellite to question that basic truth. He had purified and intensified Germanism, which was to be accepted as an ideal for all. He had suppressed un-German activities with a thoroughness which makes his American imitators look like half-hearted bunglers. I am convinced that the fanatical devotion he commanded had its origin, not in terror, but in a hope which was not ignoble. Both Hitler and Napoleon could have played the part of liberators; both could have buried ancient strife and ancient wrong; both, by transcending their victory, could have taught the conquered to transcend their defeat. Both chose force at the service of glory; and both met their Götzendämmerung.

My old friend John Doe (I once assumed his honored name, in the great crusade for the Four Freedoms) is tolerant, kindly, and not without a shrewd sense of humor. So he will smile at these platitudinous historical sermons: "True, to the extreme limit of truism: but what has it got to do with us? We are not imperialists: indeed we are the sworn enemies of all empires. We seek no leadership except as the champion of liberty for all."

As usual, John Doe, the Common Man, is profoundly right; but he is uncommonly hard to locate. If Uncle Sam is no Imperator, no Duce, no Führer, why does he so easily strike the attitudes and imitate the tones of Napoleon, Mussolini and Hitler? The sane may shrug their shoulders at Senatorial antics and flamboyant headlines: but who elects the Senators, and who purchases the papers — only the lunatic fringe? The symptoms are there, and they prove that the imperial virus is in our blood. Probe your own conscience, reader. How are you affected when you come across such phrases as: "Get tough!"; "Tell 'em (friend or foe) where to get off"; "Show 'em who is boss"; "America grimly resolved . . ."; "Allies sternly told . . ."; "Sign on the dotted line or else . . ."? What is the echo within your heart — amusement, pride, or shame? Try to imagine how this kind of leadership affects the rest of the world. The French, without whose whole-hearted support no European policy has any chance of lasting success, did not like the crack of Secretary Dulles's whip. But even Secretary Dulles was too gentle to please Senator McCarthy; and only yesterday, it looked as though Senator McCarthy might choose to become President.

The problem is a delicate one, for there is a subtle, almost imperceptible modulation from leadership to hegemony, and from hegemony to empire. We start, unimpeachably, in a righteous mood: "I love my ease; but there are intolerable evils in the world, and I cannot shirk my responsibility." The glow of self-satisfaction persists, even when selfishness and arrogance creep in: "I must maintain my privileges and assert my prerogatives as leader." There was a saving grace in Decatur's dictum: "My country, right or wrong!" For it is treason now to admit that we might be wrong. We are right, because we are THE RIGHT. What we order is right simply because it is we who order it.

Do not believe that such truculent assertions of "leadership" come exclusively from irresponsible journalists and barely responsible Congressmen, who, as a rule, are eminently misrepresentative men. We have weighty pronouncements to the same effect by citizens of the highest standing. It was Richard Olney, as Secretary of State, who said in 1895: "To-day, the United States is practically sovereign on this continent, and its fiat is law upon the subjects to which it confines its interpositions." Sixty years later, after the strenuous efforts of several Presidents to undo the harm caused by these fateful words, they still rankle in the Latin-American mind. They are worth remembering, for they candidly express the temper of many advocates of "leadership." Only the scope of our fiat has been enormously enlarged: "America today, and tomorrow the world!"

Mr. Henry Luce needs no introduction. His fabulous success in the magazine field has made him a shining example, a symbol and perhaps a portent. No one would accuse him of being thoughtless or irresponsible; and he can express himself with force and clarity. In his article "The American Century," [1] he wrote: "Hence they [the American people] have failed to play their part as a world power. . . . And the cure is this: to accept whole-heartedly our duty and our opportunity as the most powerful and vital nation in the world, and in consequence to exert upon the world the full impact of our influence, *for such purposes as we see fit and by such means as we see*

[1] *Life*, February 1941. Farrar & Rinehart, New York, 1941.

fit" (Italics mine). The phrase begins with all the trappings of high moral responsibility; it ends as imperialism naked and unashamed. And I doubt whether, for all his unrivaled acumen, Mr. Luce was aware of the transposition.

Obviously America would never submit to such "leadership" as Mr. Luce defines. But other nations also have their degree of shrewdness as well as their modicum of pride. The Olney-Luce spirit makes American leadership an absurdity. Why should others follow us blindly, if they are candidly told that we are thinking exclusively of our own interests, not at all of theirs? Common sense should induce them to bargain sharply with us (as Caudillo Franco did): "What is there in this for me?"; and also to shop round with our competitors. Thus Sweden, Finland, and, for different reasons, India, declined to enter our system. And those whom we can bribe or coerce to our side feel that they owe us no gratitude and no loyalty. If we pour billions into their economies, and build up their armaments, they have been warned that it is not for any reason "of a sentimental or ideological character." We pay them because we need them; we shall discard them when they have served their purpose. We are now backing Japan and Germany, urging them to rearm, fanning the sparks of their martial spirit. We are ready to support, with fine indifference to moral principles, both Marshal Tito and Caudillo Franco. We were at heart with Ho Chi Minh, until we discovered that the Chinese were on the same side.

Under the Machiavellian dispensation, there can be no honest dealings among the nations: we are gambling with crooks, and we should be very foolish not to conceal a few aces up our sleeves. It may be practical; but distrust and deceit mean war — cold war, shooting war, and ultimately Armageddon; for in such a game, bombs are trumps. In spite of the Kellogg Pact, we are proclaiming that war is the essential instrument of our national policy. We have, of course, an array of softer names. We are for peace, without appeasement; provided it be the peace that will enable us "to exert upon the world the full impact of our influence, for such purposes as we see fit, and by such means as we see fit." We are for peace, if it brings the unconditional surrender, nothing else, of foes, neutrals, and friends alike. But as no one will surrender except to overwhelming force, the Forgotten Soldier was right: "There is no substitute for victory." We are for peace, if it can be discussed — and imposed — from "a position of strength." All this was admirably expressed in the British song of far-off Victorian times: "We've got the men, we've got the ships, and we've got the money too." Back of Dizzy and Bismarck, we find ancient maxims and ancient fables: *Quia nominor leo*, La Fontaine's disenchanted "morality":

La raison du plus fort est toujours la meilleure . . .

History teaches us that the world has been so governed for at least six thousand years, and that, for nearly two thousand years, Christianity has been preached in vain. History might teach us also that it is high time for a change.

The root of the evil is that little men are thinking of little gains for a little while, and call it realism. Religion, philosophy, and science alike bid us take the larger view. But when will the world be ruled by wisdom? Only when rational men make the startling discovery that it is not foolish to be wise.

In the meantime — how long, and how mean? — strictly within the frame of power politics, it is a fact that *imposed* leadership is self-defeating. Ignoring France, to give only one example, or coercing France, can only weaken our grand alliance. We can, if we pay the price, "exert the full impact of our influence," make the French Parliament sign on the dotted line, arm twenty, forty, sixty divisions: but where will their fighting spirit be? The Western Allies during the Phony War, the sudden collapse of Chiang Kai-shek's armies in 1949, should have taught us that a force which has lost faith is a rope of sand. God is on the side of the big battalions, provided they be sustained by an inner power "of a sentimental or ideological character."

What is the path of salvation? Tough Rudyard Kipling, for once transcending his toughness, called it "an humble and a contrite heart." I am not qualified to speak in such religious tones. As a teacher, I should suggest: "the inquiring mind." Do not seek to lead by force, as you would refuse to be led by force. Search diligently. Search your own mind, and be ready to discard pettiness and prejudice, for they are signs of weakness. Search the minds of friends and of opponents as well, and be ready to welcome whatever source of strength you find in them. For we are here not to impose our will but to seek the truth; and the quest alone can make us free.

PART III

Free Enterprise

CHAPTER XI

Confusions

$\mathcal{T}$he discussion of economic and social problems will be much briefer than the inquiry into politics. This does not imply that I consider them as of less importance: the exact reverse is true. I admit that I had to go against the trend of my education. In my childhood, standard histories were still chiefly concerned with the high deeds and misdeeds of monarchs — republics being only the blurred shadows of kings. I learned the (abridged) list of royal mistresses, Agnès Sorel, Diane de Poitiers, Gabrielle d'Estrées, La Vallière, Montespan, Pompadour, Du Barry, as well as the rather less glamorous roll of famous and indecisive victories. But I was taught next to nothing about man's first concern in life, which is to make a living.

This was the twilight of a very ancient tradition. In economics, the bourgeois conception of property had prevailed for centuries before the last tenuous traces of feudalism were swept away. Except in a few Utopian works — including the New Testament — there was hardly any sign of social-economic thought. The *liberal* bourgeoisie simply wanted to abolish the privileges of the nobility, obsolete and annoying rather than oppressive; and the common people had no desire but to have a share in the rights and opportunities of the Third Estate. The year 1848 posed the social problem with great definiteness, and the Second Republic, in February, was called "Democratic and Social." But it was only a flare. As early as June, the Reds were crushed. At the Presidential election in December, the Socialist candidate Raspail polled 36,000 votes, against 5,400,000 for Louis-Napoleon and 1,400,000 for Cavaignac. In 1863, Paris gave four hundred votes to Labor candidates, 153,000 to the anti-Bonapartist opposition led by

Thiers, bourgeois of the bourgeois, and professed hater of "the vile multitude." In 1871, the Commune started as an explosion of wounded patriotism and Parisian pride: it was only when the end was near that it assumed a socialistic tinge.[1] For generations, the workers kept voting the Radical ticket; and the Radicals, led by *petits bourgeois,* were interested only in political progress, which for them was identical with anticlericalism. This state of mind — without the anticlerical animus — is still that of the American working classes today. The social-economic system is taken for granted, even among the most combative of the Labor leaders. Those who question the system are branded as foreign agitators. Labor is a giant among lobbies, not a party, and least of all a subversive factor.

The urgency, the primacy of social-economic problems were forced upon me when I was barely out of adolescence, at the close of the nineteenth century. The chief influence in my conversion was Jean Jaurès. But the great *political* Socialist was left behind just at the moment he had achieved leadership. At that time, there was a rebellion, among intellectual and manual workers alike, against the subordination of their socialist ideal to bourgeois politics. This rebellion worked well with the anarchistic trend of the *fin de siècle* period, under such heterogeneous leaders as Herbert Spencer, Ibsen, Tolstoy, P. J. Proudhon, and Bakounine. "Syndicalism" and "direct action" were the manifestations of that nonpolitical spirit. American Labor, even when holding aloof from politics, recognizes its legitimacy and importance: Syndicalism denies both. Reversing the famous dictum of Abbé Siéyès, it would say: "What is politics? Everything. What should it be? Nothing." This, by the way, was the prophecy of Karl Marx himself: under pure communism, the political state is to wither and disappear. I still belong to that horse-and-buggy period: how difficult it is to escape from one's formative years! If the word had not acquired such a sinister tinge in Spain, I might call myself an Anarcho-Syndicalist. I hate politics now as bitterly as I did then. My

---

[1] *Commune,* of course, had nothing to do with *communism;* it was the medieval term for municipal body, revived by the French Revolution.

conscience has never allowed me to join a party; not even the Socialist, and least of all the Communist.

So if I devote two or three times as much space to political as to social questions, it is not that I underrate the latter. But there are principles which underlie both, and which need not be discussed again. And it is obvious that the "political" field has been quietly invaded, and almost absorbed, by the social-economic. There is hardly any issue before any national parliament today — not even the race problem — that has not an economic background and economic bearings.

This is so plain that the scrupulous enquirer, ever afraid of self-evidence as a symptom of arrested thought, feels compelled to qualify the affirmation. Economics is not everything, even in the purely economic field. I have repeatedly expressed the wish that *Homo Œconomicus* did exist, and would assume control: he would not commit the same disastrous blunders as his erratic brother *Homo Politicus*. We shall see again and again, in the following pages, how man's conduct, individual and collective, is swayed by considerations that are not economic. There may be a few men, high-ranking officers and contractors, for whom war does pay, and it is right to expose them. But they could not hurl a nation into war unless the masses were ready, and even eager, to be pushed over the brink. Wars are the result of collective passions, not calculations; they are collective explosions of pride and anger; they still have the glamor of great adventures; at their cheapest, they are track meets of colossal magnitude; at their best, they are crusades. All this cannot be measured in terms of dollars and cents. The man who died in Korea did not do so in order to line Uncle Sam's pockets, or his own.

As we shall see, when national pride and economic interests clash, it is hard to prophesy which way the decision will take. From the economic point of view, Danzig was part of the Polish sphere, Fiume and even Trieste of the Yugoslav, the Saar of the French Lorraine system. All, naturally, would like to eat their cake and have it too: to combine economic advantages with nationalistic sentiment. Yet the three cities have not put the economic advantages first; in 1935 and again in 1955 the Saar chose what might very well have been economic suicide. The human mind is not a ledger; the human heart is not a cash box.

Life is infinitely more varied than the cultural patterns of the anthroposociologists, or the airy fabrics of economic theory. I am a humanist, *Homo Simplex*. I have to use theories as I have to use words: every word implies a classification, and therefore a theory. But I declined to be used by them. These farewell books of mine are not treatises, but inquiries in the form of meditations and confessions. In economics as in politics and anthropology, my definitions will cause the professionals to smile. Let them: I can afford to smile in return; for as a student of history, I was bound to note the hopeless contradictions of the system-makers, among themselves and within their own minds. In view of these *variations* (to use Bossuet's term in his controversies with the Protestant churches), two ways are open. One is to seek one more system which will be free from the faults of all foregoing systems: since Joseph Smith and Madame Blavatsky do not agree, then Bahaullah must be right. The other is to admit the vanity of all systems. The vanity of their claims as absolute and exclusive: in a limited field, they are valid, for each illustrates one particular area of reality. All systems are wrong as religions, and valuable as working hypotheses. When they stop working — and they tire easily — they should be promoted into the sedate realm of historical text books: *otium cum dignitate.*

What I am attempting here is to clear up my own mind: what do *I* mean by capitalism, communism, socialism, individualism? I have no desire to impose my own conclusions. I only hope that my honest inquiry will induce others to think out these problems for themselves.

One great cause of confusion must first be removed: there is no inevitable link between political institutions and the social-economic regime. A thorough "democracy," a People's Republic like America, may profess a vehement horror of socialism, while constitutional monarchies like England and Sweden have

no insuperable prejudices on the subject. The advent of socialism, within the framework of existing political institutions, can
be effected without a violent revolution. There was no bloodshed in England between 1946 and 1951. The chatty chroni-
cles of Angela Thirkell describe delicately the impact of the
new age on the county families of Barsetshire: but the change
is not catastrophic. If you glance at *The Tatler* or *The Sphere,*
you will see that great formal balls, garden parties, presenta-
tions at Court, grouse-shooting and fox-hunting were not suddenly abolished. So Mr. Winston Churchill could return to
power as if he were presiding over the England of Edward VII.
On the other hand, nondemocratic socialism is conceivable. It
seems to have prevailed under the Incas, and in Paraguay when
the Jesuits had absolute control. The Bismarckian empire went
farther in the direction of socialism than the liberal countries.

In good logic, all rich men ought to be political conservatives.
Their attitude should be that of Alexander Hamilton: government exists to maintain order, that is to say, the existing order,
that is to say the privileges of wealth. As a matter of fact, the
cleavage between the Haves and the Have-nots has never been
absolute. In France, the bourgeoisie, fighting for social and
political recognition, was for generations the spearhead of the
masses in the attack against the survivals of the feudal past. It
took the bourgeois nearly a century to become frankly conservative in their turn; and to the present day, many bourgeois
keep repeating with approval the radical formulae of 1789. In
England, throughout the nineteenth century, the manufactur-
ing and commercial interests, with the moral support of the
nonconformist churches, fought hard against the aristocracy,
the squirearchy and the Establishment. There always were men
of wealth on the Left, and even in alliance with the extreme
Left; while poor men, and not mere hirelings either, were
found among the ablest defenders of the conservative cause;
some out of hatred for the stodgy Philistine; some out of patriotism; some out of religious conviction. In America, Theodore
Roosevelt, who denounced predatory wealth, was not a pauper;
neither was Franklin Roosevelt, who declared war on the

Economic Royalists, and urged a new deal for the forgotten man.

Second source of confusion: the word *social* refers to the conditions of *society,* and particularly to the hierarchy of the *classes.* Now in modern Europe and in America, there is no absolute identity between the social stratification and the economic. The radical distinction between "the poor" and "the rich" is a figment. We find instead imperceptible transitions between the pauper, the indigent, the poor, the modest-but-comfortable yeoman, artisan, employee, shopkeeper, the well-to-do, the rich, the wealthy, the magnates. Baron de Rothschild could say of a friend who died leaving a few paltry millions: "Poor Untel! I thought he was well off." Furthermore, the social grading never quite corresponds with the financial rating: the Blue Book and Bradstreet's are not interchangeable. Particularly in old countries, good family, beauty, talent, the service of the State (especially in the armed forces and in diplomacy), the service of God (in the right churches), will blur and even efface the prestige of sheer plutocracy. In our own South, I have seen impoverished gentlemen consorting with other gentlemen in circles where no *nouveau riche* would be received. Money goes a very long way: unaided, it seldom goes the whole way.

Among the many confusions created by the powerful and fuliginous mind of Karl Marx, none is quite so thick as his use of the word *bourgeois.* His thought was formed at the time when the bourgeoisie became politically supreme in England and in France, and when it was despised as Philistine by the Romanticists. But the middle class, the bourgeoisie, never was wholly identified with capitalism. A government employee with a decent salary thinks of himself and is thought of as a bourgeois, although he may never have invested a penny even in the safest bonds. Bunching together as members of the bourgeois class a rich peasant, a financial adventurer, a merchant, a land-owning duke, strains the term to the breaking point. In Marxian parlance, a highly paid manager is a wage slave, a peanut vendor is a capitalist.

If we attempt to think in terms not of doctrines but of realities, we shall perceive that the essential difference is not between capitalism and socialism, but between independent and collective activities. At one time, rugged entrepreneurs fetched water in buckets from the river, and carried it to the consumer for a few pennies: this was individualism of the strictest observance. The radical change in urban life came when the water, brought from a long distance, was piped to every apartment: the sturdy water carrier ceased to exist. After this took place, it mattered little whether the water system was controlled by a single capitalist, by a company, or by the city government. Complete individual independence in water distribution had disappeared; collectivism had set in. "The revolution was not in the minds, but in the pipes."

Note that collectivism does not wholly depend on the machine. The *latifundia* of ancient Rome, the plantations of our Old South, those of colonial countries until yesterday, were run as "collectives." Even before the industrial revolution, there already were large workshops, which made it possible to practice the division of labor, to purchase materials and sell the finished products wholesale. Mines were worked, roads were built, canals were dug, before the invention of the steam engine.

Words have at least three ways of misbehaving. One is to get entangled with other words, although there is no necessary connection between them. Clear cases in point, previously discussed, are the confusions between *democracy* and *party rule*, and between *economic* and *social*. The second occurs when the same word is used for concepts which are not merely different, but antagonistic: the *culture* of Goethe and that of the anthropologists; *democrat* as a believer in equality, and *democrat* as the defender of the caste system in Dixie; *love* as brutal lust, and *love* as St. Paul's *charity*; *Christianity* as meekness, and the Christianity which has prompted massacres, and is still thirsting for "massive retaliation." Ormudz and Ahriman exchange clothes with disconcerting facility. The third way is the most elusive: the words preserve a distinct core of meaning, but they expand or shrink like Alice in Wonderland nibbling the magic mushroom. They have a maximal and a minimal connotation; and we pass from one to the other with the unconscious ease bred of immemorial habit. Economics, next to theology, is the domain of perverse ingenuity. So economic terms offer all three kinds of equivocation, with a few clever twists of their own.

Take the very plain term *business*. Does it mean to you every form of economic activity — production, transportation, distribution? Then, if it is not the whole of life, it is at any rate its indispensable substratum. If it were not for business, man would revert to mere animal existence. What is good for business is good for mankind, for business is practically synonymous with civilization. In this sense, every laborer is engaged in business; and there are two hundred million potential or actual businessmen in Soviet Russia.

But the word *business* can shrink suddenly to *buying* and *selling*: the producer no longer is a "businessman." It has a tendency to shrink further: buying and selling not actual goods (this is mere *trade*), but tokens: banking and the Stock Exchange are the citadels of such business. The financier is the man of business par excellence: he holds the producer and the distributor in fee. Instead of being considered merely as a necessary service, financing becomes the center, the very essence of business life. For a city to run its own utilities is *bad for business*. To have a concessionnaire, supported by a holding company, which in its turn is getting its resources from the banks, is a masterpiece of business procedure. This primacy of finance in business is a delusion as flagrant as the claims of monarchy and a feudal aristocracy. We can live without belted earls, and we could exist without financial barons. If the small class of *businessmen* were to disappear, business in the wider sense would not be affected.

The word *capital* also has a maximal and a minimal meaning; and the advocates of *capitalism* defend the narrower by appealing to the more general. Essentially, *capital* means *reserves*. A man (or a society) living a strictly hand-to-mouth existence has no capital. A squirrel storing nuts, a miser burying gold, are not true capitalists: for capital is more than hoarding, or delayed consumption; it means the capacity of doing something with the reserves. Every new enterprise needs capital, i.e., energy available beyond the immediate upkeep of life. If Robinson Crusoe can feed himself in a few minutes by plucking fruit, the rest of his time becomes his capital, and he can *invest* it. If a community details some of its members to gather food for the rest, those who are released from that basic activity constitute the capital of the group: they can devote themselves to extending the possessions of all. Capital, in this elementary meaning, is as indispensable under socialism as it is under plutocracy. For *capital is labor made available by forethought.* Currency and bank credits are mere tokens for that reality: it is men, not bits of paper, who build skyscrapers or power plants. Russia's series of five-year plans represents the creation of capital, and a vast investment in "capital goods."

If Russia is attempting to create and utilize capital exactly as we do, what is the difference between us? *Capitalism* has come to mean a system in which labor is working for a small class called capitalists: an aristocratic conception. In a democracy, this is an indefensible position; the word *capitalism* has lost caste, not as the result of socialistic propaganda, but because it stated the facts too bluntly. So we have been in quest of a more acceptable term. The *competitive system* was not above reproach. Competition is both incentive and waste; and the waste might easily outweigh the incentive. Many important enterprises, like public utilities, are noncompetitive; and Big Business, if left to its own devices, would end competition in favor of combines. The *profit motive* itself is a fading formula: not because the thing it denotes has receded, but because it is present everywhere, even in Russia. No man will work, under any regime, unless there is some profit in it for himself, were it only a hunk of bread: no incentive, no exertion. The minimal conception of the *profit motive* is this: a condition in which a disproportionate share of the common profit (yield above subsistence) goes to a chosen few, who deserve to be called *profiteers*, and should glory in the name. Again this is too blunt; so the Profit Motive has gone the way of Capitalism:

both slightly disreputable relatives whom we prefer to ignore. We have coined, to describe our Way of Life, the expression *Free Enterprise*: the happy union of two lovely words. Whether free enterprise is an unclouded reality in this country and at this time, whether it cannot be fostered under a setup very different from ours, are problems which will repay investigation.

Communism, finally, is also a word which covers the full range from the loftiest ideal to the ugliest reality. Etymologically, it means the sense of communal living, the desire to share in, and add to, the *common wealth.* It assumes that every group of men, and the vast earth itself, should be a brotherly coöperative society. This is the communism of the early Christians and of the religious orders to this day, and you cannot deprive it of its right name. But historically, we find that ideal refracted through the powerful and distorted mind of Karl Marx; and that caricature refracted in its turn through the confused and tragic heritage of the Russian people. I refuse either to condemn the original principle, or to defend its present associations.

CHAPTER XII

Monoliths

We are girding ourselves for Armageddon: the ultimate clash of doctrines, the decisive struggle between darkness and light. To a disinterested student, this is sheer phantasmagoria. *We* piously intone our incantations: *they*, with greater fervor and even less critical spirit, vociferate their own. And lo! It is all vanity.

The Marxians are undoubtedly the worse. They have a definite body of Holy Scriptures, the Gospel according to Karl Marx, with the writing of Lenin and Stalin as deutero-canonical. They have a permanent œcumenical council, with an infallible pontiff, ready to fulminate against heresy and define the true faith: this is known as laying down the party line. It matters little that the Gospel is a formidable fortress of erudition and dialectics, accessible only to the most determined friend or foe. Mystery is an advantage. It is easier to believe in the splendor of Truth while she remains hidden in the well so cunningly dug by Karl Marx: daylight might cruelly reveal her blemishes. To all importunate questions, "I believe in Marx" is a terse and irrefutable answer. We do not have quite the same reverence for Adam Smith, or even for Mr. Herbert Hoover.

Marx was "a man of Forty-eight": he grew up in the sultry atmosphere of continental Romanticism. But far deeper than his romanticism was his kinship with the prophets of Israel: passionate, glowing with righteous anger, drunk with millennial hopes. It is this innermost fire, not completely quenched even today, that was the secret of his power. By June 1848, the great apocalyptic dream was dispelled: there was to be no new heaven and no new earth. A wounded Romanticist, Marx unconsciously adopted, as a protective coloring, the harsh pseudo-scientific realism of the hour. He, just like the great profiteers of the period, boasted that he was not dealing with ideals and sentiments, but with facts, harsh and bare. With the splendid arrogance that was the key to his mastery, he rejected as "Utopian" all the socialists who had come before him, and as *petits bourgeois* those who, like Proudhon, refused to acknowledge his infallibility. The term Utopian would fit Fourier, and to some extent Saint-Simon. But Robert Owen and Louis Blanc were more practical than Marx himself; and even Cabet the Icarian gave an uninspired and remarkably sane anticipation of Bellamy.

It was this fanatical belief in himself that enabled Marx to capture the first Workingmen's International. He was no doubt an indefatigable collector and organizer of facts, and a formidable dialectician. But his triumph was not due to human cybernetics: it was due to his gift of identifying his personality with his cause. Such was the case with Mohammed and with Hitler, with Carson of Ulster and Jinnah of Pakistan. Marxism is not *Das Kapital*: Marxism is Karl Marx.

The Paris Commune was not a Communist insurrection: but Marx and the reactionaries agreed in considering it as such. Its defeat gave the opportunity for a drastic purge: the proletarian movement in France was crippled for a generation. The lead in socialism was assumed by Germany, where "liberalism" in politics and economics never had vigorous roots. And the German Social-Democratic Party gathered in the voters — by no means all Marxists at heart — who wished to register their radical opposition to the Hohenzollern Empire. As a result, early in the twentieth century, the German Socialist Party was a giant among its peers. It was thus able to impose its own terms upon the whole movement. So when the unity of European socialism was restored, or rather created, at Amsterdam (1904), Marxism, formally adopted as a doctrine by the Germans, became the official faith of the whole continental party. Men like Jean Jaurès and later Léon Blum, trained scholars and free spirits, could not accept the Marxian orthodoxy at its face value. But, for the sake of unity, they bowed to the paper idol.

English Labor remained uncontaminated. It was moving steadily toward socialism, but it followed its own path. Neither the Fabian Society nor the Trade Unions, in loose and almost unconscious alliance, took any great interest in formal theories. I am no worshipper of pragmatic muddleheadedness: but there are times when indifference to system is a victory for clearness of thought.

Thus Marxism became a name to conjure with; it was in the sacred name of Marxism that the Bolsheviks seized power. It may be true that no catastrophic change can be effected except through the agency of fanaticism: reasonable men, in the Russian chaos of 1917, never had the ghost of a chance. But it is far from certain that catastrophes are desirable, even when they sweep away intolerable abuses. It was not, however, through Marxism that the Bolsheviks kept power; neither was it altogether through an autocracy more ruthless than that of the tsars and immensely more efficient. Their victory was really that of pre-Marxian *socialism*, which had deep roots in the Russian soil, and was in harmony with religious aspirations in the Russian soul: the sense of working together for the common good, not for the profit of a few. It was the Workers' Republic, not the recondite pedantries of *Das Kapital*, that the Russian people defended against a long series of White adventurers, and against the crusading onslaught of Hitler.[1]

Marxism is therefore an iron mask imposed upon the living and complex realities of Russian life. There we find pride in power politics, according to a pattern set by the West and adopted by the Romanovs: a Russian nationalism and a Russian imperialism, the unholy heritage of Holy Russia. But we find also a renewed sense of dignity, when the laborer, the "common man" collectively, is sovereign at least in theory: this, to the masses, is *democracy*. Not to mention pride, as in nineteenth-century England, as in twentieth-century America, in technical progress, in vast public works, in literacy. All these sentiments, some noble, some questionable, ferment in the

---

[1] This is probably even truer of the Chinese Revolution, which is a people's movement rather than a manifestation of dogmatic Marxism.

teeming Russian world, in spite of party dictatorship and ideological intolerance. The enormous cluster of Soviet Republics is the reverse of monolithic; and that is the secret of its undeniable vitality.

Neither are we monolithic, thank the Lord! The American Way of Life, it must constantly be repeated, is nothing but the right to differ in peace, and even in friendliness. By whatever name we choose to call our key principle — we have mentioned a few such labels, capitalism, individualism, competition, the profit motive, the anti-welfare state, free enterprise — it does not constitute a "system" rigidly governing even our purely economic activities.

The religious life of the United States, for one thing, has not yet been absorbed by "capitalism," although it has undoubtedly been subjected to its influence. Neither did Christianity become a mere branch of the imperial administration when, in the fourth century, it became the official faith of Rome; neither did Catholicism simply take its place in the feudal hierarchy, or in the dynastic world that emerged out of feudalism. A church, even of divine origin, has to work among men, and through men. As a historical manifestation, it is inevitably affected by the coloring of the period; but a chameleon retains its identity. We have gone far in establishing a kind of moral bimetallism: a fixed ratio between godliness and financial success. Still, we dare not expunge from the Gospels certain embarrassing passages, which cast some suspicion on the saintliness of the late John D. Rockefeller.

Then there is an all-important sector in American life that is not fully governed by the profit motive: the family. Child-breeding is not a "rentable" or self-liquidating enterprise. Before the children can repay for their rearing (including compound interests and the heavy depreciation of their progenitors), they ungratefully start a life of their own. As insurance premiums against the disabilities of old age, they cannot be compared with the annuities that can be purchased from any reliable company. The family is not ruled by orthodox economics: I suspect that it has a slightly socialistic or even communistic tinge. Now family feelings do interfere in economic life. The son of the owner, unless he be an irremediable moron or artist, stands a good chance of becoming Vice President at an early age. We have wholly discarded the dynastic principle in public administration: but nepotism is the rule in the more sentimental business world. And wealth can be controlled by women, wives or daughters, who may not even attempt to manage the concern: the heiress who buys herself a series of exotic princes is a well-known character in American folklore. The central myth of capitalism — wealth as the reward of efficiency — breaks down in the second generation.

There is a third realm in which the rule of money is spurned, and that is the domain of patriotism. We have already stated that it does not pay a shrewd individualist to be killed for his country. It does not even pay him to serve his country as an officer, for a pittance that the assistant managers of third-rate concerns would scorn. When the honor of the country is at stake, capitalism slinks away, ashamed, and the most exacting socialism becomes the rule. Everything must be sacrificed on the altar of the common cause. Property is commandeered or destroyed without a qualm. The thought of profit, extolled only yesterday, is now branded as profiteering. (Branding, however, does not cause it to disappear altogether.) Men worth half a million a year offer to serve for one dollar. Again we sigh for the convenient simplicity of Homo Œconomicus, and his single passion for buying in the cheapest market. As Tennyson proudly said:

> We are not cotton-spinners all
> But some love England and her honor yet.

No man can be a cotton-spinner first, last, and all the time.

We are not moving toward the Profit Motive Utopia: on the contrary, it is receding from us. With our whole-hearted approval, large departments of human activity have passed from Free Enterprise to Socialism. Time was when war was definitely a business. The Grandes Compagnies in fourteenth-century France, the condottieri in Italy, were entrepreneurs of the most orthodox kind. They fought for pay, with loot as a bonus. Wallenstein was the greatest of these military contractors. Napoleon had thought of such a career for himself in the East; and perhaps Taine was right in considering him as an exalted condottiere. General Gordon, putting down the rebellion of the Christian Taipings in China, was "in the business," although he was not at heart a businessman. Fighting as a profitable trade was the ruling principle of the Tycoons, in the long confusion that followed the downfall of the Chinese Empire. Today, the merchandising of death has been limited to armaments and supplies.

We have mentioned the strange fact that for two centuries seats on the bench in France were bought like property. The judges, although they were as a rule men of great integrity, found it natural to recoup themselves with costs, fines, and *douceurs* from the litigants. These gifts of love, which went by the name of *spices*, were not bribes: as the judges equitably received from both sides, impartiality was preserved.

Tax-gathering was a thriving line of business, and on the grandest scale. The *Fermiers Généraux* (General Contractors) of the eighteenth century formed an aristocracy of wealth, taste and enlightenment. The riches they gathered were used to promote intelligent luxury. They were patrons of the arts, and they supported the *Encyclopaedia* much as Mr. Rockefeller endowed the University of Chicago. The most exquisite flower of this financial world, Madame de Pompadour, had France at her feet; and her brother Marigny was an admirable Superintendent of Fine Arts. When tax-collecting passed from the hands of these resourceful men into those of dull bureaucrats, a light went out of the world.

Political service was long considered as a legitimate source of private gain. The Roman governors and proconsuls were concessionaires who had paid heavily for their opportunity, and were resolved not to be the losers. Not merely adventurers like Concini and Mazarin, but great servants of the monarchy like Richelieu and Colbert found it natural to enrich themselves and their tribes. Young men went to India penniless, and expected to return as nabobs. Later, idealists coined the word *graft* to smear these legitimate incentives to capable management. The jealousy of the timid is eternal, and the incompetent will always have some pious phrase in readiness to revile the men who made the France of Louis XV and the America of Warren Gamaliel Harding what they were.

Again we must rebel against conventional totalitarian patterns according to which the Russian Way of Life must be homogeneously communistic (and criminal), the American homogeneously capitalistic (and virtuous). The fallacy should be patent to unbiased eyes; but there are moments when it is held a crime to be unbiased. A textbook was banned from Texas schools because it stated the incontrovertible fact that much of our economy was communistic. A clear example of the tyranny of words: one horrific term suffices to paralyze thought, and to drive plain facts into hiding. We are, in reverse, like the pious soul who found such unspeakable comfort in the blessed word *Mesopotamia*. All the activities of the federal and local governments, including the tremendous investment in atomic power, are as communistic as their counterparts in Russia. Highways, waterways, ports, the postal service, the public school system up to the state universities, are as purely socialistic as Marx himself could desire. It would be hard to give the exact percentage of such "communism": the proportion of our sundry taxes, visible and invisible, to our total income might provide a rough approximation.[2]

Much of the rest is *collectivistic*. We have alluded to the fact that the machine age had made the *isolated* individual almost obsolete. It is passing strange that men connected all their lives

[2] We should make a distinction between State Communism and State Socialism. In pure Communism (to each according to his wants), there is no immediate relation between service and payment. The most striking example is the public school system: a childless millionaire contributes heavily to it, a proletarian with twelve children does not. In State Socialism, there is definite payment for definite services: as in the Post Office, in city-owned utilities, in toll roads and bridges. So it might as well be called State Capitalism.

with giant concerns continue to preach undiluted individualism as if these were still the days of the lone pioneer. We refuse
to acknowledge the secret of our own strength: we prefer to
seek it in a vanished Walden Utopia. America's greatness is
due to large-scale enterprise and mass production: when it
comes to individual craftsmanship, the men of many nations
are fully our equals; in remote ages, many were our superiors.
In the applications of science to industry, Germany led the way;
Great Britain, France, Italy did not lag far behind; Poland and
Russia are fast catching up. The chief weakness of France, on
the other hand — beside the paucity of indispensable natural
resources such as coal and oil — lies in the invincible individualism of the bourgeoisie. The small hereditary family concern
still plays a great part in French business life, and is a great
obstacle to efficient production. With us, the modern financial
empires are collectively owned and managed: this is true even
in the rare cases when a particular family retains control, like
the Du Ponts de Nemours and the Fords. Most great concerns
count their shareholders by the ten thousands; some even boast
of their hundred thousands. For all wage earners, that is to say
for the majority of employees, it matters little whether the concern be officially labeled capitalistic or socialistic. The essential
points, so far as they are concerned, are steady work and decent
wages. They would prefer a solid state enterprise to a shaky
private one; and the bankruptcy list warns us every morning,
even in prosperous times, that private ownership is no assurance
of financial success.

More puzzling still is the blend of Communism and "Private
Collectivism," to use a term as absurd, on the face of it, as "an
orthodox Protestant," or "a Catholic nationalist." Among these
may be mentioned the coöperative societies, for production and
especially for distribution; also the non-profit-making organizations, which not seldom are Big Business: the various Foundations, the churches, the schools, even such insurance companies
as the Teachers' Insurance and Annuity Association. They are
"private" only in the sense that they are not agencies of the state.
But they are not individually owned, and they are not run for

the benefit of a few individuals. In France, vast enterprises are entrusted to authorities or boards known by the orthodox capitalistic name *companies*. They follow the pattern of private firms, but they are in reality public services. Their true nature may be acknowledged, as in the case of the principal banks and the railways. Or it may remain an open secret: the French Line is practically state-owned; and so was, for many successful years, our President Line, which had failed in private hands. The French equivalent of our TVA, a vast project for the development of the Rhône valley, is called a *Compagnie Nationale*. Our own railroads are citadels of free enterprise; they reject with horror the thought of nationalization; but they cannot open or shut down a branch line, increase their rates, offer rebates to large and valuable customers, deal with their own employees, without securing the approval of some public commission. The one privilege left to the directors is to play among themselves complicated financial war games, not in the least essential to efficient management.

The Commonwealth Club of California is composed of particularly intelligent business and professional men, and I considered it a great privilege to address them on repeated occasions. Once I teased them with a volley of local instances, which they found it hard to controvert. They soothed their conscience by smiling with friendly indulgence: a professor, like a king's jester, must be allowed his fun, even about sacred things. At that time, there were in Market Street, San Francisco, capitalistic streetcars and communistic (municipal) streetcars running on parallel tracks: now, thanks to a business mayor, they are all communistic. Only a short while before, the water supply had been shifted from the capitalistic Crystal Springs Company to the communistic Hetch Hetchy development. The round-the-world steamers of the then Dollar Line went through the capitalistic Suez Canal and the communistic Panama Canal. To send a small package, a man had the choice between the capitalistic Railway Express Company and the communistic Parcel Post. Thus the most orthodox businessman had to live in a coexistential, pluralistic world; and no shock of horror warned him when he was passing from the Eternal Verities of Capitalism to the atrocities of Communism. But if you were to suggest that one more public utility, like gas or electricity, might be run as a public service, and not for private gain, then you would be denounced as a crypto-Communist, at least a fellow traveler, and disloyal to the American Way of Life.

"Surely the life-and-death conflict in which we are engaged cannot be reduced to a shadow-fight about loosely interpreted catch words?" To this objection, I shall, now and in later chapters, suggest three possible answers.

The first is that the vastness and the ferocity of a struggle are no indications of its vital importance. Men have fought, throughout the ages, for issues which, in Bismarck's phrase, were not worth the bones of a single Pomeranian grenadier. All the dynastic wars in the past seem futile to us. So was the Crimean war — its object forgotten even before it was formally declared. Paraguay fought heroically for five years, from 1865 to 1870, against three of its neighbors; its male population was practically annihilated. There is no finer example of fanatical patriotism: like Clemenceau in 1917, every Paraguayan believed in fighting to the bitter end. But it is clear to posterity that the suicidal contest need not have been started at all, and brought no result except destruction. Even the most theological-minded among our contemporaries have ceased to hold that the first duty of man was to exterminate the monsters who were Homoiousians instead of Homoousians, or who believed in Consubstantiation instead of Transubstantiation.

The present conflict is formidable because it serves as a focus for primitive, even subhuman passions (dogs will fight to the death, without any ideological nonsense about it), and because modern technique might make it as devastating for the whole world as the War of the Triple Alliance was for Paraguay. The quiet thinker examines the issue *as if* it did not involve a life-and-death combat; and he comes to the conclusion that the world should not be set aflame for Homoousian Capitalism against Homoiousian Socialism. We have our choice: we may, indignantly, virtuously, suppress the quiet thinker; or we may try to do some quiet thinking ourselves; we are finely poised between primitivism and civilization.

The second answer is that, in the world conflict today, the Communist issue is incidental. This is a battle, not of political and economic theories, but of imperialisms, the inevitable consequence of "realistic" power politics. This is demonstrated by our dallying impartially with Franco, who is no democrat, and with Tito, who is a Communist.

The third answer, or, if you prefer, the third hypothesis, is that the anticommunist crusade is of inestimable value for the defense of economic privileges at home. In good faith, I am sure: the highest triumph of propaganda is to convince the propagandists. Any one who challenges, however mildly, our "economic royalists" is branded as the tool of our implacable enemies. Our ingrained love of liberty and order, our patriotism, even our religious sentiment, were mobilized for months in defense of the Dixon-Yates contract: a public-operated public utility would be "creeping socialism," and "capitulating to Moscow." This would be dismissed as preposterous if America were ruled by philosophers, or even if it were a full and unhampered democracy. It is plain, however, that plutocracy — profits and power shared by all, but with a heavy concentration in the hands of a few — controls both Congress and the press. It is to the interest of those Happy Few to keep the fires of hate burning. If the flames were to die, America might have another and more drastic New Deal.

These things I have said before, and I shall say them again. The reiteration is deliberate: I know that after a third and a fourth reading, those who have eyes to see and ears to hear will still refuse to use them.

~Modest Proposals~

~E~mphatically I repudiate violent subversion. I have long lost faith in all great and glorious revolutions, be they English, American, French, or Russian. The essential independence of America could have been, and nearly was, achieved without six years of war and half a century of snarling. The race question would be nearer to a solution today, if defeat had not wounded the soul of the South, if victory had not drugged the conscience of the North. I am a determined anti-revolutionist: but I cannot think of a single case in which the desires of the many for a sweeping change were the cause of an upheaval. In every instance, the responsibility lay with those who attempted to stem or reverse the natural flow. Resistance to change may be intelligent and useful: yielding to every demand is not a wise policy; every proposed reform should be examined critically. But the defense of the status quo — national, political, economic, religious — should take the form of free discussion, and never be a bar to free decision. Fighting blindly to maintain prejudices and privileges can only create a catastrophic situation. It is the attempt to suppress thought by force that calls for the counter use of force. I do not blush to offer again the most familiar example, because it is the most irrefutable: had Louis XVI not moved foreign regiments to thwart the manifest will of the people, the mob would not have rushed to storm the Bastille. This was obvious and lurid drama: but in our age there are still unreconstructed Bourbons at the helm. When Italy, France and America tamper with the free expression and the free competition of opinions, so as to check or stamp out the critics of the existing order, they are committing the same blunder as Louis XVI.

No thorough social progress is conceivable without political progress: a contented herd under a despot is not my Utopia. This does not imply that we should elect socialist politicians instead of capitalistic politicians: we must strive, as I attempted to show in the second part, to leave politics and politicians behind. On one point, I am curiously in agreement with the social conservatives — among whom, by the way, I count many friends. Like them, I am extremely reluctant to entrust public services to the slaves of the party machines. I'd rather have a business run by businessmen on business lines than see it become the prey of Tammany, the Dixiecrats, or a Pendergast crowd. And I am fully aware also of the techno-bureaucratic blight: it would infallibly turn into dull oppression, unless constantly cleansed by a stream of fresh and free criticism. Again, under any regime, the citizen cannot elude his responsibility, which is to think hard, and to voice his criticism fearlessly.

I do not desire therefore that my grandchildren should be among the Daughters (and Sons) of the Second American Revolution. In this chapter, I intend to examine a number of modest proposals, not one of them involving a sudden and radical change, every one of them based upon some definite practical experience. My method, as the reader must know by this time, is to take things as they are; and then to make a distinction between those things which should be repressed and those things which should be fostered. Disease and crimes are facts, and should be acknowledged as such. But preventive medicine, intelligent laws, an alert police force, are facts also.

There is a cure in which I have but limited faith: increased production. M. de la Palisse might have remarked that all our economic troubles would cease, if only every one had enough. All, except the trouble of knowing what is enough. M. Mendès-France, a true statesman, offered to cure the ills of French North Africa with a vast program of economic expansion. On a still larger scale, we are hoping to calm the unrest of Asia by inviting her into our co-prosperity sphere. Not many years ago, "a quart of milk for every Hottentot" was derided as foolish idealism. Today it looks as though "a quart of milk for every Thailander" were sound sense.

This is a delicate problem. So much is right about this proposition that it seems ungracious or perverse to criticize it at all. With proper misgivings, I again shall submit historical instances, not as decisive arguments, but as question marks. Is it true that prosperity is the surest remedy against discontent? It was not in the most impoverished parts of the world that the great revolutions occurred, but in England, America, France. It was not the downtrodden who rose in despair: it was the educated and well-to-do middle class that started and directed the fight. French statistics prove convincingly that the well-being of native Moroccans has greatly increased under the Protectorate: but comfort, and especially luxury, create insatiable demands. Abject poverty leads to abject resignation; it is expanding wealth that breeds dynamic discontent.

So I was not convinced when, in *The Nation* for January 21, 1950, I read these words of Leon Keyserling's, an economist of high repute: "Efforts to achieve a bigger national income are far more important than sharing what we now have." They struck me as the perfect expression of the great American heresy, and I was moved to assert the exact reverse: "Efforts to share what we now have are far more important than achieving a bigger national income." I balance the two propositions critically: I am no doctrinnaire, I am feeling my way. The following reflections will not be a counterblast to Keyserling, nor a debate with Keyserling: he might well smile at the thought, for I am not even a tyro in his field. Let us call them *Variations on a Keyserling Theme*.

Keyserling speaks of "sharing what we now have." First of all, who are *we*? The question is totally different in terms of a self-contained national economy, or in terms of One World. The global view is the Christian one as well as the humanistic. It is also the far-sighted view: ultimately, too great a contrast between destitution and plenty will cause a revolution which might well compel us to share, through the most cruel and the most wasteful of processes. In world terms, the situation is tragic. We may lose the race between sharing and catastrophe, for it is doubtful whether improvements in techniques will keep pace with the increase of population in Asia. We still refuse to face the problem stated, clumsily no doubt, but urgently, by old Malthus. If we fully accept our world-wide responsibility, it would indeed be our first goal to intensify production, and, *pari passu*, to establish a rigorous system of priorities. No luxuries until the hungry are fed; a drastic wartime economy; for the world is a city beleaguered by the unwanted.

But let us think of this country alone, as an autarky. In these narrower terms, is it true that our first concern should be for expansion, rather than for proper distribution?

Two qualifications at once rise in our minds. The first is that *glutting* does not truly increase the national income. Ill-planned, ill-distributed production may boom for a while, but leads only to a depression: the familiar paradoxes of "breadlines knee-deep in unsold wheat," fish catches thrown back into the sea, fruit rotting as not worth the picking, Brazilian locomotives burning coffee beans. Not all expansion is to the national advantage. The Southerners a few years ago wanted to expand their cotton fields, although they knew that the market could not absorb the current supply. The planters refused to submit to economic law; and, good socialists as they were, they expected the government to guarantee their prices. A well-paved path to Bedlam. We should have to erect a Fort Knox in every county, to store the hoard of produce which we can neither consume nor sell, and which we refuse to give away. In a regime of Free Enterprise (the Manchesterian Utopia that declined to materialize), cotton, silver, butter, and every other interest should take its chance in open competition, national and foreign. This would spell the end of Hooverian protection, of subsidies, of price support. We now have "planning" on as vast a scale as the Soviets, but planning twisted by the lobbies for the benefit of special interests.

Then it should be obvious that all products, even if they should find a ready market, are not of equal benefit to the community. In the "national income," sables, diamond tiaras, atomic bombs, all count for their price value in the same way as bread. This confusion might lead to a civilization of hovels and palaces, such as colonial Mexico, the India of the Rajahs, tsarist Russia, or, not quite so glaringly, Victorian England and the America of the Gilded Age. Keyserling is aware of the danger. He favors "policies affecting income flow." In blunt terms, this means equalization: the many must have more for decencies, the "élites" less for luxuries. This conception is the purest Saint-Simonianism. Keyserling affirms that it is "generally shared by economists, social scientists and thoughtful businessmen." What a pity that thoughtful businessmen should be so few!

In this, I am in full agreement with Keyserling. But in the above quotation, I omitted one crucial word: policies for expansion should be *supplemented* by policies affecting income flow. In a pauper world, this might be the right emphasis. But I maintain that, with our present high level of production, proper distribution, not expansion, is the more urgent need. Expansion per se would not cure our present ills; it might indeed make them more grievous. Above all, even if all urgent needs were satisfied, expansion would not relieve the tension, the anxiety, the insistence on material goods and material success which are the curse of American life.

I am no Rousseau, no Thoreau, no Gandhi. I abominate camping and its primitivism. I am thankful for all the achievements of modern techniques. I want them to expand, provided expansion be a healthy, normal process, and not a goal in itself. Keyserling's Utopia — fifty suits in every closet and three helicopters in every garage — does not appeal to me. It turns mass production into an idol, with the hucksters as its priests; for high-pressure production entails high-pressure salesmanship. To me such an ideal is a nightmare. I have known, I still know, a saner life, and I am not willing to forfeit it. I want freedom from worldly care. I want ample leisure for cultural pursuits. If I have these, I shall gladly let the trinkets and the gadgets go.

This, however, is not the place for my Utopia. I can only say that it would be very different from Thoreau's as well as from Keyserling's. I shall limit myself to my own field, the humanities. There I *know* that expansion is a snare. I do not want to increase the national income of commercialized art. I could do with fewer books, fewer movies, fewer radio, and television programs. I do not desire to see a statue at every street corner. I refuse to have my walls covered solidly with canvases, be they abstract or sensible. I found more enjoyment and more sustenance in the four pages of the old Paris *Temps* (confound its politics!) than in the twenty sections of a metropolitan Sunday edition. I appreciate the quiet grace of a single Hula dancer better than the precision kicking of fifty Rockettes. I am not impressed by a bulging menu: I have feasted on a single course, with a small glass of wine and a bit of cheese. In all things, material as well as spiritual, I vote for selection, quality, balance.

The two great Workers' Republics, the USA and the USSR, are both turning their mighty backs on this ideal of classical measure. Both, like Keyserling, are thinking first of all of a bigger national income. The USSR has a valid excuse: it started this century a pauper compared with us, and was ruined three times over by invasions and civil war. For decades, increased production must be its goal. But individuals and nations should know when they have enough. It is time for us to make more intelligent use of what we have.

We have seen that Capitalism and Communism were not all-embracing and antagonistic Ways of Life. Much — and the very best — lies beyond their reach. Both are *systems*, rationalizations or working hypotheses imposed upon the multitudinous facts. These are the same facts: hence the two systems have much in common.

Both, in their modern form, are *collectivistic*. Anarchism, the absolute independence of the individual, should prevail in the things that are not Caesar's: love, art, religion. In these vital fields, I resent or ignore the claims of any science to control my affections, of any clique to prescribe my taste, of any clergy to dictate my faith. For this is the realm of grace, and of freedom. But in the economic world, the share of unalloyed individualism is restricted. Even the lone craftsman, if he sells his skill, is part of society and must think of his customers. The bulk of the work, under Capitalism as well as under Communism, is done through coördinated action.

Both regimes are *oligarchic*. Collectivism inevitably creates a hierarchy of functions: planning, managing, manual labor. In both, the hierarchy is finely graded, and offers a degree of fluidity: neither is a rigid caste system, and the classes (denied by both, real in both) merge by imperceptible degrees. Yet in both, the masses are the common herd: initiative and power are the privileges of a few. There may be millions of shareholders (under Communism, all are shareholders in all enterprises), but actual control lies in a small number of hands.

Both are frankly *materialistic*. This is no reproach, but merely a definition of their proper sphere. Railroads are not run by poetry, sermons, or mystic visions: "they have no need for such hypotheses." If moral principles were involved, Communism would have the better case, for it professes to be guided by the thought of the common good. But Capitalism, in spite of its tough cynical attitudes, is no declared enemy of the general interest. In its proper domain, it wants to "do a good job" and "deliver the goods." To this end, it picks out its oligarchs on a realistic basis. When it comes to practical work, idealism must be brushed aside: let cool-headed, hard-headed energetic men forge their way to the front. And let them be rewarded with material power and material profit: if they were not attracted by such incentives, it would be sure evidence that they were not practical men, and therefore not to be trusted with the managements of economic interests. The men who reach responsible positions must be "go-getters" and "self-seekers" with a dash of ruthlessness: not theorists or evangelists. In a curiously prophetic play by Lesage, *Turcaret* (1709), the plea is offered that a man failed because he was "too kind." "Too kind!" the hero snorts, "too kind! Then why on earth did he go into business?"

From the point of view of efficiency, the capitalistic way of selecting key men has points: it is intended to make for dynamism. The Capitalistic spirit is admirable in pioneering: we need splendid adventurers. When it becomes conservative, when it seeks security first of all, when it is run by sound men in the smooth accustomed grooves, then Capitalism turns into a bureaucracy. Even in its most characteristic aspect of cool, calculating daring, there lurks a danger. "Go-getters," economic condottieri, are aggressive and even pugnacious: they are ready to shoulder other "go-getters" out of their path. Orthodox Capitalism rejoices in competition, which in its mildest form is sport, and in dead earnest is war. But both sport and war are waste, and war is deliberate cruelty.

As the "pure capitalist" is free from humanitarian squeamishness, as he is frankly after the spoils — great wealth and the prestige it confers — he will have no scruple about grabbing the prizes even when they are not the reward of actual service. Like a noted lady in Washington, they will gladly buy and sell tankers, sight unseen, through a chain of fictitious holding companies, without any thought of serving a need of mankind, the efficient distribution of oil. Commodities make and lose fortunes for people who never handle them at all. This is not looting, although looting is not precluded in business: much of our sudden national wealth was due to looting a new continent. But, if not downright looting, it is plain gambling. If you can get rich by contributing to the creation of wealth, so much the better. But if you can get even richer, and much quicker, through a poker game, this represents a higher stage of efficiency.

This inevitable demoralization of the business world has deep consequences. The power and the glory seldom go to the research scientist, not invariably to the inventor, hardly ever to the competent plodding worker. They may be handsomely paid, but they remain hirelings. The concentrated profits which dazzle imagination and give the system its physiognomy, belong to the "go-getters." In most cases, they did not originate the idea; and as a rule they leave the details of execution to technicians. Their function is to "muscle in" at the right moment. The result is all too often to place vast resources in the hands of men who are irremediably vulgar. This leads to the "conspicuous waste" described by Veblen with such pungent irony. We could well afford to keep a small number of splendid carnivora: they appeal, with a blend of fascination and horror, to the romantic souls of Theodore Dreiser and John Dos Passos. The trouble is that they set an example for a multitude whom nature intended to be tame. Small capitalists, would-be capitalists, and all the retainers of the great capitalists — lawyers, entertainers, purveyors of conspicuous waste — live by the same "Titanic" gospel. The effect is sombrely ludicrous.

We cannot be weaned overnight from the capitalistic hashish. What we can do is to emphasize the good points of the system — imagination, daring, energy — and discourage the dangerous aspects, the parasitical and the piratical. And it is exactly what we are doing. We have a vast arsenal of statutes intended to restrain the anarchy of the jungle. In spite of *laissez faire* theories, our economic life is not a free-for-all fight. Most striking in this respect are the anti-trust laws. They seek to check the natural effect of competition, which would be to destroy competition. I am thankful that we are not afraid of bigness; but thankful also that we realize the perils of irresponsible "Titanism." H. G. Wells, in *The Sleeper Awakes*, has evoked the nightmare of an orthodox economic world which, through the working of inflexible economic laws, had passed under the absolute control of a single trust.

Another familiar palliative of Titanism is the income tax. It was at one time declared unconstitutional: no wonder, for it was a curb on the great American dream, fabulous wealth. In England, it has become confiscatory in the higher brackets: the multimillionaire will soon be an extinct species. There is little difference between this curb on Titanism, and the simpler, bolder measure suggested by Mrs. Roosevelt: to set the ceiling of all incomes at twenty-five thousand dollars. This was meant purely as a war measure, at a time when the profit motive was virtuously disowned. But, until the hungry are fed and the naked clothed, everywhere in the world, the war goes relentlessly on.

The great democracies are aware of the danger, and they

have the weapons to meet it. The Free World as a whole (if there be such a world) is not yet organized for the fight. There are enigmatic characters, apparently owning several national allegiances and none, who play hide and seek in the maze of international law. We might see the rise (Sir Basil Zaharoff was a pioneer) of a curious cosmopolitan breed of billionaires, of Liberian, Panamanian, or Lichtenstein nationality, and of Greek, Hindu, Armenian, or Chinese origin. For evidently the Anglo-Saxons and the Scandinavians are not the only ones who can play that marvelous game.

Even better justified than the income tax is the inheritance tax. The strongest argument in favor of Capitalism is that it draws the best men for the job. If a man has the vision and the organizing power that will make billions for his shareholders, he should not be grudged a fee of a few paltry millions. The plea is not flawless: but even at its best, it breaks down in the case of the heirs. In the second generation of a capitalistic dynasty, we are likely to find ordinary men and women with extraordinary resources at their disposal. The result is not healthy. The evils of conspicuous waste appear without extenuation. It seems that in America the danger has passed its peak: if it were eliminated altogether, it would purify, and not destroy, the Capitalistic system. The Tycoon is welcome to be a good father to his brood: to give them a happy childhood and the most expensive education. More: it would be natural for the son of a great capitalist *to become* a good capitalist himself: certain families have produced scientists, scholars, artists, religious leaders, generation after generation. What is wrong, from every point of view, is that there should be Tycoons simply by right of birth. Hereditary wealth must go, in the same way as hereditary political power, hereditary military command, or an hereditary priesthood. Here again, England, tradition-loving and self-assured enough to be bold, has shown the way of gradual effective reform. The aristocracy and the plutocracy are preserved, but under strict control. One by one, silently, the stately homes are passing under the National Trust. A few more turns of the screw, and the sons of lords or of financial barons will have to fight their own battles, without the disabilities they would encounter in Russia, but without glaring favor.

We have seen that one of the strongest objections to the Capitalistic system is that it rewarded gambling. Fortunes can be made, not through honest contributions to human welfare, but by outsmarting the other fellow. This is a parasitical, and therefore un-American activity, on a scale which makes Monte Carlo seem as innocent and puny as a fair in Sanpete County, Utah. I know the original purpose of the Stock Exchange is not to be a den of iniquity. So long as there are securities, it is convenient to have a central market for them. The gambling element could be curbed by means of legislation which would be realistic and not revolutionary. It would suffice to have every sale and purchase considered as a *bona fide* transaction [1] *subject to a 10 per cent tax.* This would be no hardship on those many investors who keep their holdings for a lifetime. It would not hit disastrously the man who is compelled to sell, or who is buying for the first time. It would be, not a fine, but a tax. And that tax would fall entirely on surplus wealth, not on wages, salaries, or reasonable earnings. Inveterate gamblers would still have the races or the friendly poker game at their disposal, without having to travel all the way to Nevada. Business would be healthier if it were completely divorced from playing the market.

The income tax, the inheritance tax, the tax on Stock Exchange transactions are not punitive. They are the mildest of precautionary measures, to guard Capitalism against its own perils. They do not challenge its principles, or hamper its normal development. No productive activity would be restrained. There would still be handsome rewards: but no public gambling, and no accumulated power in the hands of the less competent. I am sure most businessmen would welcome such a rule of decency.

---

[1] Increasing, even to 100 per cent, the amount of actual payment (the so-called margin), has the effect of slowing the market and freezing out some of the smaller operators; but it does not touch the gambling element.

CHAPTER XIV

Drastic But Not Subversive

In America as well as in England, the proper instrument for social justice should be organized labor. The great obstacle to progress is that Labor meekly accepts the tough philosophy of Capital, which is a philosophy of combat. Businessmen fight among themselves for profit; they fight against their customers by charging all they dare; they fight against their employees, limiting their wages in order to increase their own gain. "Every one on his own, every one for his own, and against all comers." The capitalists are ruthless with a good conscience; they have persuaded themselves that this struggle for life is the key to abundance and security all round. As we have seen, they may be optimists, and believe in "the guiding hand" that turns private greed into public benefits; they may be pessimists, and hold that this is an ugly, brutal world, cranks alone maintaining that it could be otherwise.

Labor takes this world of strife for granted. In this arena, it too fights for its own interests. The strike, which is economic warfare, is held as a constant threat. I was surprised at first when I heard Mr. Herbert Hoover express warm appreciation of Mr. John L. Lewis. Then I realized that both men held the same philosophy: stand up for yourself and fight like a man. Not infrequently, a soothing Menenius Agrippa assures us that there are no classes in America; or — sometimes in the same breath — that there are classes but that their interests are identical. Practical men nod approval of these lenitive homilies, and at the same time shrug them away. Yet they convey a truth deeper than the jungle ideology. Granted that they are not invariably sincere: many a true word is spoken in 'hypocrisy. The Communists teach that under Capitalism there are antagonistic and irreconcilable classes: it is for us to demonstrate that in America this assertion is false.

But that would entail the death of Capitalism as we still half-heartedly cherish it: Capitalism in its narrowest but most distinctive sense: the right and opportunity for a few to make great fortunes. Bondholders draw their interests, shareholders their dividends: still the spectacular profits which are characteristic of the system are reserved for the elect. So long as that *de facto* distinction remains, there are still masters and men. The masters no longer own the men, but they still refuse to admit that the men are entitled to a share both in the management and in the profit. Labor is simply "employed," that is to say "used," exactly as a beast of burden was yesterday or a machine is today. If a good employer wants his workers to be well foddered and stabled, he is no more philanthropic than a good farmer with his mules. If he provides medical care, it is because the breaking down and repairs of the human engine are costly. Every well-run factory needs an infirmary for tools and a fix-up shop for men.

This sternly practical, unsentimental view, the essence of the Manchesterian creed, is not simply inhuman: it is also contrary to the plain economic facts. For labor is not merely a necessary instrument of "business": labor, not capital, is the one indispensable factor. All this is woefully elementary: but we must not blush to repeat it, until our leaders in politics, business and labor show some sign of comprehension. Imagine "capital" without labor: all the gold in the country drained into the vaults of Fort Knox, with all the shares and bonds stacked in other fabulous repositories: all this accumulated wealth would be rigorously barren. Imagine on the other hand labor without capital: a company of men shipwrecked on an island, without even a tool: the men could start at once gathering fruit. Economic activity has three bases: natural resources, skill, organization. With organization, some men could be relieved from the task of providing food, and devote themselves to less immediate needs. This, to be successful, requires planning and discipline, but not capital in the purely financial sense. It would be possible to decree: "Capital is hereby abolished," and our productive activities would not cease. But "abolishing labor" would be collective suicide.

I should say of labor what Siéyès wrongly said of the Third Estate: "What is Labor? Nothing (in the councils of an orthodox capitalistic world). What ought it to be? Everything." For management, accounting, research, planning, promotion, are but instances of skilled labor. Capital so far has managed to make them its willing auxiliaries: a middle class aspiring to be associated with the capitalists, dreading to relapse into the status of common laborers. But these skills, hired by capitalism, do not inevitably belong to capitalism. There is efficient management in the armed forces: a warship has to be run as carefully as any shop. There is research in the universities, capable of being applied to industrial uses. There is "promotion," at times of a highly successful kind, in the religious missions: certain evangelists are masters of salesmanship. And all these are not strictly identified with the capitalistic system.

Labor should realize in America, as it has in England and Germany, that its ultimate goal, is the gradual, peaceful, friendly, but none the less ineluctable extinction of capitalism as a system and of the capitalists as a class. Fighting for a larger share within the existing order, while not challenging its dualistic character, is legitimate enough: there are immediate reasonable demands which should be satisfied. But this opportunism should not blind us to the long-range policy.

Two recent developments might be an indication of a cautious but effective method of change. An automobile-manufacturing company in great financial difficulties, appealed to its labor force to accept a cut in wages, in order to save the business in which all, capital, management, labor, were vitally concerned. The men agreed to the cut. The plea of financial necessity is a favorite one with the companies, when they decline to grant the request of their workers. Labor can either accept the fact, or strike: and a strike is a brutal, costly, unconvincing argument. Now another way is open. The National Labor Relations Board ruled that in such a case, Labor would have the right to examine the books of the company. If this practice were accepted, and generalized, a new era would be at hand.

The Germans, it seems, are attempting to go one step further in that direction, which is neither Communism nor State Capitalism. The new system is called *Mitbestimmung* — co-decision, or joint control. On the managing board, Labor is entitled to full representation. With all books open, and a free discussion, it will be for Labor to decide whether the president of the company should be paid ten times as much as a member of the Cabinet, a full general, or a Justice of the Supreme Court; what balance should be kept between dividends and wages; and whether bonuses could not be more equitably distributed. I am anxious to see the results of *Mitbestimmung* in Germany. Be sure the name and the principle will not be forgotten. If the European economy is integrated through a series of Schumann and Monnet plans, *Mitbestimmung* would inevitably be extended from Germany to the rest of the continent: for Labor, no less than Capital, will have its all-European conventions. Thus Capitalism and Socialism would meet and merge on a non-Marxian basis, and in defiance of Karl Marx's prophecy. The apocalyptic vision of the Great Day of Wrath will fade away. If *Mitbestimmung* were a success in Europe, it would be difficult for America not to keep up with the movement. And even Russia, however ponderous and sluggish, might also fall into line: for after all the original Soviet system was not radically different in principle from syndicalism.

The rights of Labor, collectively asserted, imply that every laborer *is* a laborer, just as every citizen *is* a citizen, whether he be good or bad, active or passive, selfish or generous. If you move into a city, you will have to respect city ordinances and pay city taxes. If you purchase a share in a business, you become a shareholder; you are not compelled to vote at the general meeting, even by proxy; but the right to vote is thrust upon you, willy nilly, and you are bound by the vote. Dr. Ray Lyman Wilbur, a true liberal, a man of generous heart and keen intelligence, balked at the idea of compulsory membership in the unions. It seemed to him the acme of tyranny, and alien to the

American spirit. But, under his presidency, every student who joined Stanford University became *ipso facto* a member of the student body: lone wolves and rugged individualists were not recognized. You have the right to dissent from the majority; you have no right to enjoy the advantages of society, and claim at the same time the full privileges of anarchy.

Here we become aware of another danger: capital, management, labor, practicing *Mitbestimmung*, might very well think of their own industry, without due regard for the rest of the people. The agriculturists, both in America and in Russia, have repeatedly flouted the law, and attempted to force the government into surrender. Key industries like food and transportation might seek privileges in the same way as the Praetorian Guards: because they control power at a strategic point. To ward off such an injustice, the consumers should have a voice; and the clashing interests of rival industries, producers, consumers, regions, should be harmonized for the common good.

This leads to a conception of the national economy which bears an unpleasant resemblance to the syndicalist state of the Fascists, Nazis, Falangistas, Peronistas. It is the plan rather roughly sketched by General de Gaulle. Any scheme, from theocracy to Communism, can be used by selfish and brutal men. A system automatically correcting its own abuses is a Utopia. Liberalism advanced the claim that it was self-regulating: "liberty brings no evil that more liberty cannot cure." Yet we had to provide protective tariffs, anti-trust laws, labor laws, social security, to save a *liberal* economy from its inherent weaknesses. In the countries which adopted the corporative principles, the results were uneven, but not uniformly unfavorable. The disasters which engulfed Germany and Italy may well be ascribed to other causes. I remain an inveterate fellow traveler: I do not believe that any country, party or religion can be solidly and infallibly wrong. Mussolini, Hitler, Franco professed to be patriots: this is no more reason why we should turn against a saner and more humane patriotism. Hitler initiated a movement called *Kraft durch Freude*, Strength through Joy: I do not want to turn Hitler inside out and advocate "Weakness through Misery." Mussolini and Franco struck an alliance with the Catholic Church: but this will not make me consider Catholicism as the enemy of mankind.

From collective bargaining to *Mitbestimmung*; from *Mitbestimmung* to the corporative state: I know there are traps at every step. But the *Mitbestimmung* principle offers at least the possibility of converging evolution, reconciliation, coöperation, without bloodshed. Nothing need to be destroyed, except two huge horrific phantoms named Capitalism and Marxism. Today, both look appallingly strong; but you cannot imagine how tenuous ghosts appear, as soon as you have ceased believing in them.

The next Fabian path of reform is to curb the tyranny of advertising. Did I say *Fabian*? On second thought, this appears as an attempt to desecrate the Holy of Holies. For America is "sold," that is to say, enslaved, to Business, and Business is "sold" to advertising. The advertisers provide "protection" in the same way as the Chicago gangs did; and it is Utopian to dream that their rule could be broken; as Utopian as it was of the Russian democrats, a short half-century ago, to imagine that the Tsar could be tumbled from his mighty throne. "We believe this truth to be self-evident: that early to bed and early to rise will do no good if you don't advertise." When Emerson gave out his famous dictum about the better mousetrap, he showed himself for the nonce a Transcendentalist, a Brahmanist, anything but a shrewd Yankee trader: he should have known that no mousetrap sells on its own merits. We are so conditioned by our enslavement that we revel and glory in it. As in *1984*, we all bow to the synthetic grin of Big Brother. Our Big Brother is worse than any dictator of flesh and blood; he is insidious, ubiquitous, irresistible; his number is 666, and his name is Advertising. I know I cannot shake his yoke. My protest will be hushed or smiled away. Worst of all, it might be *advertised*, for the amusement of the true worshippers. They are sufficiently firm in the faith to tolerate outrageous jokes. At any rate, my own heart is cleansed from his obscene rule.

Big Brother cynically defaces the American landscape, urban

and rural. He scales the very heavens, with skywriting and searchlight displays. He has captured the two latest and perhaps greatest channels of education and intelligent pleasure: the radio and television. These are now confessedly by-products of Business; and we accept without a shudder the humiliating fact that symphonies or well-informed commentators have to be sponsored by soap or gasoline. Note that the products themselves, being of prime necessity, need no bush, and that the differences between the various brands are admittedly infinitesimal: soap is soap and gas is gas. Supposing all gasolines were sold under the same name without a word of advertising: I wonder whether one gallon less would be consumed. England has proved that radio and television could be conducted as a national, self-respecting service, not as clamorous touting, with information, music and drama offered merely as baits. But even England and France show signs of capitulating.

Advertising debases our culture. The magazines, rather than books, are the proper place for the essay, for the serious discussion of current topics, for exploration in literature. Now, one by one, the high-standard magazines of two generations ago have been forced to the wall. The rare survivors of that era have been jazzed up and smartened beyond recognition: I am sure their present editors, sound businessmen, are proud of the change. When good writers are invited to contribute, it is only because their names have advertising value. Unconsciously, they adapt themselves to the commercial standard. The style remains their own, they freely choose their topics, but the unique spark is quenched. The high-brow magazines were the bonds of cohesiveness and consciousness that created an intelligent general public. Now the popular magazines, bought by the million, are smarter, handsomer, bulkier than ever: the natural élite has been sacrificed. Neither the esoteric little reviews nor the scholarly quarterlies can make up for the loss. For they are not integrated with our common life: they are cities of refuge, *maquis*, Ivory Towers.

I know that the material results are astounding. We are offered luxury magazines, magnificently illustrated, at a price

well below the cost of production: Business is a most bountiful
Maecenas. It is suspected that this generosity does not come out
of the producers' profit: it is itself a source of profit. The cost
is invisibly tagged on to the price of the article advertised, and
the consumers pay the whole bill in the end. Some day they will
discover the trick: but most of them have been fooled for a very
long time.

Worst of all, advertising is changing the character of our
daily press. As in the radio business, information or editorial
comments are now the bait, not the central purpose. "What
does it matter, if information and comment are actually there?
Why do you not simply skip the ads?" I do not object to the ads
in themselves: as a rule, they are the cleverest part of the
paper, and not seldom the most honest. What I object to is the
subtle pollution of both information and comment. The papers
will tell us virtuously that they are absolutely independent of
their advertisers; but they are dependent on advertising. They
do not have to sell themselves to Big Business: they are Big
Business. They are "free" within that realm: exactly in the
same way as a Soviet social scientist is free, or a theologian who
belongs to an orthodox church. They may attack particular
evils: so, I understand, do the papers in Russia. They may even
insert (properly disinfected) facts which are damaging to the
whole existing order. They may denounce one particular case
of "give away": what they expose is the clumsiness, not the
essential wrongness. By and large, they exist to support the
orthodox creed: that America's business is Business; that Business is run for Profit; and that Profit demands lavish Advertising. They cannot antagonize, they cannot even question, the
Big Business principle which is the very basis of their own
existence.

The result is that we have no free press, in the deeper sense
of the term; and a free press is more vital to a free people than
a constitution. We cannot have unbiased discussion of fundamental problems, political, economic or religious. When de-
bates are permitted, they are so heavily slanted as to become
innocuous. The keenest of our commentators — I respect and

enjoy their work — unconsciously operate within the orthodoxy. We have become a single-party state. That party has many
groups and factions, but in fundamentals it is a solid rock. It is
the party of Business. Radicals do not even have to be jailed as
subversives: they do not sell, which, under the present dispensation, is silent death. There is not even a crop of mocking songs,
as there was under the absolute rule of the Bourbons. There is
no clandestine Midnight Press, as there was in France under
the Nazi occupation.

To be sure, Demos cannot be suppressed altogether by his
alleged mouthpiece; the Press was overwhelmingly against the
New Deal, at a time when Franklin Roosevelt was at the height
of his popularity. But a free debate on equal terms, before the
whole people, between Capitalism and Communism, is almost
as inconceivable in New York as in Moscow. Without ruthless
compulsion, no country could be so tragically unanimous as
Russia and America appear to be. Ruthless, yet invisible. It is
not sheer repression, of the tsarist or Old Turkish type, that is
most to be dreaded: France was free of soul before the Bastille
was stormed. We might have a few more Eugene Debs, Mooney
and Billings, Sacco and Vanzetti cases without any serious danger to our inner liberty. Our prison walls are created by the
manipulation of public opinion. You can react, that is to say,
rebel, against definite acts of injustice and violence: you are
helpless against the false unanimity created by the Press as the
vocal branch of Big Business. Even the Nine Old Men who
were our last hope are not immune against that insidious, all-
pervading, anonymous tyranny.

There are palliatives to such a situation, but no simple and
immediate remedy. Salvador de Madariaga, realizing that the
role of the Press in modern society is far more vital than those
of Congress or President, proposed that greater guarantees of
competence and integrity be required of all journalists. The
profession should be as severely guarded and disciplined as
medicine or the law. It should be possible to disqualify a journalist for unethical conduct — for taking bribes, for peddling
intellectual dope, for practicing the abortion of ideas. At pres-

ent such peccadilloes are all in the day's work of a successful journalist. Madariaga's point is well taken; but the sole result of his proposal would be to give Big Business more competent servants.

It is painfully evident that a state-controlled press, dominated either by the politicians or by the bureaucrats, would be even more deadly to freedom. It would help if at least islands of refuge were created; if the universities and the great Foundations would sponsor radio and television stations, magazines of information and discussion, and even daily papers, wholly free from the blight of advertising. On a small scale, such attempts have failed. The needed millions, as a rule, are found in the hands of millionaires. Still, the Foundations have higher standards than the business that gave them birth. As a result, they are already coming under the fire of orthodox politicians.

The ultimate solution would be the complete divorce, by law, of advertising and journalism. No open advertising should be carried by periodicals devoted to information, discussion, or entertainment. Concealed advertising, an elusive disease, would be punishable under some Pure Food and Drug Law. Much advertising, I repeat, is futile, and profitable only to the advertising agencies: it plays the part of competitive armaments in the race for power, and like armaments, it could easily be discarded in a saner world. As a guide to purchasers, consumers' reports would advantageously take the place of vociferous touting. I am advocating divorce, not murder. Advertising of the present kind could survive for generations. Let all firms deluge us with their "literature" and their "art," if it gives them comfort. Let their daily, weekly, monthly, seasonal or special issues be as bulky and as handsome as *Fortune* and *Holiday* put together. But let us bring to an end the damnable confusion between the legitimate activities of the press, and the interests of Business. So long as Business controls our thought, we cannot call ourselves free.

CHAPTER XV

Can Ethics Be Ruled Out?

It is a paradox and a scandal that, on a certain plane, no one doubts the moral superiority of communism. The family is communistic: so long as their children are under age, at any rate, no sane parents will allow them to starve. Patriotism is communistic: property and life itself are gladly surrendered. Religion is communistic. The early Christians were communists: "And the multitude of them that believed were of one heart and of one soul: neither said any of them that ought of the things which he possessed was his own; but they had all things in common . . . and distribution was made unto every man according as he had need" (Acts 4:32–35). This is not true only of the remote apostolic age: throughout the centuries and to the present day, those men and women who yearn to live the perfect Christian life renounce their private property, and, in religious orders, practice a far stricter communism than can be found in Muscovy or Cathay.

The philosophy of the Profit Motive, on the contrary, is the same as that of Mandeville in his *Fable of the Bees*: somehow good needs the incentive of evil. In blunter terms, the do-gooders are fools. We of the capitalistic persuasion proclaim: "Evil, be thou my good."

Even the most ruthless of Manchesterians, however, will not let the devil take the hindmost: our economic leaders are men of flesh and blood, not incarnations of a doctrine. There are institutions for alleviating suffering. They are not in full harmony with the capitalistic gospel, and the compromise between humanity and the rigor of the creed is by no means easy. Relief is justified, provided it is not claimed as a right. The recipients must be properly humiliated and branded as paupers; the donors must be duly praised for their gratuitous generosity. It is almsgiving with no trace of what St. Paul meant by charity. Above all, you must not preach the subversive gospel that all luxury is a crime so long as there is distress in the land. To provide barely adequate soup kitchens in times of depression is orthodox, and indeed meritorious; to assert the right to a job and a living wage is socialism, which is compounded of sin and folly. Unless things are "bad enough," it is morally wrong to help your brother. We might all too easily pass from sporadic relief, which is praiseworthy, to the welfare state, which is damnable, and from that to communism, which is very Hell.

It would be unfair, however, to assert that capitalism was born in iniquity, heir to the cynical spirit of Mandeville. It was late in the eighteenth century that it assumed definiteness as a doctrine. In its negative form, *laissez faire, laissez passer*, it was a legitimate reaction against the oppressive regulations of the fossilized guilds, against the capricious intervention of an autocratic and incompetent government. In its positive form, it was the economic aspect of the great quest for liberty that inspired the Enlightenment: down with prejudices, privileges, and arbitrary rule! It was even blandly humanitarian. What if anarchy should lead to apparent conflicts of interests? There is a Guiding Hand to harmonize them all. To the present day, the economic liberals of the softer type have in the secret of their hearts (for they do have hearts) that *Quietism*, that repose in God's wise providence, which we find in Leibniz, Pope, Rousseau, and Robert Browning. God's in His heaven, and if only Congress would refrain from interfering, all would be for the best in the best of all possible worlds. (To be sure, Rousseau believed that private property was the original sin; and his state ruled with a rod of iron; but the contradictions of Rousseau are unfathomable.) Economic liberalism (let cynics blush) was therefore born of optimism, and honestly sought the greatest good of the greatest number.

The cream of the jest — or more appropriately the tragedy — was that liberalism in economics had become obsolete even before it triumphed. It was founded on individual enterprise and individual competition at the moment when, thanks to the machine, collectivism was becoming the norm. In America, the free opportunity offered to the pioneer veiled that process for generations. It seemed that there always would be new land, new treasures under the earth, new industries, for the daring, the vigorous, and the fortunate. A man needed no capital but his strong arms, his clear head and his stout heart. That Utopia has grown very faint. But it still hangs in our gallery of heirlooms, with other period pieces such as our political and religious orthodoxies. Pleasant pictures, all of them; but they never were quite true to life; and today their appeal is purely historical.

We have passed from a predominantly agricultural stage (the dream of Jefferson), with craftsmen and merchants as subordinate factors, to the industrial stage, increasingly characterized by collectivism and mass production. It must never be forgotten that this is the secret of our wealth and power. Even agriculture and commerce are being industrialized. The small farm will become obsolete, unless it is saved through coöperatives. The small independent shop will disappear, except in remote corners, slums or villages, and in the luxury trades. Collectivism is a fact. The sole problem is whether a collective enterprise should be run for the profit of a few, or for the benefit of all.

In the case of key industries, the answer is plain. It is given unequivocally in the most conservative papers, whenever there is a threat of a strike in the railroads, the coal mines, or the steel industry. Public opinion is indignant with the men who forget that they are entrusted with a social service, that their work is indispensable to the normal daily life of the community. And, in the name of the national interest, which remains the supreme law, the government feels compelled, in a crisis, to take over these vast enterprises. To be sure, they are restored to private management at the earliest opportunity. But the principle is incontrovertible: all essential industries should by right be under the control of the community. (This does not mean that they should be abandoned to the mercies of political appointees.)

Even America reluctantly recognizes this plain fact. England, France, and Germany do so without our embarrassed hemming and hawing.

"Public utilities" in private hands are an absurdity. They are, in most cases, a practical monopoly. They cannot operate without the consent of the authorities which grant them their franchises. A man with a few dollars saved, or with good credit, can start a little shop: but in the public field, there is no such thing as private enterprise. There is no such thing as private management either. As a rule, the promoters and financiers who may be said to own the business are not the men in actual charge. Even in the most "private" sector, a Henry Ford is a miraculous exception. The technicians are hired by the companies, as they could be hired by the community.

The showpiece in the folklore of capitalism is the claim that, while private enterprise favors efficiency and initiative, public management discourages both. If "public management" means control by the politicians or by the routine bureaucrats, the point is well taken. The handsome bonuses of the private entrepreneurs would be well earned, if they made the difference between economic success and economic failure. But the situation is by no means so clean-cut. We are all familiar with poor management in private hands, leading inevitably to bankruptcy: a well-known feature in American business life, as one of our Presidents could testify. On the other hand, it is not impossible for public services to be well run. The noncommercial air lift to Berlin was pronounced a technical success. Belgian relief under Mr. Hoover was a marvel of excellent administration, although the idea of private gain was rejected with horror. And when Mr. Hoover became officially Food Administrator, still without any thought of personal profit, he did not suddenly lose his organizing talents and his energy.

Private enterprise today gets the better men, because it pays them better. But if the bulk of our economic activities became socialized, good men would have to stay in public employment, and would not cease to be good men. M. Raoul Dautry, brilliantly successful in the management of the French Northern

Railroad — then privately owned — was induced to take over the ramshackle State Railroad system, and did a splendid job of rehabilitation. Later, he was at the head of all the French railroads, nationalized shortly before the war.

I am ready to admit the value of incentives: not every man is a William the Silent, who needed neither the spur of hope nor the encouragement of success. There are three kinds of incentives: responsibility, recognition, money. The joy of honest work well done is real; the joy of honest work well praised is no delusion; the joy of honest work well paid is even more realistic. The community is not always quite so generous as private business in giving a man a free hand. Yet there is no sign that Goethals of the Panama Canal, Lilienthal of the TVA, or the marvelous cosmopolitan team that evolved the atomic bomb, were seriously interfered with by bureaucrats or politicians. The community can offer honors: rank in the hierarchy, the prestige of a public position, bits of ribbon, letters to tack on to your name. No doubt the community is more niggardly in its pecuniary rewards. But it is not necessary that the prizes offered for outstanding services should be fabulous. Old-fashioned conquerors gave their lieutenants vast estates, at times whole provinces, titles, not merely coronets but crowns, hordes of slaves: it was good business to follow Alexander, William of Normandy, Cortéz, Napoleon. Marshall and Eisenhower did a thorough job, with no material reward but a little better pay and a few ribbons. We can safely assume that they would have done just as well, if the pay had been even more modest, and if the ribbons had not been thrown in.

Accountants and efficiency managers are constantly consulted by private business: there is no reason why their services should not be more fully utilized by public bodies. France has had for centuries an admirable Chamber of Accounts. Mr. Hoover, the great doctor of ailing enterprises (except his own Presidency), offered a plan for streamlining many clashing and cumbrous government agencies: it gives the true measure of our political morality that his offer was accepted without any enthusiasm. But we can force through a reform of that kind, ultimately to the extent of reducing the politicians to impotence. I cannot imagine the shrewd and practical American public putting up indefinitely with sloth, graft, and incompetence. Why should not the community keep an alert force of inspectors and trouble-shooters? Half the energy wasted in political campaigns would make our economy run with scarcely a hitch.

It is taken as an axiom that business favors "free enterprise," that is to say daring experiment, while the deadly hand of the state suppresses it. There again, the contrast is by no means so sharp. There are not a few instances of vested interests stifling, instead of promoting, enterprise. Both the TVA and great electric developments were blocked for years by entrenched capitalists: the friends of Mr. Hoover fought bitterly against the Hoover Dam; the St. Lawrence Seaway was long obstructed by a dog-in-the-manger policy which was distinctly capitalistic. Forty years ago, I saw dial telephones tried by new companies which were mercilessly strangled by an omnipotent combine. In its own good time, the triumphant *de facto* monopoly adopted the dial system at last, with no apology to the pioneers or to the public.

On the other hand, initiative, promotion, may be divorced from the profit motive. The present Suez Canal originated with those gifted, crazy, and withal strangely practical Utopians, the Saint-Simonians. It was they who fired the imagination of a diplomat, de Lesseps, and through him, that of "Saint-Simon on horseback," Napoleon III. De Lesseps made a fortune: but this was not his prime motive. If he had been offered a handsome bribe to desist, he would have spurned it. If he had been told that the work would proceed, but to the glory and profit of some one else, he would have said: "On with the work." Judah was the first man definitely to promote the Transcontinental Railroad: he would have been satisfied if the federal government had undertaken the work directly, and not through concessionnaires. Vision, promotion, congressional assent, planning, construction, were the essential steps. The financiers who formed the companies "muscled in": we must repeat the term, as it so aptly defines the capitalistic process. They could have been dispensed with, as they were in the case of the Trans-Siberian Railway and the Panama Canal. Judah was not found among the "Big Four."

The most striking example of a great enterprise without the profit motive — it may have heralded a revolution — is the inception of atomic power. The thought first grew in the laboratories, which are even more indifferent to lucre than the cloisters. It was transmitted to the American Government by men like Leo Szilard and Albert Einstein. No company was formed; no shares were issued; a number of men were set apart by the community to do the work, and the work was done. Russia could only imitate, but she could not cap, this triumph of communistic planning and efficiency.

There is no reason why the community should not encourage initiative and pioneering research at every step, from the modest suggestion box, and the hobby room where men are free to potter and experiment in their spare hours, to vast centers of investigation, testing laboratories, proving grounds. Let there be competitions with handsome rewards for discoveries; let less time be wasted on gadgets with a mere advertising value. My plea is: liberate "free enterprise." Energetic men are now squandering their gifts in extravagant competition, frantic advertising, intricate financing, legal conflicts, political lobbying: they could be set free to seek out new paths, to increase our well-being, and — this too is "free enterprise" — to enlarge knowledge and to deepen our sense of beauty.

Collectivism for the common good can be made as efficient and as progressive as collectivism for the private gain of a few. But collectivism for the common good, ideal communism, has two definite advantages. The first is material: as I have attempted to show, the competitive system involves a fantastic waste of energy. The second is moral: I frankly admit that communism is starry-eyed. The social spirit is in harmony with Christianity, and, in broader terms, with human brotherhood; the pursuit of private gain is greed. It is dangerous for a state to reserve its outstanding rewards to men who place material success above all else, and who make selfishness the key to that success.

There are very simple words that come to you with the immediacy and the force of a revelation. I had been a socialist ever since my adolescence: the Dreyfus Case had brought me under the influence of Jaurès. But I still thought of socialism as a paradox and a Utopia: a goal definite and desirable enough, no doubt, attainable, and yet remote. In the Summer of 1931, teaching at Eugene, Oregon, I heard my colleague Edward Potts Cheyney exclaim: "I wonder why we are not all socialists now?" He was equipped for a day's fishing, and very convincing in the part of the well-preserved, vigorous outdoor man; but his rough clothes did not obliterate our consciousness that he was a most distinguished historian. I remember vividly his kind, thoughtful face, with bushy eyebrows, a face shaggy and lovable like that of a Scotch terrier. The gentle simplicity with which he uttered these words carried conviction: from that time on, I had full faith in my own faith. In that historical perspective of which Cheyney was a master, capitalism is a thing of the past, just as feudalism had ceased to be a living force before the close of the middle ages. But it was only on the fourth of August 1789 that feudalism was formally abolished in France; and its trappings survive to this day in democratic socialistic England: captains of industry masquerade as belted earls. The twilight of gods and institutions is interminable, and they linger faintly in the memory of men long after they have completely vanished from sight.

Cheyney's question is not difficult, but it is complex. There is no single answer. It is plain that the few — the very few — who actually profit by the capitalistic dispensation desire to preserve it. The French nobles before 1789 clung desperately to their privileges; so did the slave owners in our South; so do the defenders of White Supremacy today, in Dixieland or in South Africa; and the French colonists accuse the home government of capitulating abjectly to the demands of the natives. No aristocracy will confess that it is parasitical; it must believe that it constitutes an élite, that it performs an indispensable function, were it only that of setting a standard of dignity and taste. Take its leadership away, and the world will fall into mediocrity, decline and chaos.

All these élites were and are sincere. So are our plutocrats today. They hold fast to the Little Jack Horner philosophy: the succulent plums they pull out are proofs positive that they are good boys. To get rich is an evidence of virtue. Theirs is a pluto-theocratic faith: the service of Mammon is the service of God. Protestantism did not invent capitalism, but sanctified it. It amended the gospel so as to read: "Wide is the gate of heaven for those whose pockets are well lined." Any doubt concerning the holiness of capitalism appears to them as an attack on religion. Proudhon created more indignation with his Rousseau-istic paradox: *Property is theft* than with the companion blasphemy: *God is Evil.*[1] The economic royalists nursed such fierce relentless hate for Franklin Roosevelt, not because he took money away from them (they were in fact more prosperous under his rule than under Hoover's), but because he cast a doubt on their moral standards. His New Deal was a hint that rugged individualism ("Myself, first, last, and all the time!") might be hard to distinguish from gross selfishness.

With the Profiteers (again I do not see why they should be ashamed of the obvious term) go their hangers-on, those who cater to their luxury. *La haute couture* would not reach such dizzy heights if there were no millionaires. In this class, I must place, with the greatest reluctance, certain ecclesiastical and educational institutions: let us say that there is a minim of plutocratic poison in the health-giving drinks they are offering to mankind. In churches and universities alike, benefactors and trustees are rich men; and even at Stanford, where "the winds of freedom blow," it was suicidal poor taste, in the early days, to inquire too closely into the origins of certain great fortunes. Again, I am pointing to a fringe of danger, not to a pervading, incurable evil: I have taught at Stanford for twenty-seven years

[1] He clearly meant an anthropomorphic, jealous, vindictive god; not the God Who to the intellect is mystery, to the heart charity.

without feeling the least restraint on my intellectual freedom.

Add to the profiteers and their retinue the *would-be*, those who, while still in poverty, covet a position of luxury and power. A poor but ambitious lad would hate to see the privileges of the rich curtailed: he would feel as if his own future were being destroyed. This goes very deep. By the side of the determined go-getters, there are the dreamers: they may be the merest clerks, but they are "in business," and business leads (a few) to the Earthly Paradise. There are those who dream, pathetically, not for themselves, but for their children. The capitalistic world is a huge gambling den, and a gambling den is a dream factory. For the enormous majority, gambling is a waste: still there are enough cases of miraculous luck to nurse the unquenchable hope. The range is wide: from those with energy, and something definite to contribute, to those who clutch feebly at the shade of undeserved success. But the vague dreamers, who are the most numerous, are also those most passionately attached to the great gamble of capitalism, without which their lives would be stale and drab. The men who are capable of action feel that they might do just as well in a socialistic society. The supreme idol of the present system is not Work, a slow, plodding, uninspiring deity: it is refulgent Luck, that is to say, Fortune.

Then come the many who support capitalism with a weary, cynical smile. Yes, they are aware that the regime is neither the most ethical we could conceive, nor the most efficient. But we must take things as they are: striving to alter them would be sheer perfectionism. By supporting capitalism, these men, although they may remain poor themselves, feel that they understand it and aggregate themselves intellectually with it; so its victories become — vicariously — their victory. Some actually manage to hobnob with the capitalistic élite, which has always been fond of tame intellectuals. But even without this incentive, they find it a great comfort to be, in a modest capacity, on the side of the conquerors. They are the collaborationists, the Lavals, the Quislings, of Capitalism. There are many such among journalists, writers, professors. Most of them are perfectly sincere: neither self-seekers nor retained advocates. So, I am convinced, were Quisling and Laval.

But the bulk of the people who support capitalism are purely and simply conservative. Conservatism is a very natural and healthy tendency. We cannot be constantly pulling our society by the roots to see how it is growing. Practical work demands a background of certainties. I heard an eminently successful man boast that he had never questioned his beliefs since he was eighteen: my guess was that eight was nearer the mark. Order is a fundamental condition of a good life, and the only order that is neither reactionary nor Utopian is the established order. Our DAR abominate the thought of an American revolution, and most of us are in agreement with them on this point. There must be innumerable Daughters (and Sons) of the Russian Revolution; by this time, they must form the bulk of the Russian people, for no man under forty-five has any distinct memory of a different regime. Any one suggesting a change in Russia would be branded as "subversive." I easily imagine the good staid people of the USSR shaking their wise and solid heads: "No new-fangled competitive system for me! I'll stick by the good old Soviets *as God made them!*"

The conservatives of that type, be they Russians or Americans, do not realize that order is dynamic, and can be preserved only through constant if cautious change. I do not expect, I do not desire, a sudden and massive conversion in either country: intellectual or spiritual revolutions may be as catastrophic as material revolutions are: they breed fanaticism as a physical upheaval breeds violence. I am historically minded, and my hope lies in gradualness. We must realize, however, that the tempo of history has grown swifter in our era, and that it is accelerating still. If a new creed takes generations to mature, an old one, artificially preserved, may collapse in a single moment. The realization that Jupiter was not the ruler of the universe must have come suddenly to many an earnest Pagan; and it is hopeless, for the sake of Fabianism, to rig up an interim god. We must be ready for such an emergency. And I am convinced that we are. If a mighty voice were heard lamenting: "Great Capitalism is dead!" mankind would not fall a victim to intellectual or material chaos. And we shall need no Moses and no Lenin to lead us into the Promised Land: the smiling pragmatism of a Franklin Roosevelt would be a better guide.

CHAPTER XVI

If This Be Treason...

I have dared to use the word communism to mean communism, and not the devil. The overwhelming majority of my fellow citizens will object: "But we are at war with communism. To admit that it might possibly not be evil absolute is giving aid and comfort to the enemy. This is disloyalty, and punishable by law."

Such a reasoning simply demonstrates the formidable power of machine-made mass thinking, and its dire threat to the one liberty I cherish above all others, the liberty of thought. We are coaxed, we are coerced, we are intimidated, and worst of all we are indoctrinated into apparent unanimity. "This is the land of freedom; be free to think exactly on the same lines as the Committee on Un-American Activities, or else. . ." The alternatives are definite and ugly enough.

Disloyalty is an ill-sounding word. So is *infidelity*. But neither has an absolute value. When it comes to Jainism, Taoism, Cao-Daism, the Ballard faith (and a few others), I am not ashamed of being branded as an infidel. I am not in the least *loyal* to Senator McCarthy, to the ghost of William Randolph Hearst, to the fiery spirit of Colonel McCormick, to the brazen lungs of Mr. Westbrook Pegler. But then Senator Robert Taft and General McArthur were not conspicuous for their loyalty to the Commander in Chief of our Armed Forces, or to his Secretary of State. I want my country to be right; I shall never forcibly resist the law, even when I am convinced that the law is not wise; I follow my own conscience; and I refuse to "accept anything as true unless it appears to me clearly and evidently to be such." This is what I have been taught in three countries for over sixty years; this is what I have been teaching in America, quite openly, for nearly fifty years. So far, I have never been accused of disloyalty.

We are engaged in a cold war. A cold war is a mental disease: nerves, peevishness, suspicion, jealousy, dread. It may last very long: there was a cold war between England and Russia, one between Germany and France, which continued for half a century. It is fraught with danger; but it need not take a fatal turn. As it exists in the mind, it can be cured in the mind, without a physical blow: the interminable and acrimonious cold war between England and France grew perilously hot at the time of Fashoda, but ended in the *Entente Cordiale*. Officially, we are at peace with Russia; we maintain correct if frigid diplomatic relations with her; we are members of the same international organizations; we are still — technically — allies until the state of war is formally ended. Whoever claims that a shooting war is inevitable is a warmonger; whoever affirms that war can be averted through a preventive war is a moron.

Even if we did accept the warmonger's thesis, it would be singularly foolhardy to blind ourselves to the enemy's points of strength. No sane military man thinks that, because the Russians are unspeakable scoundrels, they cannot possess tanks, guns, planes or atomic weapons, with the skill to use them. Their might is no sham. We should commit the same egregious mistake if we were to nurse the thought that their civil regime is a house of cards. Kolchak, Denikin, Wrangel, Hitler, all worked on the assumption that the merest push would suffice: the Soviets would tumble down, and the Russian masses would rise in their might against a handful of oppressors. We must face the fact that there is strength in the Russian system, and that this strength has a moral foundation. The flaws are there, for all eyes to see. But it would be sound realism to consider more than the flaws.

I am by trade a historian, not a journalist. I do not close my eyes to the confused and vivid events of today; but I try to view them in the perspective of yesterday and tomorrow. "Tomorrow" — may it dawn soon! — we shall have to talk things over with the Communists. No "Operation Killer" will dispose of eight hundred million people. We should, by this time, have discovered the foolishness of hoping for the sudden and total conversion of our opponents to our own way of thinking. We should have realized the criminal fallacy that lurks in "unconditional surrender." With that haughty phrase as our sole programme, we destroyed Germany's might: now we are wooing unrepentant Germany, and begging her to rearm. Victory never is a permanent substitute for justice. After a war, or without a war, there must be a conference earnestly seeking to establish peace. We must be ready to argue our points, reasaonably; and to discuss the points of our opponents, in the hope of finding some basis of accord. To shut our eyes, stop our ears, grit our teeth and ball our fists may give us a comfortable impression of "grim determination." For a man whose lifelong business has been cautious, critical thinking, the picture is not attractive in the least. Indeed, it seems rather absurd: a cartoon, not a guide to sane living.

We have but one quarrel with the Russians: they will not play our game, yet, for nearly forty years, they have managed to get away with it. This is a scandal, a blasphemous challenge to the Eternal Verities; and as the Eternal Verities do not seem capable of taking care of themselves, we should do something about it. But the single feud is waged on three planes which, for the sake of clarity, should be made distinct.

The first is the plane of *power politics*. The realistic theory that Might is Right, so dear to tough-minded historians, that the wolf was right against the lamb, Hitler against Norway, Russia against Finland, such a theory leads inevitably to a clash. If power be the only principle that a true Machiavellian will recognize and the supreme good to which a nation should aspire, then the country whose power balances and limits ours is the enemy. This is true even if the contestants profess the same ideology, economic, political and religious. It would have taken very little to make the England of Churchill our declared foe; in Iran, in Egypt, in Israel, in China, we might easily be at daggers drawn: but England cannot afford to fight us, and we both know it; so we are fast friends. We were perfectly ready to hate the Free French of General de Gaulle: he was voted *difficult* because he was not docile, and because, to quote President Roosevelt, he forgot who was paying him. Satellites must constantly bear in mind that they are satellites: if they fail to do so, there always will be a Senator to rebuke the offender. Power means leadership, hegemony, supremacy. A great power inherits the Roman spirit: spare the humble, bring down the proud.

Both Russia and we are playing that ancient game. Russia's is an older hand than ours: throughout the nineteenth century, her enormous and baleful shadow was felt throughout Europe and Asia. Until 1900, we were content to assert that our fiat was law in the Western Hemisphere. Today we claim that this is One World, and that it should be molded in our pattern. Physically, our empire is enormously more powerful than Russia's, and we are duly proud of the fact. We have fifty satellites to her bare half-dozen. We have bases encircling the Soviet world, thousands of miles from our shores; bases which belong not to the United Nations, but to us, for us to use as we see fit. Russia has nothing of the kind. We can afford to spare half a billion to foster discontent and prepare for civil war behind the Iron Curtain: what pitiful Russian activities exist in this country would not match the advertising account of the bubble-gum industry. We are, I repeat, playing the tough realistic game of power politics. We call it (o the virtue of a happy phrase!) "discussing from a position of strength," which means dictating our own terms. For "discussing from a position of equity" might imply adjustment, the recognition that the other side may not be hopelessly wrong; and that is branded as *appeasement*.

This is primitive lust for domination; it goes back to the earliest empires; it has its roots in animal life. It has nothing to do with democracy and still less with communism. Officially, the American, the French, and the Russian revolutions, breaking away from the dynastic tradition, abjured all thought of extending their rule by force. Their sole idea was liberation, not enslavement. But the old monarchical ideal dies hard. The

French Revolution, in aggressive-defensive warfare, led to Napoleon's imperium over Europe; and Stalin's dominions, if the satellites were included, were vaster than those of the Romanoffs. The America of Mr. Henry Luce is evidently in closer harmony with the principles of Louis XIV and Frederick II than with those of Jefferson. We sponsored the Kellogg Pact, renouncing Clausewitz and all his works; we virtuously proclaim our love for peace and justice. But "realistic" historians, commentators, diplomats, as well as businessmen, sneer at those who swallow our own propaganda. We have power, and we assert our power. In this contest, we are all tarred with the same brush. Russia's treatment of Tito, because he was becoming "difficult," was on a par with our own wooing of Tito, who claims to be a rigidly orthodox Communist. The question is evidently not to be right, but to be strong.

Power politics means a universal and unceasing cold war, with peacetime diplomacy merely as an extension of war. For the sole meaning of power is the threat of violence. Now this is elaborate but undiluted barbarism. Civilization means the triumph of justice, religion means the triumph of righteousness, over mere power. I am no longer strong, I never was aggressive, and I carry no arms; yet I walked the streets of New York, and even of Chicago, unafraid.

The second level of our quarrel with the Soviets is in the field of home politics: we abominate their brutal police methods. We are the defenders of civil liberties and freedom of speech — provided, of course, they are not used to undermine existing privileges. Our "leadership of the Free World" is no doubt an admirable talking point. But this conflict of political systems is a thin camouflage for the real conflict, which is one of power. If Soviet Russia used only our subtler methods to secure unanimity, and remained strong, she would still be our enemy. If a tsar were restored through our assistance, we would undoubtedly show the greatest indulgence for his strong-arm methods in suppressing anarchy. We are seeking the alliance of Franco, although we have no illusions whatever about his democratic convictions and practices. Those who urge that we should help Chiang Kai-shek recover dictatorial rule over China are perfectly aware that he is an expert in White terrorism, and that his return to the mainland would be marked by massacres on an epic scale. If we could have used Pétain, his crusade against the principles of the American and French Revolutions, the assassination by his thugs of men like Mandel and Zay, would have been considered as amiable peccadilloes. We hailed with relief the destruction of constitutional government in Guatemala, and we gave the military junta that seized power our immediate blessing.

Both Russia and China have an aeonial tradition of autocratic misrule. It will be hard for them to acquire the difficult technique of political liberty: for even we are still fumbling. They will never acquire it under war conditions, be the war cold, tepid, or hot. For even with us, Liberty is handled without excessive courtesy in moments of "emergency": the First Amendment is the first victim of the martial spirit. Liberty grows only in a climate of security and peace. If we truly want to promote liberty in the Communist world, the initial step should be to remove all threats and pressures. *Plus fait douceur que violence*.

Many of us, however, are at war not with Russia as a great power, not with Russia as a police state, but with Communism, that is to say with socialism. It has often been stated that there are two antagonistic tendencies in government. One was most brilliantly represented among us by Alexander Hamilton: the state should be ruled by an élite, and it is the highest duty of the state to produce, maintain, and defend such an élite. In a country which has discarded monarchy and feudal aristocracy, and which frankly divorces culture and religion from practical affairs, the one definite élite is that of wealth. The daring and the vigorous should be encouraged to forge ahead, and they should be protected against the hampering, the destructive jealousy of the timid and the slothful. Translated into a less lofty idiom, this might read: "The first of all freedoms is the fredom to grab; law and order mean the police paid to protect the loot."

The other tendency is that of Henri de Saint-Simon: "The first duty of the state is to promote the material and moral welfare of the most numerous and poorest classes." It is this tendency that leads to public education, public health, social security. Let the Good Samaritan, and not the Devil, take the hindmost. Saint-Simon himself called his doctrine a New Christianity, that is to say a revitalizing, in terms of today's life, of the Christian ideal. Another name for it might be *democracy*: government *for* the people. In our own times, a blurred, fitful, pragmatic version of it appeared as the New Deal.

Now what the Economic Royalists (the term would admirably fit Alexander Hamilton) hate above all things is not Russia, a remote threat, but the New Deal, which, sharply focused for a few years, is still a menacing ghost. I have among my best friends people who are staunch followers of the Hamiltonian tradition. (I told you that I was an inveterate fellow traveler.) They did not sputter with rage at the thought of Stalin as they did for many years when "That Man" was mentioned. Russia is merely a useful bogey to combat "radicalism" and the hateful Welfare State. If they had their way, any one who once voted for Roosevelt should be branded as un-American and disfranchised for ever.

In 1849, a French expedition destroyed the Roman Republic and restored the temporal power of Pope Pius IX. This was hailed as a victory over the Red menace throughout Europe: the Papal State became the symbol and palladium of social and political conservatism. A great Catholic leader, Montalembert, said: "Now we need a Roman expedition at home." This is the true object of the present crusade. Our concern is not with Russia, alien and remote; it is not with the orthodox Communist Party in our midst, which is infinitesimal, and, if all investigations tell a true tale, particularly ineffectual. It is with the New Deal, in a deeper and wider sense than the Rooseveltian: the conscious determined striving for social democracy. Whoever questions the validity of the present system is branded as "subversive," a Red, a Communist; and, as we have made it a dogma that Communism is the enemy, a traitor. It is admirable strategy no doubt. I am impressed with the cleverness of the men who devised it. I am still more impressed with the homely wisdom of Lincoln's words: "You can fool all the people some of the time."

As a bugbear, Russia is a present from the gods. Her tradition of tyranny and violence is part of our folklore. And for the practical minded, Russia is also the perfect object lesson. "Look here, upon this picture, and on this.": compare Russia's abject poverty and our abundant wealth. On the material plane, which Marxian communism chooses as its own, does it not stand self-condemned?

The contrast is plain; the verdict is not quite so obvious. First of all, I, who am no Marxist, am not so sure that wealth is a final argument. Al Capone was a rich man, Einstein was not. Far from these antipodal heights, I am a retired educator, with a modest competence: my home has only five bathrooms, and I do not automatically accept the superiority of the man with twice that amount of plumbing. I have not espoused Poverty; but I revere the Franciscans, who have.

What are the foundations of our wealth? First of all, our "radicalism." We did start a revolution: it had begun before 1776. We rejected monarchy, aristocracy, and a state church as obsolete. Then, for the first hundred years our national life, we enjoyed the spoils of a vast, empty, and marvelously rich continent: virgin' soil, forests centuries old, illimitable grazing land, untapped mineral resources. By the time this treasure house was showing signs of depletion, we had developed a new, revolutionary technique, *collectivism*, with the lavish use of the machine. The result was enormous standardized production which, even without protective tariffs, would enable our industries to undersell the cheapest labor. We took a decisive part in two world wars. No damage was done to our home land; on the contrary, we issued from the struggle, in both cases, better equipped, better organized, vastly richer than when we went into battle. As a result, we are now striding the world like a colossus. Our virtues I do not deny: our luck is

even more patent. For generations, we called on the whole of
Europe to share that luck. Then the sons and grandsons of
immigrants pulled the ladder after them. And we decided that
land, forests, coal, ores, oil, had been conjured up by a benefi-
cent spirit, the Profit Motive, whose temple is in Wall Street.

Look on this other historical picture. Russia, landlocked, with
vast arctic and subarctic zones, lived for centuries in ignorance
and destitution, under the autocratic rule of the tsars. By 1900,
there was no comparison between her wealth and ours: she
was a sprawling pauper, America an energetic and justly proud
nouveau riche. When at last the industrial revolution was beginning to be felt in Russia, the country went through an un-
precedented series of catastrophes. The Japanese war was
merely humiliating and costly: the First World War brought
utter devastation and chaos. Then came two revolutions, civil
strife, the havoc wrought by the White condottieri, the whole
world eager to despoil the prostrate giant, the Allies at Arkh-
angelsk, Vladivostock, Odessa; Turkey, Rumania, Poland grabbing what they could; the whole managerial class in flight or
under suspicion. What the West — and the East — confi-
dently expected was irremediable anarchy and complete dis-
solution.

Like the French under the Convention, the Russians refused
to accept their doom. With no help, surrounded by distrust
and hatred, they restored order — at what price! — and economic activity — with what waste! Again, I am a student of
history; and I predict that this somber, cruel, desperate fight
for survival and revival will be acknowledged as an epic page
in the annals of mankind.

In the thirties, Russia was on the high road — austere and
arduous at first — to that prosperity which is our god, when
the threat of war compelled her to divert her resources to rearmament. Then war came: and our imagination refuses to
realize the destruction that was wrought: the richest provinces
under the Nazi yoke, the richest earth scorched by enemies
and patriots alike, the industrial cities systematically plundered,
and gutted at last when the Nazi plague receded; innumerable

dead, of wounds, starvation, and disease. Russia had no spokesman as eloquent as Churchill: but she had Stalingrad. I still
have vivid in my mind our dismay, our despair, our hope, our
pride, our triumph, as we followed the fate of that symbolic
city, a vaster and more decisive Verdun. There Nazidom was
dealt its mortal wound, although it snarled and bit and clawed
for interminable months of wanton destruction and futile bloodshed. And when Russia had sacrificed so much in wealth and
lives for the common cause, we who, through no fault of our
own happened to grow stronger and richer as a result of the
contest, we point a finger of scorn at her, and say: "How abjectly poor she is! How wicked she must be!"

The one cause of the world's distress is the doctrinaire,
totalitarian fanaticism which obstinately rejects all but a single
aspect of the complex and moving reality. *Our* conception alone
is righteous, and must prevail in its entirety; *theirs* is evil absolute, and must be utterly destroyed. Nothing could be more
opposed to the scientific spirit, or to the humanistic. It may be
starry-eyed to hope that science and humanism will ever rule
this world. My modest contention is that doctrinaire fanaticism
is unrealistic, unpractical, and therefore un-American. This is
the land of liberty, and therefore of pluralism and pragmatism.

Stuart Chase, who did yeoman service in warning us against
the tyranny of words, praises Puerto Rican leaders for having
achieved *ideological immunity*. "They are not tied up in either
Marxian or free enterprise strait jackets. They can think without
looking it up in the book; they are flexible and mentally free
to think out what needs to be done. If business can meet a need,
fine. But if business cannot, then let the government do it, or
a co-operative, or a non-profit association. The main thing is
to get it done." [1] President Eisenhower is reputed to have said:
"A house divided cannot stand; but there may be houses of
different colors on the same street." The street is this *One
World* of ours: our candid angelical white in dramatic contrast
with their blazing scarlet. But the street is also our America.

---

[1] Stuart Chase, "Puerto Rico Says Good-by to Mañana." *This Week
Magazine*, April 6, 1952, p. 48.

There we find communistic, collectivistic, coöperative, feudal, and private mansions side by side, each with its proper shade or combination of shades. Like President Eisenhower himself, I have spent all my life under communism: I have worked in the service of society, without any hope of great wealth, and I have enjoyed in return a measure of freedom from worldly care. I assume that President Eisenhower, like myself, has not a few friends among capitalists.

It is palpable that we shall not win the ideological war by boasting about our wealth, or by asserting a leadership based on sheer power. Such vulgarities (in which even well-educated men indulge) only breed contempt and hatred. Strange as it may sound, it does not pay to be tough. It is equally obvious that we cannot offer as ideals the Profit Motive, which is nothing but greed, or party politics, which fills our papers with recriminations, denunciations, and scandals. *We cannot win on the strength of our diseases.* We shall have to rely on the virtue of our essential beliefs, Liberty, Equality, and Fraternity.

But what is meant by *winning*? Is it destroying or enslaving our opponent, wrenching from him, at the point of the sword, his unconditional and permanent surrender? Or is it winning him *over*? The strategies are radically different. We have twice tasted the fruits of total victory, and they are bitter. We still have to try the formula that Woodrow Wilson borrowed (unawares) from Paul Verlaine: *peace without victory*, peace through mutual and self-understanding.

We are constantly urged by excellent authorities to adopt a more positive, a more dynamic faith than sheer containment. Associate Justice William O. Douglas pleads for a Point Five Program, that would "extend the American revolution of social justice" to underdeveloped areas, instead of "underwriting the status quo and perpetuating the conditions on which communism grew." [2] Professor Anthony E. Sokol, well versed in the affairs of Southeast Asia, says: "Perhaps the simplest and most concise way of characterizing our task there is to say that *we*

[2] Address before the National Conference on International and Economic Development, Washington, D. C., April 7, 1952.

must keep the promises that the *Russians* are making." [3] We are told shrewdly that such a policy would be the best way to *defeat* communism. Instead of *defeat*, I should prefer to say *disarm*. The men I have quoted do not quite dare to admit, even to themselves, that in presence of glaring injustices and human distress, we and the communists react in the same way, make the same promises, and have to encounter the same enemies. In other words, we cannot help being fellow travelers. Our best experts, including some prominent army men, did not like or trust Chiang Kai-shek any more than the Russians did. Franklin Roosevelt and Joseph Stalin professed the same aversion against imperialism. Unimpeachable Americans still hate Franco's rule exactly in the same way and for the same reason as they hated Hitler's: in this instance, they are inevitably on the same side as the Soviets. *We* and *they* profess to have the same goal: a government *for* the people. We have the same enemies: the upholders of ancient abuses. Our methods differ: if we met honestly, not with a dagger in our sleeve, adjustment would not be inconceivable. The Geneva Conference confirmed such a hope.

There are two obstacles: both are at the same time unsubstantial and formidable. The first is the primitive instinct of self-assertion, the heroic and brutal spirit of the dog fight. Right or wrong, our side must conquer; there is no substitute for victory. The second is the insidious tyranny of words: when the diabolical term Communism is uttered, we see red and charge like a mad bull. In both cases, civilization would be the remedy: taking thought, the critical mind, the judicial temper. But the civilized speak softly and the barbarians vociferate. After how many devastating storms and whirlwinds shall the still small voice be heard at last?

[3] *Pacific Spectator*, Spring 1952, p. 242.

SYLLABUS COMPLECTENS PRAECIPUOS NOSTRAE AETATIS ERRORES

(SYLLABUS OF THE PRINCIPAL ERRORS OF OUR TIMES)

I

ARTICLES OF FAITH OF THE PERFECT TOTALITARIAN OR HUNDRED-PER-CENTER

Omitted as too obvious. *See* American Press, *passim.*
May be summed up in the two pregnant phrases:
"My country, right or wrong!"
"America's business is Business."

II

THE CREED OF THE SOCIALIST

Socialism and the Christian spirit are one.
Thou shalt not serve Mammon.
We are all members of one another.
The kingdom of Heaven is within you and among you.
Show your faith through your works.
"They had all things in common."
"Distribution was made unto every man according as he had need."
"The Eye of a Needle."
Let the Good Samaritan, not the Devil, take the hindmost.
Socialism and Democracy are one: Government *for* the people means striving for the common welfare.
In private life, individualism is selfishness; in communal life, individualism is anarchy.
Natural resources and public services for private gain are an absurdity.

A partner is free, even under strict discipline; a hireling is
　bond, even if his chain be long.

Profit is theft.

So long as there is hunger, luxury is a crime.

When all are fed, luxury is vulgarity.

III

THE GROPINGS OF THE LIBERAL

One World, but pluralistic.

Many cultures, one Culture.

You cannot catch things as they are: they were, or they are
　becoming.

Men and societies are a welter of memories and dreams.

Beware of self-evidence: on the human plane, there are no
　Eternal Verities.

Systems do not explain: they only describe the line chosen.

Systems are the self-portraits of their authors.

Heresies are blind alleys, and orthodoxy is the worst of heresies.

Unanimity is the *rigor mortis* of a nation's thought.

Force not used for the common good is gangsterism.

The letter stands, and is dead; the spirit moves, and lives.

By thought, ye shall seek the truth; and the quest shall make
　you free.

Prove all things.

Make the world safe for differences. In material things, unity;
　in spiritual things, liberty; in all things, charity.

The Still Small Voice.

(For a fuller statement of a liberal's faith, see *Bottle in the Sea*, Harvard
University Press, 1954.)